More Praise for **Without Child:**

"At last, an intelligent analysis of the powerful societal pressure upon women to become mothers, and a searching description of how the decision not to bear a child may result from any number of choices, neither selfish nor irrational. The enormous contribution of childless women to our cultural heritage is astonishing. Laurie Lisle has written a timely book assuring us that the true definition of motherhood need not include childbirth."
—Carolyn. G. Heilbrun, author of *Writing a Woman's Life* and *The Education of a Woman: The Life of Gloria Steinem*

"Lisle's groundbreaking volume combines personal, historical and sociological perspectives. Her struggle to understand her own motivations, including her reactions to all the negative connotations associated with this allegedly 'unnatural' or 'selfish' choice is an integral part of her illuminating and affirmative narrative. Lisle's invaluable overview is infused with sense and sensibility."
—*Booklist*

"Lisle shows us a rich array of triumphant meanings arising from the lives of the childless, and on the way gives us her own moving story of self-doubt and self-acceptance."
—Ann Snitow, co-editor of *The Feminist Memoir Project: Voices from Women's Liberation*

"Laurie Lisle's wide-ranging study is a rich, sane, beautifully considered work, an invitation to tolerance and understanding on a subject that continues to cause controversy and divide women more than any other. I can't recommend it highly enough."
—Molly Haskell, author of *Holding My Own in No Man's Land: Women and Men and Film and Feminists*

D0145448

WITHOUT CHILD

CHALLENGING THE
STIGMA OF
CHILDLESSNESS

Laurie Lisle

ROUTLEDGE
NEW YORK AND LONDON

Published in 1999 by
Routledge
29 West 35th Street
New York, NY 10001

Published in Great Britain by
Routledge
11 New Fetter Lane
London EC4P 4EE

Original hardcover edition published in 1996 by Ballantine Books,
A division of Random House, Inc., New York.

Grateful acknowledgment is made to the following for permission to reprint material:

Margaret Atwood and Oxford University Press Canada: Excerpt from "Spelling"
from the poetry collection *True Stories* by Margaret Atwood. Copyright © 1981
by Margaret Atwood. Reprinted by permission of the author and Oxford
University Press Canada.

The Ella Lyman Cabot Trust, Inc.: Excerpts from the letters of Richard C. Cabot
to Ella Lyman Cabot, dated June 11, 1893 and of Ella Lyman Cabot to Richard
C. Cabot, dated June 12, 1893. Copyright © 1995 by the Ella Lyman Cabot
Trust, Inc. Published with permission.

Houghton Mifflin Company: Excerpt from "The Double Image" from *To Bedlam
and Part Way Back* by Anne Sexton. Copyright © 1960 by Anne Sexton;
© renewed 1988 by Linda G. Sexton. Reprinted by permission of
Houghton Mifflin Company. All rights reserved.

Scribner: "Parentage" from *The Poems of Alice Meynell* by Wilfird Meynell.
Copyright © 1923 by Wilfrid Meynell; © renewed 1951. Reprinted by permission
of Scribner, an imprint of Simon & Schuster.

Library of Congress Cataloging-in-Publication Data
Lisle, Laurie.
Without child / by Laurie Lisle.
p.   cm.
Originally published: New York : Ballantine Books, 1996.
Includes bibliographical references (p.   ) and index.
ISBN 0-415-92493-6 (pbk.)
1. Childlessness. 2. Childlessness—History. I. Title.
HQ755.8.L57 1999   99-20815
306.87—dc21   CIP

10 9 8 7 6 5 4 3 2 1

FOR ROBERT

CONTENTS

INTRODUCTION

I first began to think about writing this book as I approached the age of forty, a watershed birthday in regard to childbearing. I did not undertake it then for a number of reasons, but as the decade passed, it was evident that childlessness was not only a silent issue in my life but also in the lives of many of my friends. It was a situation where the *lack* of an experience was a significant event in itself. My wish to explore this subject lay dormant for a decade, gathering force, until one day, as I was making the long drive to my mother's house, the ideas for the book came pouring forth. I steered with one hand and scribbled down my thoughts with the other—almost all of them appearing here as I envisioned them that day.

As I imagined this book that afternoon, I started with my own story, that of an American girl growing up in the 1950s and groomed to be a stay-at-home mother, but coming of age in the 1970s and aspiring to another kind of womanly life, one I hoped would be interesting and joyous, but perhaps apart from motherhood. I immediately planned to research how females had viewed child rearing in past generations. I wanted to examine the nature of modern mothering and why it was so difficult to believe its ancient promise of female fulfillment. That day I pledged to describe the illusionary, perfect child of my imagination, the dream that made it troublesome to give up the idea of pregnancy. I jotted down a line about the role of fathers and husbands in the lives of females today, including my doubts about the protection of patriarchy and the possibility of co-parenting. I hoped to explore the experience of femininity outside of motherhood, a topic that had never been addressed as far as I knew. I vowed to describe my efforts to reconcile the differing demands of having a baby and writing a biography. I would end my book, I noted, by investigating what women without their own children can expect in middle and old age.

After selling the book proposal to my publisher, I began the research the way I had started my biographies—by becoming absorbed in the lives of others. I searched women's literature and letters, reviewing cases when women's celibacy and consequent childlessness was sanctioned by religion, exploring situations in which they were unable to conceive or carry, and where they chose to innovate childless marriages. I also studied the work of social scientists, eager to discover the experiences of my childless predecessors and peers. "Science" may be the wrong word for the findings of the sociologists, psychologists, psychiatrists, and social workers who have made the study of nonparents a specialty, since their various sampling and analytical methodologies are often incompatible. For instance, they do not always distinguish between their subjects' explanations for childlessness, which can range from early inchoate certainty to eventual grudging acceptance. In addition, subjects who volunteer to be interviewed are more likely to be intentionally rather than ambivalently or unintentionally without progeny. Furthermore, since the researchers tend to interview those in their academic communities, like educated white wives, it at first appears (falsely) that only the relatively privileged are willingly childfree, but United States Census Bureau figures and abundant anecdotal and other information suggest otherwise. The scientific jargon that describes the investigators' data is clinical and flat, but nevertheless the sum of their findings—interviews with thousands of the childfree and childless—offer an intriguing picture of this growing minority. (All this and other data are elucidated at the end of the book.) My reading of women's novels and diaries as well as folktales and sociological journals, my conversations with friends and recollections of my childhood, all prompted in me flashes of recognition, caused me to question the nature of free will, and finally released me from a lingering feeling of apartness.

As my notes grew and my manuscript took form, all of those who read it encouraged me to write more about myself as "a gift to others," in the words of one friend. I hesitated for a while, wondering if my own story was relevant, but realized that although my background was unusual in many ways, it was also universal in the sense that it was shaped by widespread phenomena. I was a child of divorce, for instance. So as I decided to interweave my private history with those of others, I opened my old, handwritten journals apprehensively. Would I awaken painful buried memories? Would I pity or admire the earlier version of myself in the pages? As I read my own spontaneous words written decades earlier, I found myself relieved at my intuitions and rationales about postponing pregnancy. As a younger woman, I simply had wanted to feel very strong or safe—able to protect my young—before giving birth, since the social order around me seemed harsh toward mothers and children. I also realized that as a writer I had been afraid of losing my life in motherhood—if not literally, as in the days when the physical dangers of pregnancy were grave, but in another way, by losing my ability to direct my time, mind, and energy. In contemporary America it seemed wiser for me, and more responsible toward an unconceived child, to remain childless—a dramatic turnaround of the traditional way females had survived socially by bearing sons.

Since my life is inevitably intertwined with the lives of others, I was concerned about invading the privacy of my relatives and friends as I wrote my story. But I recognized that I was taking the greatest risk of all by revealing my own feelings, so raw and unresolved at times. If I feel that most human relationships are a poignant brew of desire and disappointment, so, I am sure, do others. And many of the events I wanted to describe had happened a long time ago. As I reached the age of fifty, I realized it was finally time for me, a teller of other women's tales, to write openly and honestly about myself. My willingness to tell the truth as I experienced it has been difficult but compelling and ultimately cathartic. I certainly hope that it will be read as an offering to others.

I have named very few friends and relatives in my text for reasons of privacy and style, and I will mention even fewer here. But I wish to express appreciation to everyone who has taken an interest in this book, who has read early drafts of the manuscript, and who has shared with me their perceptions and experiences. I am especially grateful to my women friends in "Le Group," who were present for so many Sunday evenings around my fireplace during the years I worked on this book, as we tried to give one another empathy, insight, and affection. It would have been immensely more difficult to complete the manuscript without the loving support of my husband, Robert Kipniss, who also helped me refine my ideas. I am also indebted to the children in my life, the young beings whose charm, beauty, and intelligence affirm again and again the importance of this topic. My thanks also go to my editor, Joanne Wyckoff, for her intelligent editorial guidance and to my longtime agent, Charlotte Sheedy. Finally, I feel very fortunate to have explored the resources of the Schlesinger Library at Radcliffe College and those of the Women's History Collection of the New York Public Library, an institution where I was privileged to have a key to the Frederick Lewis Allen Room.

WITHOUT CHILD

FINDING THE WORDS, DISCOVERING MY WAY

The realization that I will never give birth to a child has enveloped me gradually and aroused in me an intense, combustible mixture of emotions that follows no existing script. Children have always charmed me, and during the wonderfully free decade of my twenties, I assumed I would eventually have one of my own. Then at the age of thirty-two I had "a dream about a laughing baby," I abruptly noted in one of my private, handwritten journals on the last day of January 1975, when I was living with my boyfriend and working for a newsmagazine. The nighttime reverie jolted me because I had almost forgotten about motherhood in my absorption with other forms of love and work. Although I came to believe that I faced a private struggle between mothering and writing, I was actually involved in a dilemma, even an ancient drama, that was important to members of my generation born during the 1940s. It is typical of Americans to feel tension between the symbolic pulls of the family and the frontier, and in the last quarter of the twentieth century, the issue of motherhood has become an integral part of this pressure. As I moved through my childbearing years, I never found a good way to reconcile my impulses toward intimacy and independence, my longings to nurture a child and to explore the world. Over the past two decades, these desires have been irreconcilable for me—to my lingering regret at moments, but ultimately to my measured relief.

Who are we, those of us without offspring?

When I began this investigation into what it means to be a nonmother, or a *nullipara* in medical parlance, I read a great deal of history and literature, looking for clues. I came upon the stories of numerous women who had avoided childbirth for reasons of adventure, romance, spirituality, ambition, art, idealism, duty, poverty, terror, or the desire for an education. I discovered the unusual pledge of an engaged couple in the late nineteenth century to pass up parenthood in favor of greater marital intimacy and equality as well as to devote themselves to the service of God. I came upon the passionate words of an intentionally childfree woman who only dared to publish her argument in 1905 under the pseudonym of A Childless Wife. I found numerous foremothers whose childlessness was inexplicable, but who lived extraordinarily interesting, useful, and gratifying lives. Today most of us without children do not know that the childless woman has always existed for a multitude of reasons, both fortunate and unfortunate. We are part of an old and respectable—and even inspiring—social tradition which, like other aspects of women's history, has been neglected and forgotten. This lost knowledge of archetypes and individuals, including Greek goddesses and medieval witches, Christian celibates, and Renaissance ladies, counterbalances the paucity of contemporary images of enriched and exuberant womanliness outside of motherhood.

Part of my research involved a review of the findings of contemporary social scientists. I was distressed to discover that studies done prior to the 1970s indicated that females without children were deviant and disturbed. In more current data, however, subjects were more like myself: women who had come of age in the 1970s and then, armed with educations and aspirations, had gravitated to cities in America and western Europe. As I read the sociological literature, I realized that people of my generation were childless for a wide variety of reasons. A 1983 British study, for instance, divided childfree couples into four groups based on temperament and circumstance: altruistic idealists, easygoing hedonists, partisans of a particular lifestyle, and resigned ill or older people.

In my research, I learned that rarely before have so many Americans entered into lifelong childlessness by choice or by chance. Historically, 3 to 30 percent of all women worldwide have not borne children. In 1994 almost 18 percent of American women reached the age of forty without giving birth, a number that had been gradually growing for several decades and was already much larger than the rate of their parents' generation. Much of the childlessness is now deliberate, although the line between willing and unwilling is often indistinct and wavering. Nonmotherhood as a widespread and long-lasting phenomenon has happened suddenly—in one generation—along with the arrival of modern contraceptives and legal abortions.

The topic of childlessness is so unusual, in fact, that there are no exact words or precise phrases to name or describe it. The existing vocabulary is unrelentingly negative, descending from a mythological or distant past when being childless was rare, inadvertent, and most often unlucky. Descriptive expressions for childlessness have evolved from *barren* to *sterile* to *infertile*, terminology that almost always applies to the female, not to the male. The medical term for a woman without a child, *nullipara*, comes from the Latin root for empty, void, zero, like the word for a female who has never been pregnant, *nulligravida.* In the 1970s the word *childfree* was coined, but because it suggests a flippant disregard toward children, I find it unsuitable. Other terms, like *childless* or *unchilded, nonmother* or *notmother,* have recently been invented or come into common usage, but since they all allude only to the absence of a natal child, and not to how this absence is experienced, they are also unsatisfactory. We are given or innovate a vocabulary that polarizes us for or against parenthood but never indicates the dignity of nonparenthood, which should be called something evocative and neutral, perhaps *otherhood.* Since no word or phrase yet encompasses a sense of the unique texture of living without sons and daughters of our own, I will use most of the existing ones in positive ways in an effort to evolve a more precise language.

Sociologists and psychologists tend to look for social or personal explanations for childlessness, so they are sometimes blind to the pressures of gender politics. Millions of women are not giving birth today for a number of interrelated reasons, but one of the most important is nagging ambivalence about motherhood. When a woman without a child considers having one, she invokes fantasies about her potential mothering self along with memories of her own mother and observations of her sisters and friends with children. In the early 1960s, I was disheartened at the sight of my high-spirited college roommate tending her small son, the result of an accidental pregnancy that forced her to give up school as well as her musical trio; although her little boy was adorable, she seemed shockingly subdued. Many young women are winning diplomas and degrees today, but after childbirth they are still expected to delay or drop other activities, an agenda that many resent and resist, especially those with the most education and the best jobs. This double standard is nothing new. Almost a century ago the social worker and magazine editor who called herself A Childless Wife explained that she had gained a sense of self-confidence from competing with boys in co-educational schools, an experience that left her reluctant to remain at home with children.

During times of privation and stress in the past, women have had fewer or no children for reasons of survival or even as a form of passive resistance to oppressions like slavery. In recent years, misgivings about the economic penalties of full-time child raising have been underscored by the United States government's persistent indifference to the difficulties of working parents, which contrasts sharply with the policies of European countries. In many cases a woman's choice to remain childfree is less an aversion to parenthood than an attempt to retain the potential of adulthood. In the living of my life, I came to realize that I had not just neglected to give birth to children, I had responded to very real but veiled antinatalist conditions in the culture around me. Hesitancy about undertaking parenthood is a morally responsible attitude when a man or woman determines that the odds are low for providing a child with a decent childhood in an unstable social milieu.

The rejection of parenthood is a delicate and even dangerous topic; it has an element of subversiveness to it, especially when it is the choice of happily married couples. In the past, particularly during wartime, the absence of progeny was a threat to the survival of families, ethnic groups, and nations, but although the earth is now threatened by overpopulation, few of us still dare to speak openly about our real reasons for refusing to breed. We are afraid to challenge the view of motherhood as the essential female experience. An uneasy silence exists between mothers and nonmothers, since we seldom talk frankly about the motives for our reproductive behavior or the realities of our daily lives. Even those of us without offspring rarely talk

about it among ourselves because we often feel isolated by our
private rationales. "To this day, women without children have
no common activity, no common language," Berenice Fisher, a
professor of education at New York University, has observed.
"They share a common stigma, but the meaning of that stigma
often varies for the women themselves." Certainly many of the
nulliparas and nulligravidas whom I interviewed had never
talked in depth about nonmotherhood before, and their speech
was as often painfully hesitant as quietly triumphant. And their
words made me consider the complicated origins of my own
childlessness.

Almost from birth I had wondered, either subliminally or
overtly, whether or not to be a mother. In the decade preceding
my birth, during the Depression of the 1930s, large numbers of
American women never bore children; although statistics com-
piled at the time are not comparable to current ones, it appears
that childlessness (and single-child motherhood) was near or at
its highest level in this country. Wives and daughters of out-of-
work men needed jobs, and many of them put off marriage or
postponed childbearing in order to earn wages. Patterns among
my relatives reflected those tendencies but for different reasons. My mother's older sister, an attractive "society girl" and
champion skier, stayed single into her thirties until she eventually decided to marry, and my mother, who married my father
in 1936, remained a childless wife for six years. Although my
mother said later that she had wanted to get pregnant in the
early years of her marriage, the birth of a baby certainly would
have affected her carefree way of life; snapshots taken at the
time show my parents thoroughly enjoying their little rented
house, their English spaniel's large litters, summer days on the

fishing boat named for my mother, and autumn weekends at the family hunting camp in rural Rhode Island.

After America entered the Second World War in 1941, the nation's leaders put out a patriotic appeal to civilians to enter the factories and offices vacated by those entering the armed services. More women began to earn paychecks than ever before, and by 1944 they composed a third of the nation's civilian labor force. It is revealing in light of the government's resistance to underwriting child care today to realize that during that national emergency, Washington was willing and able to open rapidly thousands of day-care centers to enable mothers to take jobs. After the armistice, however, the centers were abruptly closed and female workers were fired, effectively sending mothers and nonmothers alike back home so returning servicemen could be rehired. It was a bitter experience for those who had ventured forth to learn trades in the name of patriotism and who wanted to keep them, but their protests went unheard and unheeded as an era of virulent pronatalism began.

I was conceived just before my father joined the navy at the beginning of the war, and my mother, Lally, unlike many other mothers, stayed home to care for me. My earliest memory of her, vague in its details but emotionally vivid, is of a high-spirited and beautiful young woman who loved to sing and to twirl me around in her arms. I recently saw home-movie footage of my mother's sister's postwar August wedding that dramatically confirmed my early remembrance: my mother, the slender and elegant matron-of-honor in a long, ruffled organdy gown with fresh flowers woven into her long dark hair, was laughing and animated. As the five-year-old flower girl, I wore a circle of rosebuds over my dark bangs as well as a dress that was a miniature version of hers; I appeared lively and unafraid as I grabbed a boy cousin's hand, jumped off a low stone wall onto the lawn, and pulled him toward the sherbet and the towering, flower-decked white wedding cake.

As was the custom in my mother's family, she raised me with live-in help, first a baby nurse and then a college student, all within the embrace of her and my father's large families, most of whom lived nearby in the small city of Providence, Rhode Island. Although her sister and two brothers were in the armed services, her beloved eldest brother, who had a medical deferment, lived with his family a block away, and her father, who was retired, walked over to visit every afternoon after I was born.

When my father, Laurence (Larry), returned from the Pacific at the end of the war, he did not remain at home for long. Having had a taste of freedom and authority, he decided to leave my mother and me as well as the enveloping extended families for a different kind of life as a furniture manufacturer in a Vermont village. After his death four decades later, I discovered that his edition of Robert Frost poetry had a stanza scissored out, perhaps so he could put the lines in his wallet and reread them often; the words were about the difficulties of departing and discovering one's own way. He left behind in our house his masterly replica of an eighteenth-century corner cupboard, but he tore from my baby album a heartfelt letter he had written to me two months after my birth in the hours before his ship left San Francisco for the war zone. The letter, which came to me from my stepmother after his death, revealed a father whom I had never known. In the letter, he told me always to love my mother ("as much as your little heart will stand"), especially if he should not survive the war. His neat handwriting relayed the values dearest to him and advised me to go to my mother if I should inherit his shyness. Promising a rapport that was never to be, he wrote: "Some people, but not Lally, might be foolish enough to tell you that you have never seen your Daddy, but don't let them fool you. They told me you couldn't see, but I know better than they do, for you looked right at me and smiled and then you winked—and I winked back."

In the fall of 1950, five years after the end of the war, my maternal grandparents had a formal photograph taken of their rapidly growing family. Three of their five children had returned from serving in the military, and six more babies had been born; by then we numbered twenty-four, ranging in age from my seventy-one-year-old grandfather to a month-old granddaughter. My mother had already divorced and remarried, and among the new toddlers was my little half sister. At eight years old, I sat cross-legged at my mother's feet, in a pose identical to the boy cousin my age, wearing a lace-collared party dress, my straight brown hair neatly tamed by a barrette, gazing intently and somberly into the lens of the camera.

The ultradomesticity of the 1950s was a throwback to the Victorian glorification of maternity. For the past hundred years, since the decline of agriculture and the advent of industrialism, American women had been giving birth to fewer children. The postwar domestic phenomenon was an aberration for several reasons: women who were educated and had experienced life outside the home not only had larger families than in the past few generations, averaging 3.7 children each by 1957, but they stayed home to care for them by themselves. Middle-class American wives experienced a curious combination of comfort and confinement in that period of postwar prosperity, marked not only by advances in health care and the widespread availability of household appliances but also by job discrimination and popular notions that women could be best fulfilled through their roles as wives and mothers. My mother, who was raised by a nanny, found herself at age forty rearing me, my half sister, and a half brother who was born in 1952, with scarce help. Yet the wartime years, during which she and many other women enjoyed an unexpected amount of independence, either on the job or running households alone, had made deep and lasting impressions on them. Many, including my mother, would convey to their daughters distinct double messages that originated in their lost autonomy and aspirations—the confusing words and actions that urge conformity on the one hand and rebellion on the other—and that inadvertently helped revive American feminism when these daughters came of age a few decades later.

Growing up in the 1950s, I did not know any women without children except a few very young or elderly teachers. Most females without progeny had come of age during the 1930s and were now over the age of fifty. Childlessness among younger women was rare, consisting of only 8 percent of the daughters of Depression-era mothers. Neither did I know any mothers of young children with jobs, except for several young widows. My mother, who had left high school in 1933 during the depths of the Depression, had been told that it was wrong for girls from comfortable backgrounds to take jobs from male breadwinners. Once she mentioned to me that it was wise for a wife to have something respectable to do if her husband died or divorced her; when my father left her, she confided ashamedly, the only job she could imagine doing was arranging flowers for a florist. During my childhood I cannot remember anyone asking me what I wanted to be when I grew up. No one had to ask, because it was assumed that my only option was to be a stay-at-home mother. Even an aunt who had been an officer in the Women's Army Corps was living out that scenario. Thinking about my future was a little depressing because, although I adored my little sister and brother, I realized that the daily rounds of diapers and feedings bored me and exhausted my mother. My mother's double message to me about motherhood included excusing me from baby-sitting, since during her girlhood that was the sphere of servants. Still, I remember thinking at a young age that it was dangerous to dream too much about other ways of life, since harboring any hopes outside housekeeping would make it impossible for me to adjust to marriage and motherhood. I clearly understood that I was supposed to hold myself in suspension, essentially unformed and unjelled, in a kind of willed immaturity, because of my inevitable destiny.

During the 1950s, the 3 percent of wives without children, or even those with one child, were considered socially aberrant. A sense of secrecy enveloped them, and they were pitied as infertile or scorned as neurotic. One 1955 study, which described wives in childless marriages as introverted and maladjusted, implied that they had personality problems that resulted in a rejection of motherhood, but later sociologists have suggested that the condemnation of childlessness may have troubled them instead. The only women for whom it was possible to be childless without censure were the mentally disturbed, the genetically defective, the sexually deviant, the chronically ill, or, in some circumstances, the rare genius. The pronatalist bias was so strong then that Harvard social psychology professor Lotte Bailyn, a Viennese-born wife and mother, noted that the choices to stay single or childless existed only in principle for a professional woman. In reality, the tiny number of deliberately childless during that era were usually those of modest means with high aspirations in the arts and academia or ambitious offspring of immigrants and lower-class parents.

Against this background, meanwhile, I was in training to be a bride, the first step in an upper-middle-class milieu toward becoming a mother. The pressure came from every direction, but mainly from my mother, despite her own marital disappointments. The Bachrach photograph of her formal and fashionable May Day wedding to my dapper father at the age of twenty-one shows a stiffly smiling bride buttoned into her mother-in-law's heirloom nuptial gown and veil, flanked by six bridesmaids and two flower girls. That marriage had failed painfully, but now, in my young eyes, she seemed disillusioned again. Around 1951, while I was still prepubescent, my father and his lady friend sent me a large expensive bride doll elaborately enveloped in white tulle. My immediate reaction was to put it away in a drawer and refuse to touch it, an inarticulate but resentful act of rebellion against what I already sensed about matrimony. It was not that I did not treasure gifts from my father—I had carefully saved two simple cloth dolls he had sent me from Panama during the war. The bride doll, however, remained untouched and pristine in its tissue paper, although from time to time I wistfully gazed at its frilly loveliness, wanting to believe in its romantic promise.

Around the age of ten, as my socialization continued, my mother talked me into dropping horseback riding lessons for ballroom dancing classes at a place called Froebel Hall, which was attended by pupils from the private girls' and boys' schools in Providence. Dancing school was more a team sport in which the boys were the leaders than instruction in social correctness, however, despite our white gloves, party dresses, and Mary Janes. I remember enjoying the excitement of getting dressed up, the sound of dance music, and the warmth of low yellow lights on dark winter afternoons, but aside from that, dancing school was dismal.

In 1957 I was enrolled in a small Episcopalian girls' boarding school in a bucolic Connecticut village, the same one that my

mother and a number of aunts had attended in the 1930s. I enjoyed many aspects of this Anglo-American tradition, including
being on my own and being intellectually informed and absorbed, as well as skating on a frozen pond, reading in the beautiful library, singing Gregorian chants at morning prayers and
vespers, even the simplicity of wearing uniforms—an unflattering brown-and-white pinstripe cotton day dress, worn with a
detachable starched white collar, black bow, and brass buttons
and belt stamped with the school insignia. But there was also a
strange feeling of stagnation about the school. It may have
been because the dignified, scholarly headmistress, from the
generation of women who attained Ph.D.'s in the 1920s, was at
the end of her four-decade reign that began when my mother
was a pupil. Or it was because so few of us seemed to have
dreams other than being wives and mothers. I often felt a thick,
paralyzing boredom at meals when, wearing a white-eyelet
evening uniform dress, I sat at a long narrow refectory table,
talking about topics like the engagement of Princess Margaret.
One day I was astonished when my art history teacher, an ani-
mated white-haired German man with a passion for art, asked
us to write down our dreams for ourselves. When I recently
found this essay among my schoolgirl papers, I discovered that
at the time I still anticipated the typical future for a teenager
like myself growing up in the 1950s—that of a mother with
husband and "at least two lively, intelligent children"—but
along with other ambitions that were becoming more insistent.
After a year or so I experienced a sense of enclosure that lasted
until graduation. "I could set my goals higher than these yellow
walls," I wrote in my diary. "Something has woken up. I know
it's best for me to get out next year, especially as I see columns
of girls dressed identically marching up the hill."

In the 1950s I began to gravitate to humanistic causes as a

way to assert both my idealism and my dissension and difference from my nonpolitical family. I was first exposed to radical
thinking in 1954, when my Unitarian Sunday school held a
seminar on racial injustice, led by a reporter for the local newspaper who had just returned from traveling throughout the
South with a black colleague. A few years later, I volunteered to
do some social work with the Quakers, and I remember being
astonished by a leader's critique of the smug patriotic assumptions in an American history textbook. Shortly afterward I became an ardent pacifist. Although I did not know it at the time,
I was acting within a well-established but downplayed family
tradition of rebels and reformers, which included my grandfather's cousin, Roger Baldwin, a pacifist during the First World
War and a founder and the first director of the American Civil
Liberties Union. When I later learned about this dissenting
side of the bourgeois family pictured in the 1950 family photograph, I felt betrayed. The adults' silence about the family heritage seemed suspect; I wondered if it went unmentioned so as
not to influence members of my generation to be social nonconformists.

When I was eighteen, as my next step in being a bride-in-
training, I was presented to Providence society at the annual
winter debutante cotillion. It was one of the few times my
mother insisted that I do something I adamantly resisted; she
wanted me to meet eligible young men. By then, however, I had
absorbed enough liberal principles to feel scornful of class artifice, but after finding no support for my anti-debutante revolt,
I went along. The formal photograph taken of me shows a
young woman with defeated, slumped shoulders, adorned in
a long white satin and lace gown, an orchid corsage tied to a
drooping wrist, a stiffly pointed brassiere encasing my breasts,
and a look of irritated resignation on my made-up face. I re-

member little about the formal ball itself, except that when I was supposed to curtsy to the assembled patriarchs and matriarchs, I merely bobbed my head. The ball took place in December 1960, and I retain a vivid impression of one of the first Vietnam veterans I ever saw, a tall and darkly handsome young man who seemed disoriented, depressed, and embittered. In retrospect, I realize that I was quietly drawn to him that evening because his state of mind was a magnification of my own alienation, but we did not exchange a word. His ominous and disturbing presence, however, was a harbinger of a generational revolt that would soon overtake me.

I held to an ordinary script about my future, but my desire for an education was undermining it. At a time when not very many women were graduating from college, I was determined to get a diploma, something that few if any of the females in my family had ever done, unlike the Ivy League–educated males; most of my five older female cousins had enrolled in eastern women's colleges, then dropped out to marry and become mothers. The dark, fearful side of my mother's double message became blatant after I entered college in the early 1960s. Never having taken enough subjects to get a high school diploma, she was both proud and worried as I set out for a midwestern university. In her confusion, she sent me a newspaper article about the difficulties educated women had in attracting husbands, which left me feeling undermined and outraged. The clipping reminded me of her resentment of the college girls she had known in the 1930s, who had apparently acted superior to girls like herself, who stayed home and volunteered for the Junior League. Perhaps my mother also sensed that my stubborn resolve to graduate emerged out of a growing desire for a different kind of life from hers, a determination that was reinforced in my junior year when I read Betty Friedan's *The*

Feminine Mystique, which proposed the startling idea that wives had the right to use their educations outside their homes.

After I graduated from college, I was alarmed to overhear my stepfather solemnly state to my mother that, although I was as "ripe" as I would ever be, I was never going to get married. Inherent in his words, of course, was the presumption that all her efforts with me had failed and that I would never be a mother either. I felt alarmed, imagining that there was something terribly wrong with me, but I later understood his remark to mean that I lacked the proper attitude and mentality underneath my polite manners. I had gone through the motions of dancing school and the debutante ball, but they had not left their mark. I was not revolting overtly, but I often felt insouciant and insubordinate as well as passionate about issues of social justice; in them I found an intellectually attractive and somewhat disguised way to rebel against the milieu in which I was bored and uncomfortable. In instinctively rejecting the bourgeois and gravitating to the still-unknown radical heritage of my relations, I felt like a maverick.

The year I graduated from college, 1965, was the one when childlessness was at an all-time low in America. But unknown to me, the pendulum was beginning to swing: while I was still in college, Congresswoman Shirley Chisholm from Brooklyn, a black militant reformer and childless wife, had attacked existing contraceptive restrictions as "compulsory pregnancy laws," and she had argued that government had the obligation to allow birth control so that every woman could, in effect, pursue happiness in her own way. Meanwhile, another wife without children, writer Gael Greene, firmly defended her choice to remain childless in an article published in, of all magazines, *The Saturday Evening Post*. After graduation I joined the ranks of the growing number of college "girls" of my generation who aspired to interesting jobs. I went to work for a newspaper in Providence, rented an apartment of my own, and began to go out with some appealing men. I realized it would be prudent to start taking the heralded new birth control pill, and I made an appointment with my mother's gray-haired gynecologist, a social acquaintance of hers who had delivered my younger siblings. After the doctor examined me, I calmly asked for a prescription for the pill. Startled, he sat back, scowled, and looked extremely displeased—for I was openly assuming my right to an erotic life outside of matrimony and maternity. It was only that year that the United States Supreme Court had ruled that contraception for married couples was a constitutional privacy right, invalidating many state laws to the contrary, including the one in the heavily Roman Catholic state of Rhode Island. Still, attitudes had not yet changed and, even more important, abortion remained illegal everywhere in the country. I finally broke the long, awkward silence by asking if he would give me an abortion if I needed one. With that, he took out his pad and wrote me a prescription with the stern warning to keep quiet about it.

In the autumn of 1967, when I was twenty-five, I found a job on a small magazine in New York and moved to Greenwich Village. I soon had the exhilarating feeling that I was literally expanding in Manhattan's seemingly limitless atmosphere. I found the city, with its depth and breadth, to be the most interesting place in the world; in the company of friends, some of whom were also new arrivals, I explored the bookstores, art galleries, ethnic neighborhoods, exotic restaurants, and everything else. Under the aegis of the reformist Village Independent Democrats, I volunteered in the campaign of candidate

Eugene McCarthy, whose challenge to President Johnson's policy in Vietnam caused the president to drop out of the election.
As always, the metropolis offered hope to newcomers, but with
the liberal John Lindsay as mayor, it seemed as if Manhattan
belonged to those of us with youth, ideals, and ambition.

I wanted to be a journalist and writer and, most important,
to break my silence and fight through the verbal inhibition that
my upbringing had instilled. I was also looking for lasting love; I
was dating and hoping to marry at some time in the future, but
I felt wary of the conventions of marriage, since wedlock
seemed inevitably intertwined with being housebound. It
seemed all right most of the time, and even exciting at moments, to reject my preordained fate and put off marriage beyond the time my mother and most of my female relations had
married in order to shape my life myself. This desire was even
publicly recognized in 1970 by the President's Task Force on
Women's Rights and Responsibilities, which urged that American women be allowed "the freedom to choose the role in society to which their interests, education, and training entitle
them." I began to fling off the old beliefs that had restrained
my imagination and felt a new sense of buoyancy, as though I
could move through the air with energy and ease.

Two years after I moved to New York, I attended an event
called the Congress to Unite Women, a day of discussions run
by a group of young second-wave feminists who were picking
up where their great-grandmothers had left off after American
women had won the vote in 1921. Feminist political theory was
enabling me to give a name to much of the inexplicable pain in
my past. It was also allowing me to see childhood events with
new eyes, which, in turn, helped me to understand feelings of
inadequacy that were undermining my vitality and expressiveness. The phrase "women's liberation" was on our lips that day,

and the scores of young women in attendance talked, listened, and read pamphlets and proclamations with eagerness and excitement. The mimeographed handouts were confessional, angry, brave, and frank, as if their authors were finally finding a language of their own, one that could now be spoken without censure. Workshops were devoted to topics like marital unfairness, feminine images, the care of children, and access to jobs and education. One discussion group talked about eliminating laws and practices that forced women to bear children against their will. Being preoccupied by my relationships with men, in which I wanted love without giving up my dreams, I attended a session on love and sex, and I remember being emotionally shocked but intellectually intrigued by talk about ingrained gender inequality. When I protested to a militant woman that my amiable boyfriend was my best friend, she contemptuously dismissed my remark; shortly afterward she was proven prescient when he abruptly broke off our relationship, possibly alarmed by my new ideas. But that day I felt a contagious, optimistic spirit that was based on my naive assumption that the absolute rightness and rationality of our cause, which I and other women had suddenly come to see, would make antiquated and misogynist structures topple of their own weight.

Recently I opened an old folder of clippings from that time and found a crumbling, yellowed front-page newspaper article dated August 27, 1970, headlined "Women March Down Fifth Avenue in Equality Drive." The largest demonstration for women's rights in history, the high-spirited stroll preceded a period in American history that promised women more equality under the law than ever before. Landmark civil rights legislation had already been passed that outlawed inequities between the sexes, and professions and universities that had banned females began to open up. Congress approved the Equal Rights

Amendment in 1972, and the Supreme Court legalized abortion the next year. Women in publishing became brash, and I joined some of them in a sit-in in the editor's office of *The Ladies' Home Journal* to protest the magazine's traditional view of women. During that time of raised expectations, I took a job at *Newsweek* as a researcher, the only position other than secretary open to female applicants. I had been impressed when the magazine's female editorial staffers had picketed outside the building and sent a sexual discrimination complaint to the Equal Employment Opportunity Commission, and I hoped that more positions would quickly open up.

During that time of reform, however, legislation that would have helped mothers take advantage of the new opportunities did not become law. A number of bills intended to fund day-care programs were introduced into Congress; one, the Comprehensive Child Development Act, was passed, but in 1971 President Nixon vetoed it because of his opposition to what he called "communal" child raising. Except during the Second World War, the concept of public child care in this country had been criticized by both the political right and left: Conservatives feared that it would undermine the traditional role of women, and leftists worried that it would lead to totalitarian control of children. At the time, pregnant women could also lose their jobs because of the absence of job rights, health benefits, or maternity leaves. If a young woman wished to raise a child and have a career at the same time, there were few alternatives if she lived far from her family or could not afford a nanny. I remember visiting a private day-care center in a brownstone near the apartment I shared with the young man I eventually married; although the young women in charge seemed affectionate to the toddlers, the space was dirty, crowded, and oddly forlorn, and before long it disappeared altogether. I recall wishing that my employer had a day nursery on the premises where I could bring my baby and be with him or her at lunchtime or in case of emergency. Some years later I felt it necessary but somewhat depressing to tell a male editor with the power to promote me that I did not plan to have children.

Not surprisingly, the young women like myself who poured into the labor market during the 1970s had very few babies. By 1976 the fertility rate had dropped to 1.7 children per woman of childbearing age, the lowest in history and well below the nation's replacement rate; the childless rate, however, never quite hit levels reached around the turn of the century and in the 1930s. Those of us born during and after the Second World War were not merely reacting against being the crowded baby boom generation, we were continuing a historical trend toward smaller families that had been briefly reversed in the 1950s. Many of us, of course, were also rebelling against a cruel system that appeared to pit the well-being of a child against that of its mother; at the time, Cornell psychologist Urie Bronfenbrenner called the falling birthrate "adaptive" because of the paucity of public or private programs for young families. Paradoxically, though, pronatalist government policies were encouraging the low birthrate: By making it so difficult to combine motherhood and employment, they tended to delay and discourage childbearing. While educated women like myself had more opportunities outside the home than our mothers, it was difficult to take advantage of them after childbirth. In 1975 Lucia Valeska, a mother of three, observed that "a growing number of young women are indeed beginning to resist having their own biological children—mostly from a sense of self-preservation."

It was an era in which women and men put off or rejected matrimony in favor of living alone or together, freed from fears of pregnancy by the birth control pill and other contraceptive devices. (In 1972 the Supreme Court extended to the unmarried the legal right to contraception.) The casual nature of such arrangements was also a restraint on childbearing, as were the financial uncertainties of parenthood; many of us wanted to save money and establish careers before starting families. In the past, it was impossible for men and women to be married for very long before the birth of a child, but now we were experiencing adult privileges without parental responsibilities, an existence that was at times an intoxicating improvement over the lives of our parents. It was as if a lid had blown off. In the middle of the decade, Judith Lorber, a Brooklyn College sociologist, innocently predicted that "once women have a taste of the freedom that comes from antinatalism, productive careers, and sexual openness," it may be difficult for them to go back home again. Since it was now possible to separate heterosexuality from pregnancy, it was logical to expect that the question would arise of whether to have progeny at all. One survey found that women who did not want children in 1970 still had none five years later, but neither did a third of those who had once wanted them, indicating, in part, the pleasure people took in their lives as well as the adverse conditions for parenthood. A decade later it was reported in another study that wives over age thirty without children but with valued work and shared housekeeping arrangements were less likely to give birth than their peers. This new freer way of life grew on many of us, and we thought we were creating new ways to be womanly.

"Obituary: Motherhood" read an editorial-page headline in *The New York Times* on a Saturday in May 1972. Written by Ellen Peck, a young wife from a Roman Catholic background, it reasoned that in an era of new opportunities and ecological dangers, young adults should, instead of creating more people, direct their energies to improving the lives of those already born. Peck was one of the founders that year of the National Organization of Non-Parents (NON), probably the first organized attempt to resist the ancient pressure to breed. Armed with a mermaid insignia and a quotation from the Bible (Isaiah 9:3)—"Thou has multiplied the nation, and not increased the joy"—NON drew attention to the pervasive pronatalism in the media, the arts, and public policy. On the first day of August in 1973 and 1974, the group staged Non-Parents Day celebrations in Manhattan's Central Park, during which Non-Parents of the Year were crowned with laurel wreaths, and young women in short white outfits performed dances of liberty.

Although NON was attempting to reintroduce into mainstream twentieth-century culture a number of ideas with old theological roots, ones that had been embodied in the lives of celibate and childless Christian saints, their application to secular couples in an atmosphere of freedom and upheaval was new. It was also true that the public questioning of parenthood in the 1970s was more a change in expressiveness than in attitudes, since there have always been some nonparents and many reluctant parents. NON, however, was never able to engage the nation in sustained debate about the serious issues involved, since it did not articulate well its altruistic concerns or even the moral validity of individual rights. Despite counting environmentalists and feminists among its early members, NON was weakened by remaining unaffiliated with either cause. With about two thousand members at its peak, mostly young professionals, NON remained more of a curiosity, a playful romp, than a political movement. Consequently, the group was ineffectual in affecting ingrained attitudes or government legislation; even its founder Ellen Peck dropped out of the movement in 1977 and published a book soon afterward called *The Joy of the Only Child.* As the group dissipated, the more moderate National Alliance for Optional Parenthood took its place in 1978, but shortly afterward it disappeared as well.

The women's liberation movement played a surprisingly small role in these events. Although the movement has been called anti-mother, when scholar Ann Snitow reviewed the initial militant movement writings of the feminist second wave— what she referred to as the "demon" texts of the late 1960s and early 1970s—she was unable to find any evidence of what she called "mother-hating." She included in her analysis Shulamith Firestone's brave, impassioned, utopian work of 1970, *The Dialectic of Sex*, which blamed biological motherhood for gender inequities, looked to test-tube technology to relieve females of pregnancy, and advocated communal arrangements to free women from child rearing. Firestone and other movement women were more intent on reforming motherhood than abandoning it, Snitow argued. Likewise, social scientists have found only a weak link between feminism and childlessness. Most of the nulliparas studied in the 1970s were not involved in the women's rights movement; after they decided not to have children, however, many invoked its principles to justify their decisions. Feminism, a group of researchers discovered, made the likelihood of nonparenthood greater only when a husband and wife disagreed about women's rights, presumably because they were unable to agree about their parental roles.

In the early years of the feminist movement's second wave, when most of its leaders were young, single, and childless, they were not against maternity per se, but they tended to ignore it. When they turned their attention to motherhood, they did question its inevitability and importance for every woman, since feminism as a liberal doctrine validates individual choice. The landmark book *Our Bodies, Ourselves*, published in 1971 by the Boston Women's Health Book Collective, advocated "free and clear" decision making about whether or not to give birth. "If we don't have children yet, it is legitimate and good to wait until we feel ready, or to choose not to have children at all," the authors wrote. They did condemn the reality that so many women had to make an artificial and difficult choice between mothering and meaningful work. They warned, however, that often "motherhood is the course of least resistance" in cases when young women are exhausted by dead-end jobs and identity crises.

Movement women in the 1970s realized that children were not the problem—it was the difficult situations in which mothers found themselves. When writer Ellen Willis attended a conference on mothering in 1974 sponsored by the New York Radical Feminists, she found that many in attendance were reluctant to miss the primal experience of motherhood. An analysis around that time by social scientist Bernice E. Lott revealed that more believers than nonbelievers in women's rights called child rearing a creative and valuable activity, but they remained less interested in doing it themselves; although some disparaged child care, Lott acknowledged, they were no worse than antifeminist mothers who neglected their children, but the former were scapegoated by a guilty society. What was new and disturbing in the 1970s was that many spirited and competent young women feared being disempowered, dominated, distracted, and even despised if they took on the timeless womanly role of motherhood in America.

During this tumultuous period, poet Adrienne Rich began her own exploration of motherhood. In her confessional treatise on the subject, *Of Woman Born*, Rich, a feminist and mother of three sons, broke the long-standing unspoken taboo against revealing negative aspects of motherhood. She distin-

guished the potentially joyful experience from its troubling reality under a patriarchal system, calling it the "institution of
motherhood," whereby mothers have total responsibility for
their children but little control over resources for them. When
I read her book in 1976, I was thirty-four and still debating
whether or not to have a baby. After having invested more than
a decade in discovering my interests and developing my writing, the impact of her book was sobering. I was also brought up
short by the facts of my personal life. The man I had married
admitted that if I had a baby he would help "as little as possible" both financially and practically; his disrespect and even an-
tagonism toward parenting, attitudes that appeared to me to
reflect those in the country at large, reinforced my ambivalence. Rich's words resonated about the importance of seeking
examples of rebellious women who "embodied strength, daring,
self-determination." The year that I read her book, I decided
once again to put off pregnancy and to write a biography of the
artist Georgia O'Keeffe, who not-so-incidentally had never
given birth herself. As I turned my attention to the book, I
asked in my journal: "Is O'Keeffe a spiritual mother to me?"

By 1980 the cultural milieu seemed altered and alien. The
mood among women of unlimited possibility was gone, undermined by tensions within intimate relationships, an economic
recession that imperiled livelihoods, and Republican policies
that slashed programs for mothers and children. When the
Equal Rights Amendment failed to be ratified in 1982, its defeat symbolized the bitter backlash against social changes of
the previous decade. The ERA, by asserting gender equality,
seemed to threaten to undercut a wife's traditional dependent
role and, implicitly, the entitlement to engage in full-time

mothering. Women worried, often with good cause, about who would care for their small children. Some women, especially older ones, feared that the women's rights movement would release men from family responsibilities before females were able to make progress in the workplace. Many mothers confused anger at the conditions of motherhood with disrespect for maternity; others believed that the availability of abortion on demand denigrated motherhood. Republicans and Democrats, mothers and nonmothers, feminists and antifeminists all came to occupy enemy camps. Members of the New Right as well as elements of the mass media began to glorify stay-at-home mothers once again. Television, movies, and magazines portrayed motherhood as a panacea for loneliness and as a state of virtuous morality, whereas nonmotherhood was viewed as merely an indication of shallow self-indulgence.

As a result, women without children often felt isolated, invisible, misunderstood, and marginalized. "We are living in a period when 'pronatal' ideology is powerful, a time when being a mother, particularly a 'birthmother,' is considered the quintessential, compulsory female experience," wrote Ellen Herman in a 1988 article in the magazine *Zeta*. "Living childfree therefore means living outside the law, sentenced to solitary confinement for daring to break the rules." Strangers deeply invested in parenthood were likely to consider women without children as fair game for tactless and unwelcome inquisitions, emboldened by a sense of righteousness. The arrogant machisma of new birthmothers contributed to the imposed masochism of nonmothers. As women without children internalized the pervasive pronatal attitudes around them, even the childless playwright Wendy Wasserstein suggested in her play *The Heidi Chronicles* that raising a child was the answer to modern angst and alienation.

Although I was existing contentedly outside the old rules that decree that motherhood is mandatory, cultural messages were also conspiring to make me feel differently. I felt unable to offer a simple explanation, or even an honest one about my childlessness. This was partly because a time of turbulence had begun in my life during which my first marriage broke up; although I married again in my forties, I realized it would be difficult to conceive and carry a child, let alone raise one, because of my age. Despite these circumstances, I sometimes felt the blast of pronatalism as debilitating, and I found myself avoiding the confession that I had no child, uneasy once again about my lack of conformity to 1950s ideals, now revived with a vengeance.

In the past, pronatalism ranged in intensity from merely encouraging childbirth to legally preventing abortion to the genocide of childless women, such as happened in Nazi Germany. In the 1980s the United States Supreme Court and the medical establishment made it more difficult for poor, young, and rural women to get abortions. Parenthood became linked to patriotism, and during one anti-choice campaign, Catholic bishops displayed posters of the Statue of Liberty shedding a tear. In this atmosphere, advocates of reproductive rights only implied the right to remain childfree, they did not spell it out. Organizations like Planned Parenthood of America, Zero Population Growth, and other pro-choice forces rarely, if ever, publicly mentioned the ultimate use of abortion—the right of a woman *never* to use her uterus—out of concern that it would demonize their movement. They defined parenthood as a privilege, not a right or an obligation, but they did not dare actively advocate childlessness. The specter of the woman without a child can invoke an image of the woman who hates children, the archetypal anti-mother, the non-nurturing female. The fear of what women might do unless anchored by motherhood seems to underlie the raging abortion debate—perhaps women would no longer have children, or perhaps they would abandon men, like the childless wife anthropologist Margaret Mead discovered in a folktale who ran away from her husband but left an empty skin behind to deceive him into believing that she was still there. The concept of choice took on another layer of meaning in the 1980s as well, as antinatalist and pronatalist forces struggled: The issue seemed to be women's independence.

As this backlash against reproductive freedom gained momentum during the 1980s, at times it seemed as if it was needed to push aging baby boomers into parenthood. The percentage of those permanently without children was slowly rising, setting records in terms of absolute numbers, and there were predictions that a third of white women born in the late 1940s and 1950s would remain childfree forever. Some observers expressed alarm that a so-called baby bust, or birth dearth, would damage the economy, the nation, and even Western civilization. But the ticking of millions of biological clocks was heard, and the pronatalist pressure seemed to have its desired effect: Toward the end of the decade many women in the large postwar generation stopped postponing motherhood. In 1988 more first births were recorded than in any previous year since the United States Census Bureau began noting them in 1950, and a huge number of babies was born, almost as many as at the height of the baby boom in the 1950s. It became evident that motherhood as an institution was as difficult to reject as to reform, even under the influence of feminism.

In contrast to the previous decade, when backers of women's liberation rejected biology-as-destiny arguments, many feminists, especially those who gave birth late in life, joined in the pronatalist frenzy. Elayne Rapping, a mother and professor of communications at Adelphi University, theorized that, after the loss of the ERA and with other disappointments at home and at work during the decade, many women felt that all they had left were their bodies and their biological offspring. As they tried to dignify their retreat from the public arena, a theory arose called *difference feminism*, which emphasizes physiological differences between the genders, versus the earlier, more established, *equality feminism*, which downplays them. Backers of "difference" urged special protections for mothers, whereas supporters of "equality" minimized gender needs in the hope that fathers and others would co-parent. Like neoconservatives, the former went on to idealize motherhood as the embodiment of moral superiority, to the exclusion of males and nonmothers. Many women without children felt let down by feminist mothers, one of whom, Jane Lazarre, called the childless woman a "dark lady."

Under the onslaught of pronatalist dogma, women without children "apologized again and again for ever having uttered a callow, classist, immature, or narcissistic word against mothering," observed Ann Snitow. But feminists, mothers or not, did not express anger at the problems of motherhood nor at the prevalence of pronatalism. Why not? Snitow wondered. Because, she concluded, mothers feared being charged with lack of motherliness and nonmothers feared being accused of sour grapes. She also observed that those women who remembered the courage and openness of the early 1970s were "heartbroken" by the heavy silence a decade later. My own journey from the 1950s through the 1980s was one of stagnation, then hope, and then hibernation as the social and political mood shifted around me. I did not feel heartbroken, but I did feel a sense of nostalgia for a time when so many women seemed electrified by the potentials of their lives. In the 1980s I certainly felt a sense of being culturally alone, which I associated with being childless. However, I would find out this was a false perception.

EXAMINING THE CHOICE, WHY IT ARISES

Searching for the reply to the riddle of what women really want, Sir Gawain, a knight in King Arthur's court, discovered that it was the privilege of choice. Yet despite our desire for choice and control over our lives, the option about childbearing remains troublesome for many women; one even called it "the agony and the ecstasy of choicefullness." Two decades ago the New York Radical Feminists held a meeting about motherhood and concluded that giving birth could be "either monstrously self-indulgent or ruinously self-destructive." Social scientists, who give little credence to the role of raw instinct, have discovered that the decision to be or not to be a mother is immensely complicated, and that their subjects reveal as many reasons for avoiding as for embracing motherhood. One person's motivations for parenthood—such as wishing for a role, or for influence, identity, intimacy, pleasure, or immortality—can be another's reasons for *not* becoming a parent. Whether or not to give birth concerns millions of American nulliparas: the 42 percent of females in their childbearing years who have not yet given birth. Yet it is a quandary that neither modern science nor menopause can necessarily resolve. As I recall my own attempts to make an intelligent and heartfelt choice, I also examine the cryptic messages about giving birth from the historical past, the stark and unsatisfying options females face today, the various influences on the decision, and the differing ways women decide about motherhood.

The serious questioning of the eventuality of motherhood is for many a self-conscious, confusing, and interminable process, especially for lesbians and other single women, who sometimes have to settle insemination and custody concerns. Few take the advice of mothers like Margaret Mead, who suggested that potential parents become foster, adoptive, or godparents before becoming natural ones, or of Shirley L. Radl, author of *Mother's Day Is Over*, who advised them to interrupt their careers for a year, stay home, and read books about children before giving birth. No body of philosophical thought exists about the volition. Philosophy professor Margaret A. Simons of Southern Illinois University has described the childbearing choice as a "new feature of moral development," and a modern dilemma of young women. Simons, a wife who chose not to conceive, has observed that the option "can present a woman with one of the most profound decisions of her life, requiring tremendous emotional as well as intellectual effort to resolve."

For my own part, on the last day of July 1976, as I approached my thirty-fourth birthday, I suddenly decided that I wanted a baby. I noted in my journal that day that I had never *not* wanted a child, but my ambivalence had made me avoid the issue for a decade. This realization, which I experienced with clarity and certainty, was, no doubt, related to my imminent birthday as well as to my ennui at work and my eagerness for something new. I did not perceive my wish as a biological imperative but as an abrupt resolution of an old impasse. As I struggled to explain this impulse, I discovered it was powered by curiosity and the drive for connectedness. I noted in my journal my desire for more intimacy ("a close, loving link with another"), physicality (for my body "to prove itself in this way"), and experience (so as not "to go through life wondering what I've missed"). I added that "I'm very bored with living my life for myself," and I expressed the hope that motherhood would give me "a new perspective on life." It was also an appealing prospect at the time to lose myself in another being's needs as a way to abandon my frustrated ambition and, at the same time, to get attention and approval from my friends and family.

Doubts and problems immediately arose in my mind, however. Although I assumed I would be a caring and conscientious mother the way my own had been, I doubted that my longtime boyfriend would be a willing or active father since, I noted, he stonewalled what I called "baby talk." While I was bumping up against biological limits, I sensed that he was frightened by fatherhood as well as desperately intent on becoming successful. In the privacy of my journal I toyed with the idea of abandoning birth control, imagining the way an unplanned pregnancy would get his full attention. I thought he was a brilliant and promising novelist, and we seemed at first to share similar ideas and dreams; in fact, he felt like my lost brother. I also deeply appreciated his devotion, if not his abrasiveness, toward me. I liked our sense of being adventurous comrades, exploring Manhattan and traveling together, but now our independent pact seemed problematic. "We'd have to get married and we haven't even broached that subject yet," I wrote. I had other worries as well. I was concerned about being bored and overburdened by caring for a child alone. I dreaded that the birth of an infant would "force division-of-labor roles—traditional ones—something I've always avoided." I was acutely aware of the sym-

bolism of moving a baby crib into—and my typewriter out of—
my little white writing room in our apartment. I also worried
that not writing for an unknown number of months or years
might destroy my tentative confidence as well as my journalistic connections. After pages of soul-searching in my journal,
I finally asked myself: "Is the sudden desire to have a baby a rationalization to leave my job, to acquire a new identity and purpose, an escape from freedom?"

While my agonizing over this choice—and ultimately opting
out of motherhood—might seem to be an elitist prerogative, or
what has been derided as "childfree chic" among privileged
women like myself, childlessness exists in all socioeconomic
groups. It is true that this dilemma between chosen work and
child rearing does not seem as troublesome for all women: They
include the very wealthy, who can hire nannies for their children; working-class or single mothers, who must work for
wages; and the very poor, who qualify for welfare and cannot afford abortions. (The United States population is growing because of the fertility rates of immigrants, especially Hispanic
women, who average 2.6 children, compared to 2 for native-
born white women and 2.3 for black women.) Since the end of
slavery, African-American women have been discouraged from
reproducing and pressured to accept sterilization, giving childbirth overtones of racial affirmation. Yet in the 1940s, college-
educated black wives, especially those with Ph.D.'s, were likely
to remain childless. Even during the pronatalist 1950s, people
of all classes with high hopes and meager means decided
against motherhood. In the 1960s, a group of black women
signed a "Statement on Birth Control," in which they declared
the right to decide whether to have or not to have a baby. In response to the argument by black men that contraception is a
form of genocide, they reasoned that "birth control is the free-

dom to *fight* genocide of black women and children" because those with few or no children are more empowered.

Today the sociological pattern is the same: In a large 1985 study of male and female high school students from poor southern families, the 16 percent of girls (both white and black) who wanted no children were those with lofty ambitions. Even though black women who do not wish to have children often feel intense guilt and defensiveness about it, their childless rate is now two-thirds the white one. Carolyn M. Morell, a professor of social work at Niagara University, found that the lives of the childfree wives she studied for her Ph.D. dissertation also affirmed that childlessness was not a class issue: The three quarters from poor or working-class backgrounds had all become professionals. "And they often connected their upward mobility directly to the decision to remain childless," Morell observed. In February 1991 another scholar, Karen Seccombe, published similar findings: Childlessness "is no longer simply an elite phenomenon among financially independent or nontraditional women," she concluded.

In the midst of my struggle, I had no idea how others had resolved their conflicts in the past or even in the present. I perused Dr. Benjamin Spock's *Infant and Child Care* but felt frustrated that he never mentioned working mothers. I could imagine the losses the birth of a child might bring, but the rewards seemed less tangible. Meanwhile, I pursued other possibilities, including writing the book about Georgia O'Keeffe, since my book proposal had found an enthusiastic editor. Yet after I went to the wedding of a joyously pregnant bride, my desire for a child was rekindled. "So now I'm eager to write a book and have a baby!" I declared in my journal. "The big question is their effect on each other. If I have a baby before I finish writing the book, would it help or hurt? . . . The ideal thing is to fin-

ish writing the book and then have the kid—but who knows
how long it would take to finish the book, and I'll be thirty-five
next September. I worry about having a baby and a book at the
same time—that I'll lose motivation and ability to concentrate
on the book or that I won't be able to concentrate on the baby.
But," I finally admitted, "my concerns are more about the book
than the baby."

At times I imagined myself pregnant, proud, and strong in a
bright red sweater, but I feared that the reality would be different. In the absence of help from the child's father or a nanny,
the indifference of my employer, or the unavailability of my faraway mother, motherhood appeared as self-immolation. It
would mean, I feared, turning my back on who I had become
during the past decade and beginning again; my interests, abilities, ambitions, even my identity would mean little in the realm
of full-time maternity. Historically, motherhood was considered a way to survive under patriarchy, but now the tables had
turned: It was my earning ability, not my fertility, that
promised more security. My self-preservation instinct effectively inhibited my life-giving desire at that moment. I was
proud of my professional accomplishments—minor by the
standards of many males my age, but major compared to those
of my female relatives. Just starting to find my footing as a
writer, I did not want to give up a chance to do work that
promised adventure, challenge, fulfillment, and more independence than I had ever known.

Although I resolved to put off pregnancy as a way to play for
time, the reasons seemed deeply personal until I undertook
the research for this book. How did my female ancestors feel
about childbearing? All women suffer from collective amnesia,

asserts historian Gerda Lerner, due to the lack of intellectual continuity among females throughout the ages. "Endlessly, generation after generation of Penelopes rewove the unraveled fabric only to unravel it again," she has written. As I reflected on this fact, I realized that female wisdom about whether or not to bear children has long been distorted, lost, or ignored by history. Few old wives' or fairy tales concern the female who defines herself outside of motherhood. Furthermore, although I identified intriguing and admirable women in history without children, their attitudes toward their childlessness were mostly unwritten or forgotten; I wondered if they were courageous, or even conscious of the implications of their actions. My curiosity aroused, I persisted and discovered a few clues in old courtship letters and then within the recesses of my own memory.

Our eighteenth- and nineteenth-century ancestors in America were intensely private in their diaries and letters about even the existence of pregnancy, and few ruminated about their reasons for desiring or avoiding marriage and motherhood. Even in works of fiction they often veiled their viewpoints, as in the case of the well-born Catharine Sedgwick, an unmarried nineteenth-century woman whose sixth and last novel, *Married or Single?*, published in 1857, indirectly attempted to lessen the stigma of spinsterhood. Sedgwick, who had turned down at least six marriage proposals, lived a gratifying life as a popular writer and devoted sister and aunt. Her final novel is, like many other narratives penned by women, unreflective of the reality of her life: Although its characters debate the pros and cons of marriage, the story ends conventionally as the heroine reluctantly marries. Yet a subtle, subversive intent was at work by simply raising the question of whether or not to marry. While few female novelists created rebellious feminine protagonists, probably because of pressures from publishers and cautious self-censorship, writers like Jane Austen, Sarah Orne Jewett, and Edith Wharton did quietly question the status quo by simply suggesting the possibility of choice.

I found a rare exception to the usual historical reticence about childlessness in the literate and lengthy courtship letters written in the late nineteenth century by a young Boston couple, Ella Lyman and Dr. Richard Clarke Cabot, who came from intellectual and established Boston families. Ambivalent about giving up her independence to marry, Lyman finally did so after almost six years of courtship. During their engagement, she and Cabot worked on a prenuptial document that they called "the paper on marriage." Then, in 1893, the twenty-nine-year-old physician suggested to his fiancée the unusual prospect of a childless marriage: "In reading over the paper on marriage I feel the duty of pointing out one whole set of considerations which perhaps you have never thought of and which will more and more come to be a factor in every marriage choice—an essentially modern factor.

"I mean marriage without children.

"You assume, as almost everybody does, that the earlier years of married life will of necessity be taken up in the care of children. You ignore the possibility, *which lies wholly in our own hands,* of not having any children. I conceive that two people might find they could be better servants of God by living and working together in a house of their own and belonging specially to each other, who yet found it expedient not to have any children—either because they could not afford it, or preferred to carry on their own work each of them in a way that would leave no time for children. I have thought of this for years and talked it over with married people of both sexes, but I never suggested it to you before because I thought as you considered marriage longer you would think of it yourself and come to the idea more easily in that way than in this."

He went on: "If anyone says that marriage is justified only for the sake of children and exists for that and means that only, I deny it in toto. I am very sure that there are many who need marriage in the sense of a close and constant partnership such as can be best obtained by living and working together, and for whom there is no reason why they should not decide not to have children. The idea is so familiar to me and I am so sure that it is rational and will be carried out, that it does not seem to me revolutionary and outlandish."

What is interesting in Cabot's letter to his wife-to-be is his visionary thinking. The son of a biographer of Ralph Waldo Emerson, Cabot had graduated from Harvard summa cum laude in 1889 with strong philosophical, rationalist, and religious interests. As a medical doctor, he was undoubtedly aware of modern contraception methods and the possibility of preventing pregnancy. His proposal indicates his idealism about his work and his respect for Ella Lyman's intellect, which had been sharpened during two years at Radcliffe, as well as his desire for a deep intimacy with his future bride. His letter also reflects an idea that was and remains radical—a mother's and father's equal responsibility for the daily care of their children. This is particularly intriguing, since the young couple could have afforded a governess, and in any case, child rearing was always assumed to be a wife's concern, an activity that affected her life much more than his.

"Now I want to tell you just what I think of marriage without children," the twenty-seven-year-old Ella Lyman immediately wrote, in an open-minded and unsentimental response. "It hurts to think about it, as all things hurt which are deep down and must be pulled up and handled somewhat brutally, but that is no matter," she began. She was in the difficult position of those whose mates are uninterested in parenthood, but she was willing to examine her maternal desires honestly. Her immediate response was to be protective of her beloved mother, a member of the well-known Lowell family who had given birth to seven children. "I want you to realize, and realize without condemning her, that if Mamma saw your letter she could never forgive you. I say this not because I do not think it only right and wholesome to be frank . . . but because we have no right to condemn or ignore the other feeling till we have wholly understood it." After that caveat, she concurred with her fiancé that "marriage does not and ought not to exist merely for the sake of children, that it may be right to marry with the intention of not having children, that there is no reason for not taking our lives into our own hands in this respect as well as in every other, that this changes the relative sacrifice which women make as compared with men, all this I agree to and believe."

I was surprised by the couple's enlightened thinking about such an emotionally laden area as parenthood, and by their belief that it could be governed by free will. As I turned to the contemporary canon, I found disturbingly little that was positive or substantial about the childbearing choice. What little information exists must be gleaned by reading between the lines of letters or observing the texture of others' lives, and it is often an equivocal and ineffective counterweight to pronatalism. In fact, much modern thinking and theorizing, like the Freudian tenet that maternity is necessary for female maturity, is destructive. In the early 1970s, I underlined a passage about the gradual emergence of childlessness as a respectable option in *The Future of Motherhood*, a book written by feminist sociologist and mother Jessie Bernard. She noted that human behavior often changes before the rules for it do and, she wrote, "we are only now working out the script for nonmotherhood." The continuing muteness about serious aspects of motherhood and nonmotherhood makes the decision immensely more difficult. The playwright Tina Howe, who wrote a drama in 1973 called *Birth and Afterbirth* about a debate between a mother and a nonmother, recently observed that what was once a public dialogue has become an interior monologue. So all too often the decision not to give birth—the rejection of what traditionally has been considered the fulfillment of femininity—is made alone, uneasily, and with little conviction about the outcome. Many of us without children believe that our behavior makes perfect sense in the contexts of our lives, but we remain uncertain as to why. During her indecisive years poet Irena Klepfisz explained that "I was unable to articulate to myself or to others that I was following other instincts." We have no support from collective knowledge and thus little confidence in our childlessness.

Our own daughterhoods are imperfect guideposts in our choice because of the powerful influence and idiosyncratic nature of each woman's mothering. Sara Ruddick, a philosopher and mother, has written: "It is because we are *daughters*, nurtured and trained by women, that we early receive maternal love with special attention to its implications for our bodies, our passions, and our ambitions. We are alert to the values and costs of maternal practices whether we are determined to engage in them or avoid them." Certainly as an older sibling I was vividly aware of my own mother's experience of motherhood. I intuited her pleasure in her pregnancies, but I also felt her anxiety and anger after her babies were born. As I remembered her earlier gaiety, I felt her sadness as my own.

When we wonder if we want to be mothers, it is difficult to locate alternate scripts because our mothers are usually disqualified. Unless a natal mother has more nonmaternal than maternal virtues, it is easier to go along with the known experience of our mothers and grandmothers than to emulate other women's stories. Scholar Lorie E. Hill has made the interesting point that since most of us are raised by females who have children, "no children grow up and experience the day-to-day life of a childless adult." In my own case, the reality of my mother's daily life was far more important to me than all the stories I read about childless heroines like Florence Nightingale. So as children, we are sometimes strangely blind to those around us who live alternate and appealing lives—childless relatives, cultural figures like Martha Graham, or fictitious characters like Auntie Mame. We may have aunts without children, but our relationships with them are not primal; an infertile friend of mine has ignored the appealing model of a beloved great-aunt who was married but mysteriously not a mother. Even Georgia O'Keeffe, who had a number of affectionate and admirable maiden aunts, so identified with her mother that she assumed, until well into her thirties, that she would be a mother too. Then, during the year her older husband Alfred Stieglitz gave her a solo show and his daughter was institutionalized for postpartum depression, she made peace with her childlessness.

After we find ourselves living lives that are diametrically different from our mothers', we may remember early influences that were instrumental. Poet Honor Moore, the daughter of a bishop and the eldest of nine children, recalled that the unmarried people at the family's Christmas dinner table had an exciting "different aura . . . I thought it would be all right to be like that—to go through life trailing that sort of mystery." Others remember grown-ups without children as giving them more intense and imaginative attention than other people's parents. I interviewed women who recollected glimpses of alluring nonparental lives, like the exotic peripatetic travels of the wife of a foreign service officer or the exuberant but dedicated life of a woman seeking the Episcopal priesthood. Sister Rosemarie Greco, the eldest in an Italian family, found the nuns—doctors, principals, poets, and missionaries—at her Catholic school better educated as well as more powerful and adventurous than the mothers she knew. "They were in missions," she recalled, "and they were taking canoes across dangerous rivers to reach people in the jungle."

In my case, I have belatedly understood that a strong influence in my early life was a grandmother who was a mother but not motherly in any ordinary sense. My maternal, step, and paternal grandmothers had very different personalities, but they did have one thing in common—none of them tended their children after they gave birth in the early decades of the twentieth century. My father's mother, Gaga, a tall, dominating matriarch with sharp, hooded, hazel eyes and soft, wrinkly, fuzzy cheeks, was the third daughter of a Massachusetts lumberman. The former Miss Helen Josephine Sawyer often traveled with her sisters: A 1940 photograph shows four elegantly dressed matrons in elaborate hats and pearls with a grinning Clark Gable and a demure Claudette Colbert on a Hollywood set. In her youth she had been a golf champion, and as she aged she retained the physicality of an athlete and an abundance of what she called "pep." She also had a vigorous creative drive, and she carved in wood and painted landscapes of rural Rhode Island with skill and seriousness. Motherliness had never seemed to interest her. On the governess's day off, for instance, she would have her chauffeur stop for a female friend and her children, then drive them all to the zoo. The mothers would talk in the backseat while the chauffeur entertained the children.

With me she was different, however, perhaps because she

had become a little lonely. After she lost her husband and I lost my father, she energetically moved into the void in my young life. I spent many weekends with her, playing with an old doll's house and climbing into her big bed in the mornings, where she read children's books to me until her maid brought breakfast on a tray. She told me tales about her nineteenth-century childhood and showed me photographs and artifacts from her travels—an embroidered oriental robe, a collection of jade elephants, a wooden model of a Chinese junk. I loved to day-dream at her mirrored dressing table and adorn myself with beads and bangles, especially the tinkling anklets from India. On Sundays, the maid's day off, my grandmother, who did not know how to cook, made popcorn for me in an explosion of noise and excitement.

Her one anxiety was about upholding proper social appear-ances, a concern that gradually put a distance between us as I became a recalcitrant teenager. After I left for boarding school, she wrote me weekly letters in her powerful black script about my cousins, her garden, and the weather; the reg-ularity of the letters revealed the real message—that our al-liance was intact. But even her conventionality eventually seemed questionable to me. She worried aloud when I did not marry at an early age, yet when I introduced a proper beau to her in my twenties, she forgot to put in her false front tooth, as if to scare him off. She represented a forceful form of femi-ninity to me, a benevolent contramother, an Amazonian fairy godmother, a female who did exactly as she wished in a sense of spirited willfullness, a woman whom I had never seen hu-miliated. In old age she still towered over me on long thin legs, and at the time of her death, at the age of ninety-two, only her knees and her memory for names had failed her. I came to realize that her legacy to me, nurtured by our many hours together, was profound—an example of nonmaternal and independent womanliness.

As I agonized about whether or not to give birth, my paralysis, I later realized, was understandable. For more than a century the necessity of choosing between a calling or children has been a theme in the lives of middle-class women in America and Europe. Mother Nature, capitalism, patriarchy, and other forces have been blamed for this conflict. In the 1970s it certainly was an issue for me, since I was existing in a twilight zone between the ashes of patriarchy and the advent of co-parenting. Recently, when I began to examine young women's lives in America today, I initially felt hopeful that many of them had been able to avoid the choice between motherhood and the childless state by doing it all. But I also felt concerned that the balancing act seemed so difficult to pull off.

In the past the decision to marry, which went along with the assumption of continual childbearing, was not always easy for an educated or exceptional young woman. Boston intellectual Margaret Fuller, who in 1848 at the age of thirty-eight had a son by an Italian revolutionary while reporting on Italy's war for independence, observed: " 'Tis an evil lot to have a man's ambition and a woman's heart." American feminist writer and mother Charlotte Perkins Gilman, who lived from 1860 to 1935, wrote about the educated woman's unsatisfactory choice between "world service" or "home service." Martha Carey Thomas, who became the president of Bryn Mawr College, confessed to a niece in the 1870s about an excruciating choice between her work as an educator and a man she loved: "I knew myself well enough to realize that I could not give up my life's work, but I thought of him for three years night and day and then suddenly I was free." Around the time of the First World War, artist Wanda H. Gág wanted children out of curiosity, the desire to draw them, and the impulse "to reinvest my aesthetic urge in another human being"; after struggling for several years between art or offspring, she chose artistic over physical creation, since drawing was her greatest joy, while the pleasures of motherhood were hypothetical.

For his part, reformer and novelist Floyd Dell—who lived in Greenwich Village in the early twentieth century, where he had a love affair with the poet Edna St. Vincent Millay—saw his female friends facing "an indecent choice between childlessness and something too much resembling martyrdom." Around the same time, in 1905, A Childless Wife explained that she had desired offspring but changed her mind after marriage. She and her husband were social workers who earned little money; if she left her job to raise children, she wrote, it would "destroy both my earning power and my social usefulness" and, she added, her husband would also have to give up his humanitarian work in order to support them. "I hope and work for a social readjustment which will give to the woman of the future all that I have and motherhood as well," she continued. "And, meanwhile, I deny the right of any one to criticise [sic] me who is not doing something to lighten the pressure of those social conditions which have forced this dilemma not only upon me, but upon thousands of American women."

In 1924 psychologist Lorine Livingston Pruette published a survey of almost four hundred middle-class teenage girls in New York and Tennessee in which she found that 61 percent desired vocations and the rest wanted to be housewives. The girls had no conception of combining work and mothering: "She must, whatever her choice, subdue or thwart one part of her being in order to satisfy the other part," Pruette wrote; Pruette later advocated part-time work as a way for wives to pursue other aspirations. Around the same time, seventeen professional women—lawyers, artists, journalists, and educators—wrote personal essays for *The Nation* magazine. In those essays it was revealed that only five of the women were mothers because most were unable to reconcile children with a career. In a 1930 book, *The Retreat from Parenthood*, Jean Ayling addressed the falling birthrate among educated Britons and called for a restructuring of professions to make parenting easier. Also an advocate of a "Child Rearing Organization," she argued that children's interests "are seriously damaged by the fact that so many women are presented with the choice between career and cradle; and that the insistence on a sterility qualification for women who undertake professional work is as prejudicial as the insistence on whole-time motherhood for those that breed." Then in *The Second Sex*, published in 1949, Simone de Beauvoir, who considered it impossible to combine a career and child raising in France prior to the Second World War, also decried the necessity for choice. A few years later, Swedish sociologist Alva Myrdal and English writer Viola Klein suggested in *Women's Two Roles*, published in 1956, that women do one, then the other—tend children until the youngest is nine or so, then pursue meaningful work outside the home—but they ignored the impact of this long delay on the ability to find rewarding jobs.

Over the years, the decision to have children has become less absolutist, since it has become easier to marry and have fewer children. Twice as many accomplished women in *Who's Who in America* were childless in 1926 as a generation later. Nonetheless, law, government, and custom still assume that motherhood and work are separate spheres. In the mid-1970s Adrienne Rich wrote that the modern woman "has with good reason felt that the choice was an inescapable either/or: motherhood or individuation, motherhood or creativity, motherhood or freedom." She continued: "The depths of this conflict, between self-preservation and maternal feelings, can be experienced—I have experienced it—as a primal agony." During that decade, when I was in my thirties, I recall explaining to a female friend my devil's dilemma between writing and mothering without a supportive husband; as a writer with a child, I would have more time to write and the ability to live inexpensively; as a mother who wanted to write, I would have less time for writing but more need for money. Facing alternatives that young men in my circle did not, it was during those years that I often encountered male hostility or indifference by merely *naming* my impasse.

Whatever path we take, it separates us from other women. The housewife is likely to disapprove of the young mother who holds a job, condemning her materialism or ambition. The woman without children may envy or criticize a colleague who has them, imagining that the other woman is either supremely competent or neglectful of her job or family. Both the stay-at-home mother and the childless careerist pity the exhausted employed mother of young children, but they are also threatened by her. Although the full-time mother and the nullipara are alike in the sense that they do not try to reconcile two roles, they feel their differences acutely. Like myself, those who do one or the other find it impossible or unappealing to combine both for reasons of temperament, opportunity, inclination, or ability. Meanwhile, many mothers tend to deprecate nonmothers for being selfish, emotionless, or unwomanly while secretly envying their privacy and freedom. Poet and mother Sylvia Plath was one who scorned the childless woman's supposed single-mindedness and high standards—"Perfection is terrible. It cannot have children. It tamps the womb." A working mother, for her part, may have veiled contempt for those who do one thing or the other. She scorns those who, she believes, take the easy way out, but she comforts herself with the thought that they will eventually have their regrets.

Antipathy can quickly develop among friends, colleagues, even sisters, after one becomes a mother. Mothers and non-mothers she knew "could not tolerate each other's ambivalence" about their ways of life, explained Jyl Lynn Felman, a lesbian short-story writer. "In our terror we required absolute loyalty without question." In my own case, I published my first book, the O'Keeffe biography, and my sister had her first baby within months of each other, events that were equally meaningful to each of us. As my manuscript grew, I felt an increasing sense of satisfaction, even elation. Meanwhile, my sister told me about her awe as her abdomen slowly swelled. My moments of anxiety about publication were similar to hers about the approaching responsibility that would edge out her artwork. But while her gestation appeared to require patience and passivity, mine demanded the forging of a tenacious willfulness. Publication finally ended my three years of intense and grueling work and abruptly made my time, though temporarily empty, my own again. For my sister, childbirth commenced a rigorous routine, perhaps the hardest work she had ever done, laced with marvelous moments. When her daughter was a few months old, I flew from New York to California to visit them. One day, while the three of us were visiting an art museum, I was thrilled to see the first copy of my book in the museum bookshop. A little later, as my sister nursed her daughter in the ladies' room, she suddenly blurted out that "a baby is better than a book." I was deeply wounded by her remark, particularly since I had encouraged her to have a child and she saw my difficult dilemma. Years later she explained that she had been frightened at becoming a mother and was jealous of me.

During the decade of the 1980s, the do-both ideology began to gain ground among middle-class women; the stagnating male wage made it imperative for both feminist and old-fashioned wives and mothers to earn money. In fact, with roots in European and American social feminism, balancing work and family had been advocated by feminists ranging from the eighteenth-century Englishwoman Mary Wollstonecraft to the founder of the National Organization for Women, Betty Friedan. It is interesting to note that the black mother and grandmother who has always done it all has been regarded as an emasculating matriarch, whereas the white mother with a job is presented by the media as a glamorous and indefatigable young woman with briefcase in one hand and baby on her hip. Many women blossomed in their expanding roles, but others had trouble. My sister wept when she realized she would never have the uninterrupted hours to be a painter; sometimes she also felt guilty when she took time away from her children to pursue a landscaping degree. And Sylvia Ann Hewlett, an economist and mother, admitted that she had failed maternally and professionally—not dramatically or drastically, but in terms of "painful trade-offs, underachievement, hundreds of small, disappointing compromises."

As I struggled to understand how I could do everything, to stretch my income and my time to embrace both a baby and a book, I was haunted by the story of Sylvia Plath. In the 1950s she had desperately wanted to have children with her husband, British poet Ted Hughes, believing that if she didn't, her writing would be "a hollow and failing substitute for real life, real feeling, instead of a pleasant extra, a bonus flowering and fruiting." After her daughter and son were born, however, her marriage ended. These three events eliminated her inhibitions and enabled her to mine intense negative emotions, thus allowing her to produce her most powerful poems. Poetry was no longer "a pleasant extra"—it had become her reason for existence. "Read something interesting about Sylvia Plath," I noted in my journal in early 1981, "that motherhood aided her final burst of ego and magnificent poetry. Of course, then she killed herself. As if after having the poetry pour out in a pure stream—her experience of seeing God—it was impossible for her to return to reality. Did the burden of child care and shame of abandonment enter in? The fear the flow would stop? Normality seemed unbearable after being touched?" I did not know the answers, but I felt chilled by their implications.

Female grief, guilt, anxiety, and anger seem to emerge from suppressed feelings of envy, fear, frustration, and resentment—emanating from each woman's dissatisfaction with the limitations of her own life. In her efforts to be a good mother, my sister worried about being considered a "dinosaur" for staying home and a "doormat" when she postponed her career. The divisions between women—including whether we are financially dependent or not—remain debilitating. "We should expect and willingly acknowledge the differences between us, in our senses of who we are and what constitutes our woman-identity, without succumbing to the temptation to justify our own identity by denying our sisters," philosopher Margaret Simons has written. "We should celebrate the resultant spectrum of values with its vibrant oppositions as a sign of our flourishing explosion out of the narrow confines of our traditional sphere, even when those values at the same time express an authentic preference for motherhood over competitive careerism, for nurturant woman-loving lesbian identity over heterosexual marriage, for professional involvement in social change over domesticity, and for loving our loving-men over lesbian separatism." Even though the differences between women are deeply entrenched

in our country, we can attempt to eradicate them within ourselves and with others.

Inevitably a choice is made by each childless woman through
inner conviction, delay and default, or acceptance of infecundity. A third of the intentionally childfree are certain at a young
age that they never want to become mothers, according to
Jean E. Veevers, a Canadian sociologist. They find the decision
easy—it is seemingly made for them—but they have difficulty
defending it. As young girls they felt an inchoate but unshakable certainty about not becoming mothers that probably arose
from their mothers' experiences as well as their own inborn
temperaments and emerging identities. One such woman I
spoke with, a married African-American literary agent, made
this choice around age six because, as the third of four siblings,
she felt overwhelmed by her family's turmoil. Another, a petite,
pretty novelist and wife, suddenly announced to her mother at
the age of fifteen, in a moment of utter confidence, that she
was not going to have children; sure of her daughter's sincerity,
and perhaps regarding her statement as a personal rejection,
her mother ran from the room crying. Another woman thought
about having children for the first time after she eloped in the
1930s and then firmly rejected the idea. "There was never any
real choice at all," she said. "It was always that I wanted freedom, and I didn't want to be tied down by a child."
   Women whose motherliness is integral to their sense of self
have no trouble embracing motherhood. One of my sisters-in-
law, a mother of three, believes with utter conviction that she
was born to bear and care for children. Her intense desire to
nurture small beings is an expression of her innermost nature,
and her chosen work as an elementary school teacher affirms it,

although she prefers to be a stay-at-home mother. Her strong maternity has an inevitability to it: As a child she mothered her younger sister and the smallest sisters and brothers of her playmates. When she became a teenager, her obsession with her yet-to-be-born children took her to Vermont cemeteries where she looked for old-fashioned names for them on tombstones. As she moved through her adolescent years, she felt that if she did not become a mother, she would rather die.

Far more common are ambivalent women like myself, a group that is growing. In 1992, 15 percent of American women between the ages of eighteen and thirty-four were still unsure whether they would give birth, while another 13 percent never even bothered to answer the census-takers' question about their intentions; statisticians regard such hesitancy as tantamount to permanent childlessness. It is hardest for the ambivalent, since the uncertainty can last from menarche to menopause, the better part of four decades. Yet it is detrimental to vacillate too much and become childless by default: A 1984 study found that "delayed parents" (people who had not yet become parents) were more dissatisfied than either parents or the childfree. My conclusion evolved erratically over the course of ten years, from my mid-thirties to my mid-forties. "My pattern involves rich dreams, a lot of initiating action, cautious movement and preparation toward change, then either change or last-minute withdrawal," I mused in my private papers when I was thirty-four.

Deeply conflicted, in early January 1981, at the age of thirty-eight, my desire for a child was aroused once again at a heartfelt, candlelit Christmas christening. In the letdown after finishing my book, I again wondered if I should attempt motherhood. My husband had softened his opposition to parenthood, but gynecological troubles had raised the possibility that childbirth might be problematic. Nevertheless, I felt a reckless impulse to try. "One night I go to bed with a diaphragm in, the next night I go without—I lose courage, gain courage, the rational and realist is in charge one night and the hopeful and emotional the next," I confessed in my journal. I again expressed the egocentric hope that a child would revitalize my life; enveloped by ennui, I was eager to experience creative energy once more. "I feel the impulse comes out of strength—a feeling that I am a strong womanly woman—as well as from a touch of intellectual and emotional boredom," I wrote. "Perhaps that's another reason I desire to become pregnant—to be creative on that front at least, to have my own genuine experience instead of vicariously living another's as a biographer, and to slow down the intellectual pressures (everyone is always asking me what the next book will be). I want to get to that other place from where I can launch the next book with total self-expression—with passion, fascination, excitement, commitment." Looking back, I am perplexed by my idea that mothering would lead me back to writing, since few mothers of small children manage both well, but I would never give it a try. After I celebrated my third wedding anniversary, I noted in my journal: "Yesterday I felt all kinds of twinges in my womb, and my breasts were very sensitive and I wondered if I was pregnant. Then my senses came back to me and I realized that in less than twenty-four hours all that couldn't happen, a microscopic blob couldn't do it, and I was going to get my period on the early side."

As we try to decipher coded cultural myths and messages about motherhood, the ones scholar Jean F. O'Barr has likened to "medieval maps," factors like birth order are surprisingly influential: firstborns, including only children, are twice as likely to be childless as other siblings. As a firstborn myself, I find this intriguing; it is sometimes said that we are more driven than younger siblings because we carry parental aspirations, but perhaps we are just over- or underexposed to the problems of child rearing. Among the ambivalent, half the couples in one study easily agreed on childlessness; among the others, the strongest and least unsure partner had his or her way. Those with the most tangled emotions rely on logic to come to a resolution, like Ella Lyman or the Arizona wife who proudly defended her choice as a rational and intelligent result of "hard, grueling work," a process that one observer has called "self-understanding and self-discipline." Social scientists have classified the intentionally childless as repudiators who decide against parenthood, or postponers and aficionados who affirm their present way of life. Several have noted that the latter take many affirmative actions before rejecting motherhood. Social worker Carolyn Morell even resists using words like "choice," "postponement," and "forgo" in the discussion as too presumptive of the inevitability of motherhood and the inferiority of childlessness. Psychoanalyst Roberta Joseph, for instance, explained that it had taken her years to create an ideal life; the decision not to change it (by having a child) was "a less dramatic choice than to change it radically, but a profound choice nonetheless."

When I was given a prescription for the pill in 1965, I believed that the option to conceive was entirely in my hands, but it eventually became easier to avoid conception than to allow it. A number of women, both mothers and nonmothers, have testified that they never felt their choices were made with complete freedom. One believes that her drift into childlessness was a result of many smaller decisions as well as chance, compulsions, and circumstances. "If a choice has been made, it is at such a deep level that it feels like no choice at all," she said. Also, there is no real option if there are few or poor alternatives to motherhood, or if the downside threatens to drown us. Those of us who feel that we are connecting with inner convictions and core values, that we are fully exercising volition, have fewer regrets. Paradoxically, it can be liberating to finally free ourselves from the choice or the illusion of choice. Eventually, after I was in my forties and in a second marriage, I determined neither to block nor encourage fertility but to let Mother Nature decide for me. Perhaps I bravely abdicated control because, biologically at least, I sensed it was too late. Finally I arrived with a sense of inevitability at the age of fifty as a nulligravida, a woman who has never been pregnant.

THREE

SEARCHING HISTORY, REMEMBERING OUR MAIDEN AUNTS

As many of us approach middle age without children, it is important to place ourselves in historical perspective, to find relevant female ancestors, to enlarge the frame, and ultimately to connect to a feminine tradition outside of motherhood. Once I felt as though I was outside of history because I had no child to give me a sense of continuity with the past or connection with the present. I felt somewhat apart from the human family, uprooted and ungrounded, and sometimes even ashamed of myself. When I undertook this study, I decided to search my own genealogy for foremothers with whom I could identify, a quest that was not without its difficulties. I looked into one possible ancestral narrative after learning of a collection of thousands of sixteenth-century letters from Tudor England, *The Lisle Letters*, that chronicled the daily life of a landed family from 1533 to 1540. At first glance I was intrigued by the companionate marriage of Honor and Arthur Plantagenet Lisle. As I read further, however, I realized that the Lisles were at the time middle-aged with children from previous marriages, disqualifying them from my search of the family tree.

Nonetheless, through exploring history in other places, I

59

have discovered many interesting, even inspiring, narratives
about nulliparous females throughout the centuries. I have also
detected a historic pattern of advances and retreats in women's
control of their reproductive lives from the Roman Empire to
the modern world. I was surprised to discover that the avoidance of motherhood, usually by means of religious celibacy or
early forms of contraception, often elevated the existences of
women; childless females often had greater independence, better health, even more wealth and status than mothers. The
wedded nonmother, however, was in a more tenuous position
than her unmarried counterpart because of her violation of the
wifely expectation to bear. The Old Testament, for example,
portrays its so-called barren matriarchs as passive and even piti-
ful wives yearning for sons; Sarah, the wife of Abraham, finally
conceives because God decides, in biblical parlance, to open
her womb. In eighteenth- and nineteenth-century America, a
minority of women desired liberty from the restrictions of marriage and motherhood. Many of them, as symbolic, surrogate,
or spiritual mothers, made significant contributions to their
families and to society. Then, in the late nineteenth century,
when the birthrate began to decline, a fierce social and political
struggle erupted for and against the rights to birth control and
abortion, a struggle that continues today. Indeed, as I examined the lives of childless women in the early years of the twentieth century, I was dismayed to see how little has actually
changed from a hundred years ago.

As I searched the past, I realized that ancient female archetypes include the mistress, helpmate, sage, artist, warrior, and
virgin, only the last of whom is by definition childless. The
mythological maiden is distinctive in her absence of biological
offspring, a fact that separates her from most other females.
These prototypes of the modern nonmother appear in pre-

Hellenic myths as independent goddesses, like the aggressive Athena, the meditative Hestia, and the able Artemis. These goddesses are virginal only in the sense of being without progeny, not necessarily because they lack eroticism or male companions; common usage indicates literal or biological virginity with the modifier *intacta*. Not mothers and rarely wives, these goddesses are virginal in the symbolic sense of having psychological integrity, personal identity, and social independence, exemplars of feminist ideals.

These early self-possessed goddesses were more androgynous than those in later Greek and Olympian traditions, even more so than females in modern psychological interpretations of "the feminine." Artemis, a fierce huntress with bow and arrow, was also a pleasure-loving performer of ecstatic dances in the forest. Her wide-ranging abilities, from warfare to midwifery, as both a defender and destroyer of life, are evident in her representations as maidenly and motherly figures. Although proudly childless, Artemis has been portrayed as many-breasted because of her acts of surrogate maternity. A guardian of both chastity and childbirth (*artemisia* is a medicinal herb once used to induce labor), she was also ruthlessly self-protective: After a hunter violated her privacy while she was bathing in the nude, she transformed him into a stag, to be destroyed by his own hounds. Artemis-like heroines abound in history. They include numerous Christian saints and rulers, such as Elizabeth I, England's Virgin Queen, who used her marital eligibility and the tradition of courtly love, which placed the virgin on a pedestal, as sources of royal power. When the subject of the need for an heir came up, she managed to sidestep it. Her virginity was also more symbolic than real; she relied upon the counsel, affection, and companionship of men, one of whom had an adjoining bedroom.

There have always been women who turned away from continual childbearing in an attempt to have more control over their lives—not, however, without great difficulty and often eventual disappointment. In the days of the Roman Empire, for instance, widows and unmarried women ran estates for men away at war; they became involved in politics, philosophy, the military, and the arts. Some refused to marry, others divorced with alacrity, and many took lovers as readily as men, all of which resulted in a sharp decline in the birthrate and a rise in childlessness, according to later disapproving male historians. Nonmotherhood was regarded as a way to increase personal authority, perhaps through greater wealth or legal rights, and when one mother lost a son to death, the Roman Seneca tried to comfort her by saying that "childlessness gives more power than it takes away." This rare exercise of female authority and autonomy was extremely unsettling, however, and in an attempt to rein in women and increase the population, laws were passed in the third century A.D. that eliminated inheritance rights of single and childless persons.

If one looks at other societies and other times, the same pattern of rebellion and resistance emerges. The early unestablished Christian church proselytized females to win converts—virgins, wives, widows, and prostitutes—and had novitiates take vows of chastity. Membership in the church endowed women with more sanctity and sovereignty than was available to them in secular society. Joining the church, as well as later established orders of nuns, gave chaste women the chance to use their intellects, express creativity, and exercise leadership. Visionary mystics and martyrs, mostly unmarried, from Joan of Arc to Mother Teresa, found a way to obtain learning, dignity, influence, peace, and praise by forswearing childbirth. Even for highborn women, Christian conversion was a way to avoid a woman's biological destiny: For instance, Constantina, the daughter of Constantine the Great, the first Roman emperor to convert to Christianity, took a vow of celibacy in an attempt to elude motherhood; she eventually married but died a year later, possibly in childbirth. In the second century A.D., when orders of independent celibate women were officially accepted into the church, ecclesiastical fathers started to chastise these women for such sins as prideful behavior, rejection of veils, and mingling with the populace.

For young women who married, either by their own desire or the design of their parents, the ability to control conception was, of course, much more of a challenge. Perhaps the earliest form of wedlock without children was spiritual marriage, whereby a pious husband and wife agreed to refrain from carnal relations altogether or during the church's penitential periods. Spiritual unions originated when church fathers tried to impose them on married priests to encourage a celibate clergy; they were sanctioned by the church as the path of the Virgin Mary and her husband Joseph, the parents of Jesus. Its result, of course, was fewer or no children. Often initiated by wives, chaste marriage was a rebellion against the separation of the sexes in religious orders and "a revolt against the reproductive imperative" as well as "a fight for physical autonomy and self-definition." In the late fourth century, a wife and mother named Ecdicia took a vow of sexual abstinence in order to transform her carnal marriage into a spiritual one. She persuaded her husband to take the vow too, hoping that the pledge would release her from marital obedience. Perhaps Ecdicia reasoned that if she controlled her fertility, she could also rule her person—but in the familiar pattern, her husband and the church patriarch Augustine, to whom she appealed, did not endorse her plan.

Although it did not necessarily increase a woman's power, chaste wedlock did at times improve a wife's lot—specifically, when it was a consequence of the ancient practice of forced marriage for highborn girls. The eleventh-century princess Salome of Galicia, the devout daughter of the king of Poland, was betrothed at the age of three, took a vow of chastity with her intended at nine, and was married at thirteen; as a result of her early religious leanings, her seventeen-year marriage remained unconsummated. The fourteenth-century French nobles Elzear and Dauphine also had a long-lasting virgin marriage. Friends from childhood, the children were betrothed when she was twelve and he ten. On their wedding night she recited the lives of saints to him until he fell asleep. Elzear knew beforehand of his intended's desire to keep her virginity, and he tried to suppress his sexual drive through self-mortification and fasting before eventually taking a vow of chastity. His family wanted heirs, so the young couple had to conceal their celibacy; when his relatives concluded that Dauphine was sterile, they tried (unsuccessfully) to poison her. The wedded couple lived together for almost twenty-five years, sleeping in the same bed but not touching and remaining dressed. They adopted three orphans, devoted their lives to charitable works, and finally established "a profound spiritual rapport" as well as a "frictionless intimacy and consummate friendship."

Actually, intended or unintended childlessness throughout history remains enveloped in mystery, since low birthrates are often ultimately inexplicable. Members of the upper classes in Greece and Rome, for instance, are thought to have raised few children in order to maintain their positions. It has also been documented that for at least four hundred years, European nobility with irreversibly declining fortunes restricted their fertility to retain their land, wealth, and class privileges. Primogeniture, the right of the eldest son to inherit the entire family estate, meant that younger children could be costly. Parents were unlikely to marry off more than two children: Daughters needed dowries to compete for eldest sons or to enter convents, and younger sons needed educations or means to join the church or the army or to marry an heiress, according to one early-eighteenth-century account. Unwanted offspring were usually abandoned, a matter that will be discussed later. In the sixteenth and seventeenth centuries, 20 to 40 percent of English aristocrats did not marry, and 10 to 20 percent of the wedded ones had no children. Similar figures exist for Italians in Venice and Florence. The fear of downward mobility during this time was real; in the sixteenth century, for example, impoverished members of the Russian gentry were forced to sell themselves and their children into slavery.

As I read accounts about childless women in the Old World, I gradually realized that many were procreative in nonbiological ways. One of them, the Old Testament's intellectual and virginal Leah, was "out of reach of the passions," but she possessed "the seed of wisdom" and the ability to give birth to "beautiful ideas worthy of the Father who begat them," according to biblical scholar Mary Callaway. Others seemed emotionally crippled by their place in society, not necessarily by their childlessness. In seventeenth-century England, for instance, Margaret Cavendish, Dutchess of Newcastle, a shy, eccentric lady-in-waiting to the queen and childless wife who wrote, in the words of Virginia Woolf, "hare-brained, fantastical" poetry, plays, and prose, was discouraged and undisciplined because of a lack of education. In "Female Orations" the noblewoman penned a bitterly ironic statement, which was part of an imaginary dialogue between an insubordinate and a conventional woman: "Ladies, gentlewomen, and other inferior women . . . our words to men are as empty sounds; our sighs, as puffs of winds; and our tears, as fruitless showers; and our power is so inconsiderable, that men laugh at our weakness. . . . But we have more reason to murmur against Nature than against men ... for women are witless and strengthless, and improfitable creatures, did they not bear children." As all these narratives make clear, the nullipara in history has left us with a heritage that is both troubling and inspiring, one composed of expansive archetypes and constrictive stereotypes. The single woman, called a "femme sole" in the American colonies, from an old French expression meaning a woman alone, has often appeared in mythology, folklore, biography, and literature in an idealized or demonized form, a saint or a devil, but rarely as normal or fulfilled.

After looking at the ancient world and the more recent European past, I located my American maternal genealogy, which one of my mother's older brothers had researched exhaustively, beginning with seventeenth-century English settlers who lived in villages in New Hampshire, Massachusetts, and Rhode Island. In the early days of the American colonies, there was no upper-class antinatalist tradition as in Europe. In a vast, verdant, and underpopulated continent, families were large and opportunities abundant, and the topic of whether or not to give birth to children rarely came up in American courtship letters. Women as breeders were essential to the family, and singleness was viewed as a state of sin. As I perused my family tree, I noted that while the occupations of the males were often noted—ship captain, minister, clerk, or tradesman—the callings of the females were assumed. The twenty-one Abigails and the numerous Hannahs, Hesters, Rebeccas, Rachels, Lydias as well as Patience, Thankful, Temperance, Prudence, and even an ancestor named Experience Bliss, were there in name only, noted for the number and names of their offspring. Those who did not bear children were usually identified by given name only, not even by birth and death dates. Even though I would later learn that my nulliparous antecedents were relatively numerous, they were ignored, invisible, and lost from family records.

In my efforts to unearth the stories of foremothers without offspring, I discovered the charming account of the life of an Artemis-like woman to whom I was not related, Elizabeth Haddam Estaugh. Born in 1680 in England to a Quaker family, she was a willful and idealistic girl. When she was six, the Quaker minister William Penn, who had proselytized in the New World, visited her father's home and described his experiences in America, eventually leading Mr. Haddam to buy property in New Jersey and plan to emigrate because of religious persecution. But when her father was unable to undertake the journey, the twenty-one-year-old Elizabeth went in his place—enabled by his power of attorney and accompanied by three servants—making her perhaps the youngest female landowner in the colonies. Before long she met up with a young Quaker minister, John Estaugh, and as an example of her unusual willfulness, she proposed to him; they married but for unknown reasons never had children. A century later, however, Elizabeth's tale attracted the attention of another childless wife, Lydia Maria Child, who published it in story form, which, in turn, inspired Henry Wadsworth Longfellow to write about Elizabeth—and her bold marriage proposal—in his *Tales of a Wayside Inn* ("I have received from the Lord a charge to love thee, John Estaugh"). When John Estaugh was ill or away preaching, Elizabeth managed their land as well as that of other English Quakers. One of her nieces lived with them for eight years before returning to England; then they adopted a nephew who married and settled permanently in America, making his children their grandchildren. Elizabeth became a renowned healer and wealthy landowner, and she was remembered as "A

Woman Remarkable for Resolution, Prudence, Charity." Her nuptial union remained a very happy one: "I'll venture to say, few, if any, in a married State, ever lived in sweeter Harmony than we did," Elizabeth wrote in a posthumous book about her husband, which was published by Benjamin Franklin.

Although Elizabeth Haddam Estaugh was probably inadvertently childless, I was fascinated to find out that seeds of revolt against the female reproductive role were planted during the American Revolutionary War. In the late 1700s, female academies were opened in anticipation of expanded roles for women in the republic after the revolution. The impetus for women's education, however, had little to do with gender justice or a desire for learned females. In the new democracy, it was believed, knowledge and virtues like selflessness and self-restraint would be important. Such moral qualities were invested in females, who were then expected to practice "republican motherhood" and instill these values in male citizens. The ability to read can be subversive, however, since it cannot be completely controlled, and some American women took seriously the new ideas in the air about freedom and individualism. (It was also during that era, in 1792, that English philosopher Mary Wollstonecraft, who later died in childbirth, wrote A *Vindication of the Rights of Woman*, the first forceful challenge to male supremacy.) The Declaration of Independence cited the right to "life, liberty, and the pursuit of happiness"; but the first of these was threatened by the dangers of childbearing and the second by the inequities of marriage.

It is not altogether surprising that some educated American girls were excited by the new ideas about the rights of individuals. Touring America in the early 1800s, French diplomat Alexis de Tocqueville noted that American women, in comparison to European ones, were freer before marriage but less so afterward. "In America the independence of women is irrecoverably lost in the bonds of matrimony," he wrote in *Democracy in America*, adding that public opinion relegated the wife to "the narrow cycle of domestic interests and duties, and forb[ade] her to step beyond it." Meanwhile, the confidence of young girls inexplicably became the caution of grown women, he observed. A wedded woman in America understood that "a spirit of levity and independence in the bonds of marriage is a constant subject of annoyance, not of pleasure." Perhaps it was the country's puritanical and religious beliefs that forced "a constant sacrifice of her pleasures to her duties which is seldom demanded of her in Europe," he theorized, but more likely it was the fact that she bore seven or so children that was responsible for her submissiveness. Since Tocqueville did not really understand this transition from lively daughter to obedient wife, his theories about why paternal "discipline [was] very relaxed and the conjugal tie very strict" are unconvincing. It seemed to him that the American female gave up her independence voluntarily, even with "a sort of pride" and "without a struggle and without a murmur when the time comes for making the sacrifice." But Tocqueville did note a tension between women's elevated moral role and their dependent inferiority within the family. He added significantly that the most virtuous women expressed compliance, but that "the others are silent."

Tocqueville's last observation was particularly perceptive; quiet expectations of loss, struggle, and even incarceration and death within matrimony were commonplace in American courtship letters of this era. Death in childbirth was so common that it was customary for a woman in her first pregnancy to write a will and, in later ones, to record her wishes for her existing children. It was not uncommon for a man to marry one sister after another as each died in childbirth. Even in the early twentieth century, one out of thirty women died in childbirth, and almost everyone had a relative or friend, or knew of one, who had perished that way. In 1905 the woman with the nom de plume of A Childless Wife noted that she had lost six acquaintances during delivery in the past four years, including her husband's sister. A pregnant woman also faced the possibility of excruciating labor pain and physical mutilation due to primitive medical techniques, which might result in lifelong incontinence, painful intercourse, and other problems. According to one scholar, "most married women, and some unmarried women, had to face the physical and psychological effects of recurring pregnancies, confinements, and postpartum recoveries, which all took their toll on their time, their energy, their dreams, and on their bodies."

Tocqueville seemed unaware of the large numbers of American women who were rebelling at that time against the restrictions of wedlock. To be married, "the 'I' must surrender girlhood, which is shown to be life," wrote the poet Emily Dickenson. In what was called "the cult of single blessedness," many delayed or rejected marriage for the sake of "self-cultivation" over "self-sacrifice." They wanted knowledge of themselves as well as of the world, independence, and the opportunity to develop their interests and abilities as a way to serve their country and God, according to historian Lee V. Chambers-Schiller. In her study of more than a hundred unwed women who lived between 1780 and 1820, she concentrated by necessity on literate, white, native-born, well-off Protestants from northeastern states, because these women wrote about their lives or were written about. Many stayed single by choice or because of a poor selection of partners—many young men had left for the western frontier, or, in later decades, had died during the Civil War. Most of these females aspired to have their own incomes and homes as well as an ongoing intellectual life. Few achieved all these ambitions, but all of them avoided the perils and penalties of matrimony and maternity. As I read the words of these unmarried New England women, I easily identified with them; indeed, I believe that, under the influence of my own teenage idealism and intellectuality, had I lived in that period, I would have been one of them.

The relationship of childlessness to liberty continued beyond the American revolutionary era. In the nineteenth century, females had more equality in celibate sects than elsewhere in society. By eliminating procreative roles, for instance, Shaker women became involved with "production and leadership rather than consumption and submission," according to Sally L. Kitch. The ethos clearly had its appeal: Many Shaker converts were young women of childbearing age, some with small children, some of whom were probably escaping the dangers of repeated pregnancies. Unwed women were also well represented among Quakers and other faiths that preached and practiced the equality of women; a number of accomplished women, such as social worker Dorothea Dix, educator Elizabeth Peabody, and writer Catharine Sedgwick, were congregants of the Unitarian minister William Ellery Channing, who "upheld, advised, exhorted and soothed" them. One forebear who was not silent about the penalties of wedlock was Lydia Maria Child, the childless wife and writer who objected to the view that marriage was the end of a woman's "season for gaiety." Likewise, Catharine Sedgwick, the novelist who turned away suitors and called the single state "not a condition to be dreaded, scorned, or pitied, but infinitely preferable to the bankruptcies of married life." Writer Louisa May Alcott, whose mother had eight pregnancies in ten years, also chose to stay single; she wrote in her diary on February 14, 1868, that she and other unwed women believed that "liberty is a better husband than love."

A generation later Ella Lyman of Boston expressed her delight in her singlehood to her suitor, in words that clearly express her strong enjoyment of her liberty as well as her closeness to members of her family. "I have told you, I think, as clearly as I can, why I cannot now marry. It is love of my own life which at times makes anything else seem like tearing up my roots; and independence of temperament which makes marriage not a need as it would be with many people," she wrote in the same letter in which she tentatively accepted his idea of childless marriage. "My social atmosphere is so rich and yet free, I have in an unusual degree the maximum of doing what I want and the minimum of what bores me, and I know and love it through and through; I am close to people whom I know and draw life from and yet my solitude is my own." Since she entered a marriage to this suitor the next year, intending not to have children, it is likely that the agreement was an innovative way to retain the important advantages of girlhood within the intimacy of marriage. What is interesting about her story is that whereas generations earlier, women turned to celibacy to preserve their senses of self, now they were beginning to turn to childlessness, as do many childfree couples today.

Although such women without children did not sacrifice themselves to motherhood, they served society in other ways. In the tradition of nuns and female saints, regarded in orthodox theology as virgin brides of Christ, unwed women were supposed to engage in what was called "social mothering." In the early nineteenth century, it was believed that, like a secular Protestant priesthood, single "ladies" could better serve God and mankind and their own moral development if they were unburdened by children of their own. Families depended on unwed females to assist sisters in childbirth, to nurse ailing parents or invalid kin, to keep house for widowed fathers or bachelor brothers, and to care for motherless siblings, nephews, nieces, and cousins. If no relations were in need, they were expected to volunteer to care for orphans, the poor, and the ill outside the extended family. In fact, social mothering was virtually the only outlet for well-bred spinsters, whether they were altruistic by nature or not. They were pressured to meet humanistic needs with little or no monetary reward in order to fulfill their so-called feminine natures; no such standard applied to working-class women, of course, the vast majority of whom were servants, seamstresses, or agricultural workers in 1890.

The social mother was even more highly regarded than the natal mother prior to the Civil War. The maiden aunt, for example, was deemed an exemplar of high-minded motherhood; she was considered capable of mothering with objectivity and moderation, avoiding maternal overidentification and overindulgence. Ideally, the unwed aunt balanced "unconditional love tempered by strict expectations of good behavior." An unattached aunt, in this view, also had the moral courage for handling family tragedies. This seems to have been the case with E. M. Forster, who wrote a biography about the maiden great-aunt who raised him, a devoted yet strong-minded person. Unlike an elderly grandmother or an employed governess, an aunt usually had a more permanent or esteemed place in the family. Also, she was often more vigorous, since she was spared the rigors of childbearing, and sometimes she was more affectionate, since she had respites from caretaking, like Miss Caroline Fox, or "Little Aunty," a nineteenth-century English aristocrat who was kinder to her nieces and nephews than their natural mother, described as "far from a fond mother."

If unwed women of this era were temperamentally disinclined to be nurturers and wished instead to study, write, paint, or travel abroad, they usually encountered little understanding or opportunity. If they lived in the family home, which was customary, they struggled to integrate their duties as daughters with the demands of vocations. Often they suffered inner conflicts, as in the case of Elizabeth Peabody, who experienced an "intense struggle between the need to cultivate the self and the ideology of domesticity"; she resolved the tension by devoting herself to the education of young children. Catharine Sedgwick, for her part, spent much of her time working for the reform of women's prisons instead of writing. But not even social motherhood always spared an unconventional nonmother from bourgeois censure in the early years of the twentieth century. My great-aunt Dorothy, for example, a single social worker who worked in women's prisons and in a Hawaiian leper colony, was considered by my mother's brother, the family historian, as scandalously "independent and left-wing"; furthermore, my uncle did not know what to make of her when in old age she lived on a Maryland farm with someone he called her "feminine friend."

The idea of women ruling their bodies has always threatened the social order, perhaps arousing fears of their desires for chastity, licentiousness, or childlessness. Certainly when I tried to get a prescription for the birth control pill in 1965, I had to threaten a gynecologist with the possibility that without it I might ask him for an illegal abortion. In the past few decades, of course, the widespread use of the pill and legal abortion have made it possible for women to consider marriage and motherhood as two entirely different matters. When I demanded the contraceptive pill, I never imagined giving up sexual intimacy or marriage if I did not have children. Lifelong virginity is rare if not extinct today, and most people feel entitled to an erotic life. But the specter of freewheeling sexuality is still profoundly disturbing to many segments of society, and this fear of promiscuity helps fuel the anti-abortion movement. In view of the enduring agitation over abortion rights, it is enlightening to put the long struggle over female fertility into perspective.

Throughout history efforts at limiting births have been widespread, persistent, and often effective; they have included the practice of abstinence and withdrawal and the use of vaginal sponges and abortifacient herbs. Information about such techniques was developed by wisewomen and midwives, who passed it along from generation to generation in the face of rigorous attempts, including witch hunts, to suppress it. The knowledge would be lost and rediscovered again and again in an attempt to protect a wife's health or a family's prospects. One woman who had such information was portrayed in Geoffrey Chaucer's fourteenth-century account of Alison, the Wife of Bath, a wealthy, worldly, and lusty woman who, although married five times, had no children; her knowledge of the "remedies of love," she explained, make love "moore for delit than world to multiplye."

In the absence of contraception or the practice of continence, results were predictable. In the early fifteenth century, after twenty years of marriage and fourteen children, Christian zealot Margery Kempe finally bargained with her husband for the end of sexual relations, even though they enjoyed "great delectation" in each other, she wrote in her memoirs. She explained that she became celibate for reasons of faith, but clearly she had no other way to avoid pregnancy, which interfered with her desire to preach the gospel. Because women in earlier times had more frequent pregnancies and shorter life expectancies than their modern counterparts, child rearing often occupied a female's entire adult life. If a mother was unable or unwilling to raise her offspring, the alternatives were infanticide or abandonment, or, if she had means, turning them over to wet nurses, servants, and governesses. Uncontrollable childbearing was a tyranny for many women. In 1818, after giving birth to three children in as many years, the teenage Mary Shelley wrote the novel *Frankenstein*, a Gothic tale about a scientist who created a headstrong monster, which has been interpreted as a disguised description of a body prone to rampant fertility.

It was not until the nineteenth century that American women began to control the number of children they bore. Few feminists considered the avoidance of motherhood possible or even desirable, since there were few other dignified alternatives for women, so they attempted to elevate it. Arguing that having fewer children would make women better mothers, most advocates of what was called voluntary motherhood urged periods of sexual abstinence within marriage. They disliked and distrusted contraception because of several Victorian beliefs—that women's eroticism was satisfied by motherhood, that only conception justified intercourse, and that continence gave women more control over men. Reformers also feared that birth control devices would encourage male promiscuity and thus spread venereal disease, leading to sterility as well as disability, dementia, and death. They also worried that if the link between sex and matrimony was severed, young men would never marry. Abstinence was also respected in many circles as a way of preserving the life force and following in the footsteps of Jesus Christ. Even the scientifically enlightened Dr. Richard Cabot hinted at his idealistic acceptance of sexual restraint within marriage in his aforementioned courtship letter: "Of course you know that I recognize the physical side and feel its pressure like the rest; but it can be set on one side, and it often ought to be and will be more and more often in the future, and if you and I are not the apostles of the future who is?" he asked his intended.

Nonetheless, various ways of avoiding unwanted births besides abstinence were widely advertised in American newspapers after the Civil War. In 1867, after returning to England where he was vicar of Whenstead and chaplain to Queen Victoria, the Reverend Foster Barham Zincke noted with horror that in New York City there was a place to get contraceptives and abortions: It was "a large establishment ... from whence the high priestess of this evil system dispenses her drugs and advice, and where she also receives those who need her direct assistance." The reverend was also offended by the existence of seemingly carefree childless wedded couples in cities throughout America. He realized that the use of contraception would continue and even spread, despite the fact that it was denounced by churches, legislatures, and medical societies: "We cannot expect that it will die away, as long as the motives which prompt it continue to be felt as strongly as they are at present."

As the desire for smaller families took hold in America, the fertility rate for whites dropped by half during the nineteenth century—from an average of seven live births per woman in 1800 to three and a half in 1900, the lowest anywhere in the world except for France. People became alarmed that the American race seemed in decline, but others dismissed such concerns, pointing out that medical science was keeping more infants and children alive. The declining fertility rate was affected by many factors, including urbanization, parental ambition, and the elevation of women. The first wave of feminists had demanded female education in the name of enlightened motherhood, but almost a third of the early graduates of women's colleges never became mothers—they stayed single or got divorced—and others produced only one or two children, a pattern that would persist throughout the twentieth century. In that era, many females were forced to choose between the use of their educations and the enjoyment of erotic lives. Ida Husted Harper, a suffragette, predicted that if the price of learning was nonmotherhood, many would pay it. "The society of little children has much in it that is sweet, but it is not mentally stimulating," she wrote. The belief took hold that the use of the female brain diverted blood from the reproductive system, leading to infecundity, dysmenorrhea, and other gynecological problems.

As the rate of childlessness headed to an all-time national high of 27 percent of females during the years 1885 to 1915, the earlier value placed on virginity was forgotten. Enforcing the cult of motherhood required the intimidation of females who did not conform, like feminists who defended the right to remain childfree: Eliza Duffey, for one, wrote that "an unwilling motherhood is a terrible, a cruel and unjust thing." If maternity satisfied a woman's emotional and erotic nature, the pronatalist argument went, then single women or childless wives were, by definition, unfulfilled and incomplete. Unflattering images arose of the angular spinster, strident feminist, and mannish orator. Words like *spinster, old maid,* and *bluestocking* became epithets, while the valuable roles of the social mother and the maiden aunt were ignored. When Ida Harper defended the right not to be a mother, an enraged man wrote to her that "all the 'crimes against women,' for which men are punished, are offset by the unpunished refusal of women to bear children." And George N. Miller, author of a novel called *The Strike of a Sex,* which was published in London in 1891, imagined the worst—the fearful specter of childlessness: Woman "will have this ownership of her person or she will allow the race to lapse from the face of the earth."

Childlessness within matrimony was an explosive topic, even to the eminently rational Ella Lyman, who thought that many people were "sentimental and unreasonable" about parenthood. When she responded to her fiancé in 1893 about the possibility of marriage without children, she also expressed her concern that the idea might catch on too easily. She began by writing that she was unsure how many people secretly wished to avoid parenthood because they felt it was "wrong to speak of it freely." Despite her belief in the desirability of being nulliparous for "exceptional or very poor women," she worried about advocating or even mentioning the possibility—"the *extent* to which people ought to marry resolving not to have children, I don't know"—because it was a volatile and subversive idea. Like the option of suicide, she went on, the concept of childlessness is "dangerous" and might be "used for selfish ends, illegitimately, and for escape from pain." And if it was "used at all commonly it would endanger the race and tend to preserve the cowardly and irrational," she reasoned.

An inevitable backlash gathered momentum. It became forbidden to send birth control devices and information through the United States mail. Abortion, which had been legal and commonplace earlier in America, became illegal state by state during the last decades of the nineteenth century. In 1905, at the height of the wave of European immigration, President Theodore Roosevelt, in an address before the National Congress of Mothers, attacked the so-called selfishness of women who refused to have large families; he compared their duty to bear at least six children to a man's duty to fight for his country. The social worker who called herself A Childless Wife challenged the president's words that year: "We are not selfish and pleasure loving," she responded, explaining that if she and her husband had children, it "would be detrimental to our usefulness as members of society . . . and make us lower, not nobler, people." The president's concern had overtones of anti-immigration and ethnic prejudice, because it was his constituency, the daughters of the New England establishment, who had the lowest birthrates; as many as 30 percent of New Hampshire women were nulliparas at the turn of the century. Fears of "race suicide" led to hysterical opposition to contraception and childlessness, which reached fever pitch during the patriotic frenzy of the First World War.

In 1916 Leta S. Hollingworth, a married educational psychologist without children, described in *The American Journal of Sociology* the intense pronatalist tactics and rhetoric surrounding her—the illegality of birth control, the fact that sterility was grounds for divorce, the censure of anyone who said something negative about motherhood, and the circulation of false myths about nonmotherhood. She noted that at least fifty-five magazines and newspapers had published pro-birth articles in the past year, and all but one were written by men. Calling the pervasive propaganda full of inaccurate "bugaboos," the psychologist gave as examples the statements that only children are inevitably troubled, that birth is dangerous after age thirty and, astonishingly, considering the high childbirth mortality rate, that mothers with the most children live the longest. Finally, she naively predicted that the irrationality of pronatalism would destroy itself. "Belief, law, public opinion, illusion, education, art, and bugaboos have all been used to reenforce maternal instinct," she wrote. "As soon as women become fully conscious of the fact that they have been and are controlled by these devices, the latter will become useless, and we shall get a truer measure of maternal feeling." Meanwhile, the right to contraception became a key demand of a large reformist movement made up of labor union and women's groups. "No woman can call herself free who does not own and control her own body," wrote birth control pioneer and mother Margaret Sanger in *Women and the New Race*. "No woman can call herself free until she can choose conscientiously whether she will or will not be a mother."

Despite the ringing rhetoric and the real availability of choice over childbearing, the educated female at the turn of the century, now called the "New Woman," usually wanted to earn a wage and mother a baby too, but like many others before and after her, she found it difficult to do so because of discriminatory laws and traditional customs. Floyd Dell, the writer and bohemian who lived in Greenwich Village at the time, recalled that his girlfriends regarded motherhood "not so much the crown and glory of a woman's life as one of the most interesting of its adventures." They found it "unfair that modern life should put so high a price on the adventure of motherhood," he explained. "But they did not intend to be bluffed out of the adventure by however high a price. They wanted babies." Yet despite the bravado of those young women, they did not always end up with babies; Dell realized that for many of them, pursuing professions and raising children simultaneously remained only "a heroic theory." Since many of his intellectual or artistic female friends married for love, not for financial support, they finally "accepted childlessness as the not necessarily tragic price of companionship with the lover of their choice." I was fascinated to find in Dell's observations the themes that continue to dominate the childbearing dilemma of many women today. Yet the failure of women during the next few decades of the twentieth century to break patriarchal rules to solve the old either/or dilemma is deeply disturbing in its implications for the future.

From the end of the Civil War to the beginning of the Great Depression, dreamers had come up with visionary ideas for "a grand domestic revolution" to lighten the burden of housework so mothers could broaden their lives. Most theories tended to abolish the family home and replace it with apartment hotels with shared housekeeping services; Charlotte Perkins Gilman, for instance, invented a fictional Herland and an Orchardina in her novels—female paradises where no one did private housework. Feminists and other thinkers drew on innovations in utopian communities and ideas of the Greek philosopher Plato, who had envisioned nurseries managed by both men and women. For three generations, reformers advocated ways to streamline cooking, cleaning, and child care, much as factories had modernized home cottage industries, advocating kitchenless homes, mechanized housecleaning, infant nurseries, and other innovations. The concept of group child care had generated much interest since the mid-1800s, when children of working mothers were often sent to orphanages and foster homes; in 1860 Elizabeth Peabody and her sister opened the country's first private kindergarten in Boston, and a generation later, in 1893, a model child-care center operated in the Children's Building at the World's Columbian Exposition in Chicago.

Ideas for collective housing took hold in England and on the east and west coasts of America, especially among members of labor unions. A few of these buildings were erected; many more were not. In New York City in 1919 an architect drew up plans for a communal apartment building, and backers selected a site on Washington Square in Greenwich Village. A twelve-story prototype was planned with a basement kitchen to be run by people educated in the domestic sciences, while teachers trained in child psychology would instruct preschool children in Montessori lessons in a rooftop school. The concept, however, like many others of its kind, did not attract enough financial support for a number of reasons, including the preference of many husbands for the personal homemaking services of their wives. As a consequence, the building never went up.

Nonetheless, such inspired thinking continued to be relevant in a democracy with large middle and working classes and a small servant class. A living arrangement with a "baby garden" would enable a young working couple to have children who otherwise might not be able to afford them, noted *The Milwaukee Leader* on April 24, 1914. A few years earlier, in 1907, a working-class childless wife who lived with her husband in a boarding-house with fifteen other families, most of whom also had no offspring, wrote in *The Independent* that she did not dare give birth because motherhood would reduce or eliminate her wages, and she wanted to be able to educate her child properly. This woman, who was evidently politically aware, claimed that she "would rather commit suicide than beget children without hope, destined from birth for wage slavery and exploitation. . . . The master class can't force me to furnish food for its factories," or, she might have added several years later as the First World War got under way, soldiers for its armies. It is interesting to note that the childlessness that Reverend Zincke, the English churchman, had regarded as frivolous a few generations earlier was considered to be moral by this wife.

After the end of the First World War, a backlash gathered force against the collective housekeeping movement, partly as a way to keep women out of a tight labor market. The War Department even accused women's advocacy groups of being part of a "red web" intent on destroying America through socialism. This powerful opposition took its toll. Although the suffragettes were victorious and women won the right to vote in 1921, in the years afterward newly enfranchised female citizens did not vote to further the cause of freeing themselves from housework. The alliance between the women's and birth control movements fractured during the 1920s, ending any radical realignments with regard to child care. Crystal Eastman, a mother and lawyer, stated dispiritedly at the time that "if the feminist program goes to pieces on the arrival of the first baby, it is false and useless." Ideas about ways to free women from domesticity survived for a while, and determined individuals designed personal solutions for themselves. Georgia O'Keeffe and her husband, the photographer and art dealer Alfred Stieglitz, for instance, spent winter months starting in 1925 in two small rooms on the highest floor of a New York residential hotel, which had a cafeteria and housekeeping services; O'Keeffe, then in her late thirties, was painting with great intensity, and she needed to be able to devote all the limited daylight hours to art.

Around the same time, influenced by ideas about collective domestic arrangements, the elegant and expensive Hudson View Gardens apartments were built in the Washington Heights section of northern Manhattan. The group of Tudor-style buildings was constructed, with a restaurant, maid service, grocery store, laundry, nursery, and supervised playground. But the designer and developer disavowed feminist intentions, ones that would enable mothers to have lives outside the home, so the private units contained kitchens, and the child-care services were for occasional use only. Over the years visionary alternatives to privatized housing and housework were forgotten by subsequent generations of women. Although my great-aunt and great-uncle lived in Hudson View Gardens for many years with their daughter, and my maternal great-grandmother from New Hampshire spent her winters there, my mother, despite her dissatisfactions with domesticity, was unaware of the building's innovative origins and, therefore, was never able to make use of its concepts herself or even to share them with me and my sister. The communal living movement finally ended in complete defeat during the Depression, when the United States government began to subsidize single-family housing in suburbia, a trend that isolated mothers even more, and one that continued after the Second World War in the form of mortgages to veterans. Ultimately, my search of women's history was inspiring to the extent that I came across interesting childfree individuals, but also disheartening, since so many social movements failed to give mothers and nonmothers real options in their lives.

UNDERSTANDING OUR MOTHERS, ENLARGING MOTHERHOOD

While nulliparas stand in antithesis to mothers, women without children are nevertheless deeply influenced by their mothers and grandmothers as well as by their own unexperienced motherhood. We watch our sisters and friends care for their children, and this too, colors what we know about mothering. As I have explored motherhood from the slightly sideways angle of a nulligravida, I have come to understand some of the friction between birth mothers and nonmothers. And I have concluded that the conventional concept of "Motherhood" needs to be changed, opened up, and expanded into a broader and more realistic one.

We think back through our mothers if we are female, Virginia Woolf has observed, and nulliparas first learn what it means to be maternal in the modern world from our mothers. Even though not all women are mothers, and all mothers do not have daughters, every woman is born a daughter, even if she is not raised by her natural mother. Grounded in our memories of childhood, we often cannot see beyond a mother's shadow for years. Her presence is especially strong if she is the only caretaking parent, like mine was, an experience that often fuels intimacy and overidealization, then sharp disillusionment, making adolescent rebellions painful and urgent. I have vivid memories of my mother's life as a mother—hours she found pleasurable and purposeful, minutes she found exhausting and entrapping, and moments when she expressed intense love and, more rarely, sudden impatience. I, like many daughters, tend to remember in disproportionate measure the times when she failed my endless emotional expectations. One day after her remarriage, when she was pregnant and moving into a new house, she suddenly cut off my braids in a fit of frustration at her lack of time to plait them. I deeply resented losing my long brown hair, so much like her own, but I missed even more our ritualistic time together. This incident aside, it was partly the very heartfelt fullness of her mothering that made me hesitate before giving birth myself, wondering if I could give as richly as she.

The influence of a mother on a girl's desire for motherhood is a complicated one. A number of contemporary researchers have suggested that childless daughters received a poor impression of maternity from their mothers, and this is undoubtedly true for many. It is still unknown exactly what early events, if any, predispose a woman to nonmotherhood, but it may be that lack of maternal or paternal warmth causes young girls to hold low expectations for family life. Some people theorize that daughters with ineffective mothers are likely to worry that they would inevitably become inept mothers, even though such consequences are unproven. In numerous other cases, girls with troubled mothers vow to become the loving parents that their own were not and, in effect, to nurture a child of their own as if it were themselves when young. Many childfree daughters have excellent mothers, but for a number of reasons they choose not to emulate their mothers' maternal roles; instead they attempt to forge unusual, nonmaternal, but sound feminine selves in

other ways. Many, for instance, had loving mothers who struggled as single parents or who stayed unhappily married for the
sake of their children. Sometimes a young daughter feels that
her mother's life would have been better without her and her
siblings, a realization that invokes guilt over her own role, grief
for a beloved mother, and apprehension about suffering in the
same way. Other girls identify with a maternal figure's independence, her achievements, or her thwarted desires for them; in
the latter case, a female parent often encourages a daughter to
fulfill vicariously the adult's wish for another kind of life.
"Mother's multifaceted personality, not just her 'good' or 'bad'
mothering, has an impact on her child's female identity," psychologist Mardy S. Ireland has observed from her study of a
hundred childless women, of whom only a quarter had an "unsatisfactory" parent. The data ultimately suggest that our girlhoods at our mothers' sides are only one of many childbearing
influences upon us, and our choices are shaped by our own
characters and circumstances as much as by our mothers'.

A myth that has particular poignance for me is that of
Demeter and Persephone, in which a mother is powerless to
protect her daughter from returning to dark and threatening
Hades every winter. Since a girl usually identifies with her female parent, a mother's helplessness not only humiliates but
also "mutilates" the daughter, Adrienne Rich has observed. We
do not understand, Rich continues, "why our mothers did not
teach us to be Amazons, why they bound our feet or simply left
us" since we needed them to discover our womanly strength;
we sensed they were on our side, but all too often we still felt
"wildly unmothered." Many of us have seen our mothers unable or unwilling to take risks for us that would result in punishment for them. After I argued with my stepfather for the first
time when I was about twelve, I rushed weeping to my bed-

room, while my mother followed me upstairs. As I lay on my bed, feeling both fearful and freed by my outburst, she rubbed my back in an attempt to calm and comfort me. But her quiet words were about the need to be conciliatory to her temperamental husband, regardless of who was right. I felt deeply let down by her at that moment because she did not applaud my courage; in retrospect, of course, I realize that she could only teach me her own way of appeasement. Later in life, however, I would wonder if I would be able to protect my own hypothetical daughter from the anger of her father.

It has been widely assumed in modern psychiatry that children do not need to separate psychologically from the parent of the same sex. But what if that parent's life is not entirely worthy of emulation? Matrophobia, the fear of becoming one's mother, is sometimes experienced by a daughter who feels pity or painful empathy for her female parent. For a daughter who fears following in her mother's footsteps, the most obvious way to resist identification with a distraught or depressed mother is by not becoming a mother herself. As a young girl, Gloria Steinem, for instance, cared for a mentally ill mother and later avoided pregnancy because she feared becoming overwhelmed again by caretaking or ending up broken-spirited like her mother. Likewise, Nancy Friday, the author of *My Mother, Myself: The Daughter's Search for Identity*, decided against parenthood to avoid turning into her fearful, widowed mother. "Alone, I can control the helpless mother who lives inside me," she explained. "A mother myself, I would become just like her." Social worker Wendy A. Haskell, in a Ph.D. dissertation about maternal influence on daughters' desires for maternity, found that when mothers were unable to tolerate their daughters' disobedience, the teenagers' rebellions were secretive, short-lived, or subdued; perhaps because such girls could not draw away naturally from female parents, they reacted later in a more extreme way by resisting motherhood itself. Reading this analysis, I realized that I went along with my mother's few wishes for me as a young girl because I wanted to please her, perhaps driving my revolt underground. Whatever its genesis, Adrienne Rich has properly called an unhealed estrangement between a mother and daughter "the essential female tragedy."

Like the fertility goddess Demeter, who gave birth to the childless daughters Persephone and Artemis, homemakers who reared girls in the 1950s were more likely to see their daughters reject motherhood than were mothers who held jobs. It is as if the female offspring of those stay-at-home mothers could not imagine the successful integration of motherhood and employment because they lacked day-to-day examples of it. Certainly when I contemplated having a child, I was unable to reconcile the notion of being an ever-present mother with my dream of being a peripatetic journalist. My concern, like that of other daughters, was also affected by the discontent of my housewife mother with her domestic life. She was restless with constantly cooking and cleaning up; when I was about twelve she confided to me that she did not want to spend the rest of her life washing dishes. Other mothers with a houseful of children and a husband at work were overwhelmed by parental responsibilities; as a result, their older girls often grew up as so-called little mothers, who aspired to be free of mothering and even to be mothered themselves.

In literature and in life a maternal figure is usually considered a conservative influence on a daughter, someone who connects the younger female to a traditional way of life. Adventurous fictional heroines often have mothers who are mysteriously absent, weak, or deceased. A mother is viewed as binding her daughter to a dutiful role through the bonds of love and loyalty, so only the literally or figuratively unmothered daughter can set out on a journey, as the eponymous Jane Eyre did in Charlotte Brontë's novel, the tale of one motherless daughter penned by another. Many girls born in the 1940s and 1950s grew up reading Nancy Drew novels, stories about an audacious girl with an absent mother and an admiring father who bravely solves mysteries. In the real-life case of Catharine Sedgwick, her mother suffered from depression and her father was often in Philadelphia at constitutional congresses. She was raised casually and affectionately in the late 1700s by five older siblings and the family's black servants. Her unusual upbringing gave her a taste for independence, such that at the age of twenty-three she declared that she did not plan to follow in the footsteps of other young women who are "frightened to death by the terrors of maiden life." Indeed, it is surprising how many female artists, including Georgia O'Keeffe, Frida Kahlo, and Louise Nevelson, began to create with utmost seriousness and determination only after the deaths of their mothers. Such evidence has made me wonder about the subtle effect of my own mother, who is now in her eighties, on my writing. In the past I have struggled with the delicate process of writing about other female models; now, when delineating our relationship, I have feared that revelations of any disappointments would overshadow my expressions of gratitude for her steadfast and generous love.

At various times a mother may either subvert or support a daughter's nontraditional aspirations, but more often she does both at once by sending out a double message. Mothers like mine often give daughters conflicting signals about defiance— subtly encouraging it but also indicating misgivings about its price. After one of my mother's babies died, due to a malformed heart, on Mother's Day during her second marriage, she vehemently refused to allow any of the rest of her children to observe Mother's Day again. Although she cited her dislike of the sentimental hypocrisy and commercialization of the holiday, her attitude always seemed to be less an expression of lingering grief than one of inexpressible anger about motherhood. Raising daughters to gender inequality and colluding in their socialization creates repressions and tensions in mothers. "It is understandable that such women fight insight as others fight bodily assault," Sara Ruddick has observed. Stories about mothers overtly teaching daughters insubordination to an unjust social order are rare, as when Oriana Fallaci told an unborn girl child that "you'll have to struggle to explain that it wasn't sin that was born on the day when Eve picked an apple: what was born that day was a splendid virtue called *disobedience*." If she had not miscarried, would she have told her daughter this—or would her words have been tempered by fear for her daughter's fate?

Some mothers distance themselves from daughters in an attempt to save the latter from their own dependent fates—by making themselves recede, they reason, they will let their daughters go free. At the age of three I was described by a nursery school teacher as a fearless child, but shortly afterward I suddenly became withdrawn. One reason was the departure of my father, whose desertion, ironically, caused exactly what had once concerned him the most. "Perhaps you will take after your Dad, and be inclined to be a little shy," he had written in the letter to me right after my birth, along with advice about coping with the problem. In any event, believing that I was too timid, my mother began to firmly push me away, discouraging confidences and refusing to let me cling to her. While she was inculcating Yankee virtues of self-reliance and emotional restraint, in my father's absence she was also instinctively playing the usual paternal role of enforcing independence. Other child-less daughters, according to contemporary sociological data, re-port the same kind of parenting—remote rather than coercive. Permissiveness was about the best tack my mother could take as I grew up: Because of her inexperience outside the home and her intuitive, inarticulate, and unanalytical nature, she was utterly unable to give practical advice. When I became a teenager, this translated into a rare degree of tolerance, respect, and trust from her. As I became more educated and experi-enced in the world, I wondered if I was living out a frustrated desire of hers for another way of being, perhaps for the ani-mated and autonomous young woman I had glimpsed in an old home movie of her sister's 1947 wedding.

If I am living out an aspect of my mother's unlived life, we both have had turbulent feelings about it. Psychic distance be-tween mothers and daughters can arouse deep but vague feel-ings of loss and isolation on both sides. A mother, sensing a daughter's growing distance from her, can invoke the right to grandchildren. My mother never did that, but she found her own gentle strategy: She placed on a shelf a small faceless clay mother-and-child figure that I sculpted for her in school, as if it were a lost part of me.

Likewise, a daughter can feel distraught about her separate-ness from her mother; literary historian Elaine Showalter has theorized that Virginia Woolf became depressed after finishing each novel because publication was a reminder of her deep dif-ference from her deceased beloved Victorian mother, who had had seven children. In my case, although I always felt instinc-tively, unconditionally, if somewhat distractedly loved by my mother, when I became absorbed in writing the life of Georgia O'Keeffe, I worried that my mother might think I admired the artist more than I did her. Although the birth of a sibling's child can arouse the fear that one has nothing comparable to offer one's mother, I was glad for her sake that within months of the publication of the biography, my sister gave birth to our mother's namesake and first granddaughter. And although I have gone my own nonmaternal way under her loving glance, I have felt sad about our lost chance for connection as well as her anxiety whenever my life has taken a new course. Still, unlike my sister, I felt entitled to be different, perhaps because my mother set me so firmly on the road to independence at a young age.

Many daughters without children, despite any angst they suffer because of their unusual lives, believe that they are better off than their mothers. Out of this perception can come compassion as well as the ability to emulate their mothers' skills and strengths. After recognizing the dissimilarities between my mother and myself, I began to see our similarities, and then we drew closer. My mother is an imaginative and inspired gardener, so when I planted my own flower garden a decade ago, we developed a new vocabulary. "What's blooming?" she would telephone to ask, and our conversation would digress into multisyllabic Latinisms, my eager and ignorant questions, and her vague and idiosyncratic instructions. Large shipments of fine garden tools and cardboard boxes of plants leaking loose dirt arrived unexpectedly from her, and my garden began to overflow with her botanic tastes—gigantic white iris with yellow tongues and tall lacy purple meadow rue, for example—and hers became adorned with wind chimes and sculpted creatures from me.

Other daughters and mothers who have divergent lives can also arrive at tender and understanding relationships. In her Ph.D. dissertation, which examined 284 nulliparas between the ages of thirty and forty, Constance A. Logan discovered that daughters who had decided not to bear children had somewhat better relationships with their mothers than those who remained unresolved; the former, who were more likely to be married and stepmothers, experienced less intimacy with their mothers but also less conflict and more sympathy for them. And as the daughter heals, so does the mother. As if in forgiveness for my not following in her footsteps, my mother recently sent me a tongue-in-cheek article about the so-called disadvantages of childlessness, which was actually a paean to life without children. In the end, the childless daughter, as a result of untangling her complicated childhood closeness with her mother, is capable of developing an inner sense of maternal richness that can enable her to act as her own mother, even to experience her own rebirth, as she matures.

As those of us who are nulliparas advance through the years from fourteen to forty, the desire to give birth like our mothers usually waxes and wanes with age and opportunity. A conflicted or changing wish for a child belies the old assumption that all females have a compulsive maternal instinct, as opposed to moderate or reasonable parental desire, and that instinctive or ingrained behavior rules us. The longing for motherhood may also vary in intensity within the women of one family. While my mother, born in 1914, always assumed she would have children, and my little sister, born in 1950, became a mother with trepidation, I passed through ambivalence to decide against it. As a young girl I never liked baby-sitting; yet as a doting eldest sister and the daughter of a warmhearted mother, it feels natural to me to tend a child, and I fall into it easily, sensing and meeting a youngster's needs and feeling pleased by doing so. In my own case, a biological argument becomes highly suspect when I realize that when I was in my twenties, at the height of my fertility, I wanted freedom more than babies.

Nor is there one type of motherliness: In my own extended family, for instance, one sees an astonishing range of mothering styles, from the laissez-faire to the overinvolved; in fact, one member of my family without progeny seems more nurturing than some of the birth mothers. It is also interesting to note that almost all the mothers became pregnant the first time by accident, then allowed motherhood to shape their lives. Such variety among the females in only one family inevitably raises more questions about the strength, and even the existence, of a universal, inborn maternal drive. The widespread belief in the existence of such a blind reflex, however, makes childlessness suspect, and the intentionally childfree are made to wonder if they are lacking some essential gene.

The enduring practice of infanticide at the hands of mothers, as well as maternal and paternal indifference and abuse, also raises doubts about the prevalence of an overwhelming natural drive to protect one's young. Throughout history infants have been abandoned by whim and in times of trouble: The Greeks and Romans regularly exposed unwanted offspring to the elements, and European women have left their children in gutters or on the doorsteps of convents and monastaries. Orphanages and foundling homes have for centuries reared the sons and especially the daughters of unwed women, impoverished wives, and derelict parents. Nor have mothers always nursed their babies; in 1780, for instance, a French police chief reported that less than a thousand of the twenty-one thousand infants born each year in Paris were being breast-fed by their mothers. The widespread, long-lived, habitual practice of sending newborns away to wet nurses was, in effect, a form of infant slaying, since so few survived the neglect or outright killing that often went along with it. Throughout the centuries, the murder of the young has been so commonplace (although forbidden by religious and secular law) that casual references to it are found in old English ballads, in which babies are described as being strangled by hair ribbons or thrown into the sea. In the songs, servant girls kill their newborns in order to keep their positions, and respectable maidens do so to retain their reputations. Only sometimes do the mothers grieve: one song states that a girl "has slain it in her sorrow," and in others dead children return to talk to their mothers like unforgiving consciences, but another exults that "you'll ner get more of me."

Despite such evidence, psychiatrists and psychologists have attempted to prove the existence of a universal, protective, procreative female instinct. It seems more wishful thinking than scientific fact. Erik Erickson observed that prepubescent girls emphasize womblike "dynamic inner body space" (and boys outer space) in activities like playing with dolls' houses, which, he concluded, express an innate desire for pregnancy. By that age, however, girls have been readied for their future reproductive role, so their play may already be affected by their expectation. Likewise, the influence of hormones on maternal desire also remains inconclusive. Studies by John Money and Anke Ehrhardt have found that girls inadvertently exposed to excess amounts of the male hormone androgen in the womb from drugs, foods, or chemical disorders were uninterested in playing with dolls, and by the age of sixteen, only half expressed a wish for motherhood. Some researchers saw the influence of nature in the results (that female hormones underlie a mothering drive); others, however, saw the impact of nurture (parents knew about the androgen exposure and did not expect their daughters to be normal females).

Other arguments in favor of a maternal instinct have their

flaws: If bearing children were merely second nature and immune to reason, it seems likely that human beings could not refrain from reproducing again and again. The urge to parent is obviously subject to social inhibition, since people have always attempted to limit the number of their offspring. Virtually all women in developed countries suppress their reproductive capacity for most of their lives, and in the present generation, women in many developing nations have averaged three instead of six children. In fact, it usually takes very few babies to satisfy maternal desire. A twenty-four-year study of rural wives raised in the 1950s, who had intended to have several children but ended up with none or only one, found that all were contented, particularly those with one child. Most social scientists have come to believe that parental desires are acquired, not inherent; in fact, anthropologists rarely talk anymore about raw instinct in human behavior.

In debating the existence of a maternal instinct, it seems misleading to make a distinction between homosexual and heterosexual women, since it is not known whether these two groups experience hormonal differences. Regardless of sexual orientation, some women want to mother more than others for a variety of reasons—to have a family, to experience pregnancy, to enjoy children. Although it is a long-standing assumption that lesbians will not become mothers, and one estimate indicates that two-thirds do not, it is the lack of opportunity, threat of custody battles, and fear of homophobia that are the most likely restraining forces. Until recently, schisms within the homosexual community have divided parents from nonparents: Politicized nonmothers criticized lesbian mothers who accepted the inequities of the maternal role, who gravitated to friendships with married mothers, and who were more preoccupied with their progeny than with gender issues. In recent years, in the wake of the gay rights movement and the availability of artificial insemination, there has been less divisiveness and an increase in both the visibility and number of lesbian mothers, many of whom have made innovative co-parenting arrangements. Yet motherhood outside the traditional family, whether lesbian or not, has the unfortunate effect of putting more pronatalist pressure on all women without children.

Some observers wonder if people pass up parenting because of their personalities, or if they develop differently because they are not parents. In the early years of marriage, before children are born, one social scientist has found that young married individuals test more alike in personality than after some become parents. Since females usually have children at an early age, the impact of mothering (or not mothering) on them is a powerful one. "We learn, often through painful self-discipline and self-cauterization, those qualities which are supposed to be 'innate' in us: patience, self-sacrifice, the willingness to repeat endlessly the small, routine chores of socializing a human being," Adrienne Rich observed from her own experience. Likewise, philosopher Sara Ruddick, who formulated a theory about how the act of mothering leads to specific habits of being and thinking, has written that "out of maternal practices distinctive ways of conceptualizing, ordering, and valuing arrive. We *think* differently about what it *means* and what it takes to be 'wonderful,' to be a person, to be real." Defining maternal thinking as a way of looking at life, similar to religious or scientific reasoning, she writes that it is made up of its own kinds of "reflection, judgment, and emotion." Its elements have evolved from the ways of training small children and include an emphasis on the importance of peacefulness, cheerfulness, and steadfast love.

Some of these theorists as well as others have noted that it is possible for completely different kinds of experiences to elicit the same kinds of behaviors. After Sister Rosemarie Greco joined a religious order in her twenties, for instance, she underwent three hours a day of prayer and meditation, an unusual, distinctly nonmaternal way of life for a young woman. Nonetheless, this Roman Catholic nun evolved into an ebullient, serene enabler—much like the one described by Sara Ruddick—in her role as the director of a spiritual retreat in Connecticut. Although Ruddick's theory has come under attack for its culture-bound assumptions about the nature of mothering, her ideas do recognize the importance of learned behaviors as opposed to instinctive ones.

Along these lines, it is also interesting to reflect on the long-standing relationship between mothering and pacifism. Mother's Day was established after the Civil War as an antiwar protest, setting up a political link between the moral authority of motherhood and peace. Yet an 1896 poem, "Parentage," by Alice Meynell, an English poet and mother of eight, blames parents for the deaths of young soldiers: "These, who were childless, are not they who gave / So many dead unto the journeying wave / . . . Not they who doomed by Infallible degrees / Unnumbered men to the innumerable grave. / But those who slay / Are fathers. Theirs are armies. Death is theirs— / . . . And she who slays is she who bears." In this century, Alva Myrdal, the Swedish sociologist, mother, and winner of the Nobel Peace Prize, noted that not all pacifist women were or wish to be mothers (any more than all militarist women want to be childless). More recently, Sara Ruddick has written that nonviolent values arise not from any inherent womanly qualities but from anyone's practice of "maternal preservative love." But journalist Katha Pollitt has disputed Ruddick's assumption of the peacefulness of child rearing, citing maternal violence and mutilation (presumably the circumcision of pubescent African girls); she has imagined that nurses, historians, and gardeners might be better advocates of peace.

Observed from the outside, maternity appears to be more a social than a biological construct, since it is desired only under certain circumstances and usually disapproved of in others—for example, when females are teens, unmarried, lesbian, or on welfare. In the Middle Ages, in fact, women who gave birth outside of wedlock were suspected of being witches who had had intercourse with the devil. Mothers are also supposed to gestate children of their own race; when I am with my niece, who looks like she could be my daughter, we get benevolent smiles, but when I am with my godchild, who is African-American, we get shocked stares at the possibility that I could be her mother.

The reality is that regardless of whether they are parents or not, many people have protective feelings toward the young, even toward those who are not their blood relatives. The Money-Ehrhardt research mentioned earlier found that both men and women with abnormal levels of gender hormones parented adopted children successfully, even genetic males with female genitals who were mistakenly raised as females. The desire to parent can also be stimulated simply by being near newborns or little children, as young fathers have sometimes discovered. A childless friend of mine was once walking on a crowded city street with her young stepdaughter and another little girl; when the girls began to cling to her for safety, my friend had a sudden visceral knowledge that she would, if necessary, protect them fiercely, "like a mama bear." Her spontaneous feeling is a human one, experienced by men or women with or without children, and it has little to do with the urge to bear or raise progeny.

When American women are asked by social scientists why they bear children, they offer social, altruistic, and narcissistic reasons. Sociologist Nancy Chodorow has proposed that women give birth because of a socially induced need for intimacy, not because of natural instinct, gender socialization, or pronatalist pressure. Affected by nature and nurture, males and females have, as anthropologist Margaret Mead has observed, "a willingness or an unwillingness to breed that is deeply imbedded in the character structure." The evidence indicates that not only is mothering apparently not instinctive, it is not even essential to every woman's well-being. In fact, analysts at the Wellesley Center for Research on Women concluded from studies of mothers and nonmothers that motherhood is not even key to female self-esteem. Viewing the feminine personality as adapted for mothering because we all have ovaries, wombs, and breasts is simplistic. It is important to cast a wary eye on generalizations about the nature of women and to realize that our individual differences, inborn or imposed, are deep.

Our mothers and grandmothers may have told us that motherhood can invest all female lives with prestige, influence, meaning, and authority. As a result, young girls rarely want to abandon it without the confidence that there is something else to take its place. At times, those of us without children have felt terror that we have given up too easily the ancient power of maternity, the promise of intimacy, the pleasure of nurturing. Yet the desire for this adventure can be dangerously seductive because motherhood is actually an indirect, fragile, and often ephemeral experience that relies on the dependence and loyalty of others. But while motherhood is placed on a pedestal, mothers are often treated poorly, a contradiction that can cause anxiety and paralysis in potential mothers. Good mothering is expected and bad mothering is condemned, even though birth mothers often have too much responsibility and too few re-sources for their children: "I do not believe that the price of motherhood should be freedom and the right to self-ownership; no one needs these more than the mother," declared A Child-less Wife. As those of us who are nulliparous look around, we realize that all too often mothering has meant diminishment. In the 1960s writer Gael Greene assumed that she would have children until she saw friends with babies feeling imprisoned and resentful, and "fighting a furious battle" against changing, in ways they disliked, into their mothers.

Motherhood, like any intense and intricate passage, is rife with ambivalence, as mothers tell it. Delight in a child can co-exist with dislike of domestic routine. It is the smiles, not the cries, of babies that entrap their mothers, Margaret Mead has observed, or "the silken chains of motherhood" that ensnare them, in the words of writer Anna Quindlen. A friend of mine confessed that she felt more imprisoned as a mother of a de-sired small daughter than as a novitiate in a convent. French writer Marguerite Duras, the mother of a son, has described mothering as a masochistic passion, a "colossal swallowing up which is the essence of all motherhood, the mad love." Like-wise, Sara Maitland, an English writer, has also testified: "Emo-tionally, psychologically, politically, socially my daughter has forced unwelcome changes on me. I feel bullied and victim-ized—intellectually, emotionally, and practically—in precisely the ways I swore I would never be by any man. And I chose that oppression, and I do not regret it; indeed I embrace it with love and joy." And novelist Margaret Drabble has even said that children are "the compensation for feminine surrender," a ca-pitulation that some women find worthwhile and others do not. In the mid-1980s, 25 percent of the American mothers in a poll said the reality of motherhood matched the romantic myth,

20 percent said it did not, and the remaining 55 percent were ambivalent.

Those of us without children are also alert to the words that mothers have written about the "shadow side" of motherhood. Because of its inevitability and the attendant bodily dangers, maternity has not always been romanticized, except by religious celibates in the Christian church. Elizabeth Cady Stanton, nineteenth-century feminist and mother of seven, advocated the primacy of womanhood over wifehood and motherhood, the last of which she called "an animal function." For her part, Charlotte Perkins Gilman, in her 1892 autobiographical novel *The Yellow Wallpaper*, expressed a hysterical sense of maternal suffocation. Then in 1933, Dora Russell, mother of two sons and wife of iconoclastic English philosopher Bertrand Russell, challenged conventionality in her book *Children, Why Do We Have Them?* by asking: "Why especially should the modern young woman, with the whole world opening to her, be summoned back to the cradle and the nursery just because some cranks had announced that children were more interesting and important than had hitherto been thought?" Despite the desire for intimacy that motivates many females to conceive, mothers of young children can feel isolated, since youngsters cannot share adult thoughts and interests. The motherhood myth, according to Jane Lazarre, a mother of two and author of *The Mother Knot*, "leaves out half of the truth." Similar writings, particularly those of Adrienne Rich, influenced me against motherhood in the 1970s, as I realized that enrichment and anxiety, elation and despair, passion and rage, joy and depression were the everlasting emotions of mother love.

Women without children have especially sensitive antennae to what our sisters tell us about motherhood. As I observed my younger sister's entry into parenthood, I was aware of her happiness in her daughter and son as well as her sense of rightness about being a mother. But as I reread my journals from the 1980s, I found them replete with references to her darker feelings as well as my reflections on them, which reinforced what I knew about our mother's maternal experience and influenced me against any late-life effort to become a mother. When my sister gave birth in 1980, she had been terrified because there was no turning back. "There was no idea of owning your own life if you were a mother," she later explained. Balance and detachment were impossible, she felt, and she experienced a painful, anxious, and exhausting compulsion to be with her young children all the time, part of which was her need for passionate emotional connections, which had been lacking in her early life. She also felt it would be disloyal to live and nurture differently from our full-time mother. After talking to my sister on the telephone in the spring of 1984, at the time of her thirty-fourth birthday, when my nephew and niece were four months and four years old, respectively, I observed in my journal that she was depressed about losing the parts of herself that she had jettisoned in order to raise them. Although she had lashed out at me four years earlier about a baby being better than a book, she was in fact upset about losing the dedicated life of a creative artist. Despite such misgivings, I admired her devotion to her children, her creativity as a mother, and her intuitive openness with them. Yet half a year later, I noted that her discontent had had its effect on me, now almost forty-two, and I realized that I would probably not give birth myself.

Mothers and fathers try to avoid or repress their uncomfortable ambivalence, of course, for their own sakes as well as for those of their offspring. One of the ways they have done this over the centuries is by idealizing the maternal and denigrating the nonmaternal. The contramother caricature reflects the ancient cultural fear of the nonnurturing woman, the virago who is angry, demanding, egocentric, or isolated. An archetypal polarity exists between the saintly mother and the evil one, the selfless madonna and the selfish careerist, the life-giver and the life-destroyer. It can include madwomen and unnatural or black mothers like Medea, who killed her own flesh and blood, or cruel stepmothers, like the one in the tale of Cinderella, who favored her own offspring. Stepmothers in literature and in life are scapegoated as the bad mothers, since an unloving stepmother is less threatening to children than an unloving mother. In fact, the love of the mother is so important that in many legends the real mother is absent from the narrative, not only because she diverts her daughter from an unconventional script, but "because the only mother good enough to be a Good Mother is a dead one."

While these exaggerated archetypes are damaging to mothers, they are even more destructive to nonmothers. As the earth mother has come to represent nurturant virtues, the barren woman has been invested with opposite ones. Certainly powerful anxiety is associated with a female who chooses, or permits, childlessness, perhaps rooted in the unspoken fear that one's own mother might have chosen childlessness. The monstrous nullipara is often the ultimate bad woman, as in the parable of Snow White, in which a childless queen regards a beauteous stepdaughter as a feminine rival and tries to have her murdered. Fearsome anti-mothers in literature include Shakespeare's ambitious Lady Macbeth, who calls on spirits to "unsex" her and expresses her willingness to beat out the brains of a nursing baby, and Ibsen's Hedda Gabler, a childless wife who is idle but bored, restless but fearful, cowardly but reckless, and who destroys the manuscript (his child) of a former lover. These archetypes are also sharply etched in Hindu figures—the amorous Parvati, a full-breasted beauty, and the bloodthirsty Kali, symbol of death and destruction with her emaciated breasts.

Although these are exaggerated fictional and mythic figures, Margaret Mead has described in *Male and Female* a continuing, pervasive, cross-cultural fear of the female "who denies or is forced to deny childbearing, childcherishing," adding the twist that she is feared even if her childlessness is inadvertent. In contemporary culture women who are not mothers are often portrayed by the media or in movies as damaged or deviant, as in the film *Fatal Attraction.* Such attitudes can make us feel that we are "just not *nice enough,*" as a childless wife admitted to me. I have occasionally sensed such suspicions from others; they have made me feel ashamed, misunderstood, angry, or sad to be alienated from those who are mothers simply because they became pregnant and I did not. The false overstatements are harmful to both mothers and nonmothers, since no flesh-and-blood female can be as good or bad as a mythical figure. What is more, they arouse guilt and anxiety in *all* females and act to keep us silent.

Of course, the anti-mother archetype has another face: that of the saintly nonmother who devotes herself to the well-being of others. Over the centuries, as we have seen, there have been women without children who were called "social mothers," "symbolic mothers," and "spiritual mothers." Even if a woman chose celibacy, she was likely to spend much of her life rearing younger siblings, nieces, nephews, and cousins in the multigenerational extended family; if she joined a religious order, she often cared for orphans and foundlings, or if she took one of the few paid positions open to females, it probably involved the physical care or instruction of youngsters. In fact, in the nineteenth century, maiden aunts were called "almost mothers" and "more than mothers" by relatives searching for ways to describe those who mothered but were not mothers. In our century, many nulliparas have quietly continued this nurturing tradition, but attempts by reformers and feminists to make an informal motherhood more inclusive of all women have run into resistance.

This is still true today, despite the fact that our definition of the term *mother* is rapidly expanding. Besides birth mothers, procreative science has given us the ovum mother, the womb mother, and the surrogate mother. Ethicist and lawyer George J. Annas of Boston University recently observed that for the first time in history, children can have two biological mothers, but it is possible for youngsters to have a number of psychological ones as well. Society offers women the roles of adoptive mother, foster mother, godmother, lesbian co-mother, stepmother, and step-grandmother, as well as the informal caretaker called the "other-mother" in African-American communities. Some of these women are legal or natal mothers, but others are nulliparas who are mothers only in a moral sense, as mentors, and who should be acknowledged as such. Adrienne Rich, for one, has stated that *rearing* a child, whether one's own or not, essentially makes a woman a mother; she felt that her black nanny, who had no blood children of her own, was definitely a mother.

The expansion of the meaning of motherhood is important for a number of reasons, including the fact that maternal love can be imperfect as well as indifferent or even hostile. Some birth mothers, in fact, are better symbolic than caretaking parents, and they should be allowed to be so without censure. When Charlotte Perkins Gilman's daughter was nine, for instance, the girl went to live with her father and childless stepmother while her mother turned to writing brilliant philosophical treatises about ways to improve social conditions for mothers and children. Attacked in the press for being "an unnatural mother," Gilman strenuously defended her form of maternity: "The unnatural mother cares for Children—all of them—and knows that she can best serve her own by lifting the standard of child-culture for all."

Many of the "great mothers" in literature are not gestational ones, Adrienne Rich has observed, but like the older single women depicted in the novel *Jane Eyre*, they nurture, inspire, assist, and challenge younger women. "For centuries, daughters have been strengthened and energized by nonnatal mothers, who have combined a care for the practical values of survival with an incitement toward further horizons, a compassion for vulnerability with an insistence on our buried strengths," Rich has written. The poet has also made the point that a girl child often has a birth mother who represents conventionality or relatedness and a symbolic mother who stands for rebelliousness or adventurousness. A young woman may identify first with one and then the other, but it would be better, Rich goes on to say, to integrate the values of both mature figures in an attempt to achieve authenticity and strength and thus, she implies, to move toward the transformation of the institution of motherhood.

Among such nominal nineteenth-century mothers were Eliza Farrar, a childless writer and European-educated wife of a Harvard professor, who was a mentor to the brilliant young Margaret Fuller, and Catharine Sedgwick, who called herself the "virgin mother" of her niece and namesake Kate and who, at the age of fifty, led her nieces on a hiking trip through Europe. Instead of rearing any children of her own, Ella Lyman

Cabot spent her time teaching ethics to young people and directing the King's Chapel Sunday school in Boston. Countless other nulligravidas and nulliparas have sheltered, inspired, and instructed youngsters in expert, warmhearted, and imaginative ways: Jane Addams founded the famed Hull House in Chicago, Juliette Gordon Low created the Girl Scouts of America, and Lydia Maria Child edited the first American children's magazine. In this century the unmarried child psychologist Anna Freud (who liked to say that she had three mothers—biological and psychological ones as well as a caretaking *Kindermutter*) directed a war nursery in London during the Second World War and later a famous psychoanalytic institute for children.

One woman friend of mine in this long-standing, nonbiologic mothering tradition feels that she is passing on to her nephew, stepchildren, and goddaughters a quality of attention that is both intense and detached. It is a form of attentiveness that she first experienced from an aunt, a pilot during the Second World War, and from a Manhattan businesswoman, a college friend of her mother's, both of whom were wives without children. Her friendships with these older women when she was a teenager fed her self-esteem and enabled her to take herself more seriously. Unlike her mother, who felt responsible for as well as very invested and involved with her daughter's behavior, the mentors listened to my friend intently but without parental judgment, treating her as a younger but immensely interesting equal. While a mother naturally tends to identify intimately with her own issue in a way that can restrain a child, a modern nonmother, much like a nineteenth-century maiden aunt, has the ability to react to youngsters differently and in ways that can benefit them immensely. "The intellectual activity of motherhood is seeing limitations and boundaries," my friend observed. She also noted that closure or censure was not a habitual kind of mental activity for her, with the result that she easily encourages experimentation and adventurousness in young people.

A number of visionary ideas have been proposed during the past century about how to restructure and redefine motherhood, some of which made room for the nullipara. One point of view holds that only professional breeders should bear children, a notion that seems distasteful and discriminatory. In the name of enlightened motherhood, for example, Charlotte Perkins Gilman advocated that children *not* be reared by their natural mothers but by trained or gifted caretakers because most mothers were too isolated or ignorant to rear children well; she also may have been thinking of mothers like herself, who were temperamentally unsuited to raising children. Likewise, several generations later Margaret Mead predicted that rearing children would become a vocation to be pursued by a diminishing number of highly motivated people, some of them nonparents. In her own case, Mead raised her only child in a "combined" household of families and friends in a Greenwich Village brownstone, an arrangement that left the divorced anthropologist free to take field trips and provided her young daughter with a number of other affectionate "mothers."

Other researchers, writing in the freewheeling 1970s, when the inevitability of parenthood was being questioned, pointed out problems with parental self-selection: Two research projects concluded that young women with the most mature and admirable personalities, who presumably would make the best mothers, were not the ones who were bearing children. A 1977 study by Linda Silka and Sara Kiesler, for example, found that young women with few or no children who favored the women's liberation movement had more rationality, independence, and capacity for attachment than women who opposed it. Another analysis by Bernice E. Lott, published in 1973 in *The American Psychologist*, indicated that pro-liberation women were the most adaptable while anti-liberation ones were more rigid, fearful, and cautious. Lott explained that if the culture assigns child raising arbitrarily to all women, then makes that activity a self-sacrificial one, those who go along will be the females with the fewest alternatives. Whatever the validity of these studies, they imply the value to children of inducing all kinds of women to be involved with them.

Another line of thinking has advocated that everyone undertake some child tending by pairing each child, adopted or biological, to every adult, with or without offspring. An intriguing alternative to the traditional family, as explained by sociologist Judith Lorber, it includes a utopian model that has a male or female parental figure backed up by a national child service consisting of schools that provide medical services, enrichment programs, and occasional overnight care, as well as communes for teenagers. Inherent in the concept is a way to integrate the needs of both dependent children and independent adults. "The result could be true sexual equality and greater individual choices in all areas of life without the sacrifice of the joys of parenting and the emotional security of children," Lorber has explained. Other innovative ideas include sociologist Jessie Bernard's proposal to draft youths into child care, as well as the practice of polygamy, as suggested by Elizabeth Joseph, a lawyer and one of a Utah man's nine wives, all of whom tend one another's children. Although most of these quixotic ideas are unworkable for many reasons, including the unwillingness of everyone to parent and many mothers' belief in their superiority as parents, they assume the importance of including a wide variety of personalities, including those of nonparents, in nurturing the next generation.

In 1975, the same year that Lorber's proposal was made, Lucia Valeska expressed a similar idea: "All women who are able to plot their destinies with the relative mobility of the childfree should be encouraged to take on at least one existing child, part time or full time," she wrote. "Love that child, teach her something she might otherwise never learn, show her respect she might not find elsewhere." But Valeska discovered to her dismay that women in feminist collectives without offspring did not willingly share child care. "Of course the privileged, be they men in power or your so-called childfree sisters, will *never* give up their advantages out of the goodness of their hearts," she wrote angrily at the time. Valeska, a lesbian whose former husband ended up with custody of her three children, declared that "*my* children must become *our* children." She went on, hopeful that the discord between mothers and nonmothers was not as deep as it appeared: "If the childfree raise existing children, more people than ever will 'have' children. The line between biological and non-biological mothers will begin to disappear."

Since stay-at-home mothers often suffer from solitary mothering, and women without children often regret their separateness from toddlers or teenagers, it would be valuable to erase the line between them. But child-rearing arrangements that might allow more part-time mothering have rarely found much support from family members, corporations, or government agencies. And because few good alternatives exist, there remains a tenacious belief that unsalaried birth mothers are the best caregivers. Two decades ago, Lucia Valeska recognized that it would take the strenuous efforts of mothers to galvanize reforms. But busy and isolated in their homes, most mothers today remain inactive politically and interested only in more realistic private solutions to their baby-sitting needs. Meanwhile, young women who still hope to have children seem to be more outspoken about inequalities in the workplace than about inequalities within the institution of motherhood. Although more of their older sisters are doing it all, the younger women are not blind to the difficulties, and many remain uncertain about whether to become mothers. Yet despite the de facto existence of some full-time breeders in our country, the growing trend toward more part-time parenting for all is hopeful. Still, as we recall our early years with our mothers and recognize the struggles of our sisters, it becomes evident that the concept, the construct, of motherhood needs to be released from the limits of biology to encompass wider visions for everyone's sake, especially the children's.

FIVE

DREAMING ABOUT A CHILD, LOVING CHILDLIKENESS

Many people have lingering fantasies about an imaginary child, a son or daughter they never bore, inadvertently or not. A father of daughters may yearn for a like-minded young son, or a mother of sons may desire a companionable daughter; I remember hearing one young mother of a son and daughter daydream about giving birth to yet another infant, one she realistically knew she was unable to raise. While the imaginings of parents with existing children have the bittersweet edge of experience, the reveries of nonparents—especially the reluctantly childless—are likely to be highly romanticized, since they are infused with the force of the unknown. It is ironic that while those among us who are infertile may cling to idealized fantasies about unborn children, many parents are forced, often by circumstances, to be neglectful of their flesh-and-blood progeny. The intentionally and unintentionally childless, however, may be able to transform their phantom children into something else, perhaps into life-affirming attitudes within themselves and toward others. It is important, for example, to cherish childlike qualities like curiosity and creativity wherever we find them, particularly in the real children around us.

115

When I was in my early thirties, I used to visualize a dark-eyed daughter, brunette and delicate, who was a combination of the best physical features of myself and my boyfriend; this dream child was, of course, charmingly intelligent, quiet and obedient, loyal and adoring, and my ever-present little friend. Her potential existence was so real to me that from time to time I used to thumb through a dictionary of girls' given names for those that phonetically fit with my boyfriend's surname. In my imagination, her reality would re-create the intimacy of my earliest years with my mother, but our relationship would have its own uniqueness. Her care, I thought, would also be absorbing and a distraction from the boredom of work. Although unarticulated at the time, my assumption was that a little girl's presence would also overcome the existential loneliness in my life. This pleasant fantasy of mine, however, was inevitably brought up short by my other desires and by the realities of my life, and then her image would drift away.

The literary imagination has also produced chimerical children, some born and others not, like the baby daughter in Toni Morrison's novel *Beloved*, whose mother murdered her in order to save her from a life of slavery. There is an interesting use of the dream-child motif in the 1962 play *Who's Afraid of Virginia Woolf?* by Edward Albee, who had no biological progeny. In the drama, a middle-aged married couple without offspring fight viciously over an imagined being called "The Kid"—about his upbringing, appearance, paternity, and very existence—in a sadistic game called "Bringing Up Baby." The husband, George, is an ineffectual history professor at a small college, and his homemaker wife, Martha, the daughter of the college president, is an enraged virago because her husband has not lived out her ambitions. In the vacuum of her life, she has created a phantom son who perhaps, in her mind, could let her live vicariously through him. When arguing about their non-existent child, George and Martha are obviously, though unconsciously, describing the lost innocent, trusting, and hopeful aspects of their love for one another, before they became hardened, cynical, and mutually destructive. The invented child is now used as another weapon with which to maim each other. As a younger childless couple arrives on stage, the dialogue reveals that the girlish wife used a false pregnancy to trick her husband into marriage but is pathetically fearful of a real one. George had warned Martha against talking about "The Kid" in front of others, but she defiantly announces to the company that their son will turn twenty-one the next day. Toward the end of the drama, angry at her betrayal, George announces to Martha in the presence of their gullible guests that their son is dead. Her reaction is one of tremendous grief and rage at the end of her illusion, which filled such an emotional void for her.

The disappearance of a dream child is undoubtedly less traumatic than the loss of a real son or daughter to miscarriage, abortion, stillbirth, or early death, but it is a real bereavement nonetheless. A sense of sadness may be fleeting or persistent, mild or severe. Some of those with no biological descendants, especially the infertile, must mourn an imaginary creature like a living child lost to actual death—"the small smiles missed, small hands and feet unseen, silky skin untouched, and the first step not taken," in the words of one nonmother. Abandoning an unobtainable and idealized rapport with an unborn being has its own poignancy and power, particularly if it is built on unrealized aspects of ourselves. In one theory, a woman's hope for the birth of a male child is a hidden wish for an active and assertive self, while a mother's desire for a female child is an expression of her desire for more empathy and relatedness in her life.

My own experience partly confirms and partly contradicts this notion. When I first considered getting pregnant, my journalistic career demanded that I be aggressive in the fiercely competitive arena around me, but it was a requirement that often repelled me. I had a growing urge for more gentleness and closeness in my daily life, and I assumed that a daughter would provide it. But this female creature of my imagination also had characteristics of my favorite 1940s cartoon character, Little Lulu, the mischievous brat with black ringlets and Mary Janes. She was my childhood alter ego both because my relatives nicknamed me Lulu and because I admired her daring naughtiness. Besides being my little friend, my daughter would, in my reverie, be the reincarnation of the fearless, adventurous small girl whom I had left behind after the earliest years of my childhood—a fiction too oversized for any real child to fulfill, of course.

Other willingly childfree women besides myself have had intense imaginings about their unborn children, as well as about themselves as mothers. An abortion in the 1930s occasioned much complicated grief for diarist Anaïs Nin, a childless wife who was pregnant by her lover, the writer Henry Miller. Her late-term illegal abortion was long and difficult, even life-threatening, because of her ambivalence about it, she believed. "All of me which chose to keep, to lull, to embrace, to love; all of me which carried, preserved, protected; all of me which wanted to imprison the whole world in its passionate tenderness; this part of me would not thrust out the child, nor this past which had died in me," she wrote in a passage from one of her famous diaries. When the fetus finally emerged, she insisted on seeing it. "As I looked at the dead child, for a moment I hated it for all the pain it had caused me, and it was only later that this flare of anger turned into great sadness. Regrets, long dreams of what this little girl might have been. A dead creation, my first dead creation. The deep pain caused by any death, and any destruction. The failure of my motherhood, or at least the embodiment of it, all my hopes of real, human, simple, direct motherhood lying dead, and the only one left to me, [D. H.] Lawrence's symbolic motherhood, bringing more hope into the world. But the simple human flowering denied to me."

When I myself awoke from a surgical procedure at age thirty-eight that would make pregnancy problematic for me, I wept for the receding memory of my dream daughter. As my journal reminded me years later, I had once envisioned motherhood as a way to revitalize myself during stagnant phases of my life; others whom I talked to or read about also imagined or experienced motherhood as a yearning for an unexpressed self, a second chance at life, for the opportunity to create someone like themselves, only better. It is evident that fantasy constantly infuses our feelings about children. When Italian writer Oriana Fallaci asked to see the embryo she had miscarried, she was surprised to find that the creature she had so richly fantasized looked like "a little fish," a realization that released her from her imaginings. The same year that I had surgery, I read a newspaper story about the discovery of five infant skeletons in the attic of an elderly unmarried woman's house after her death; she had remorsefully strangled at least three of the out-of-wedlock babies, and, unable or unwilling to bury them, had wrapped them in newspapers and placed them in an old trunk. Shocked but fascinated by the macabre article, I realized that on some level the account reminded me of the named but unconceived child buried in my memory, the little skeleton entombed in my psyche.

Although I had a richly imagined child, I resisted having a real one during the years when I was presumably most ripe for pregnancy. By midlife, whether or not I got pregnant did not matter very much, if it really ever had, since I had been against it or unsure about it for more years than not. After marrying again in my forties, I gave up birth control but still did not conceive. I never found out if I was technically barren or not, since I never went to a fertility specialist. A little mystery remains in my mind, however, since a gynecologist once discovered what he called "dead tissue" in my uterus after a dilation and curettage. Had I been pregnant? I'll never know. I'm glad, though, that my ability to conceive and carry remains unknown. It leaves me with a sense of agency, authority, and the assumption that I was capable of childbirth. For the infertile, however, the passage to childlessness is much more difficult and presents dangers if it remains unresolved.

Obviously the imagined son or daughter is hardest for the reluctantly childless to give up because they had always expected the fantasy to become real. They are not alone in their anguish. Besides those who have difficulty begetting or bearing children, there are others who are inadvertently childless because they are older, single, unsettled, or sterilized. Promiscuous, poor, disabled, or retarded women, as well as those of color, have often been surgically sterilized against their wills, sometimes as the price for an abortion. Others have lost a child to death, adoption, or court order in instances of bitter divorces and deep alienations.

The loss of existing children to early death has actually been a common human experience. In past centuries, when child mortality was so high that half of those born did not live, relatives used distancing and rationalizing to deal with their losses. Many of the accounts from bereaved parents are deeply moving, like the following one from the diary of a New England wife. In May 1871, Annie Holmes Ricketson left New Bedford, Massachusetts, with her husband, a whaling captain, for a three-and-a-half-year voyage. At the age of thirty, she remained without offspring since her first baby had been stillborn four years earlier. Six months' pregnant at the time of the departure, she gave birth a few months later in Portugal to a three-pound female infant, who died shortly afterward. As was customary, Annie dressed the little body in baby clothes and, adding a pink ribbon, had it photographed before burial. "Now my little one is an angel with the angels in Heaven," Annie wrote sadly in her diary, calling on her religious faith to justify the tragedy. "It is much better off than it would be here in this wicked would [sic] of ours."

Although infant mortality has been drastically reduced, there remain many would-be parents. Many are unable to adopt. While fifty thousand American infants and older children are adopted each year, there are about a million infertile couples interested in finding a child. A year or two after my second marriage, when it became apparent that I was not getting pregnant, I telephoned an adoption agency, called Thursday's Child, only to learn how difficult it would be for an older, recently married couple to adopt a healthy American infant. I recall being told by a rather unsympathetic person that the prospect of adopting a foreign child was also virtually impossible, since only one or two Third World countries would even consider an application from a couple over the age of forty. Private, unregulated routes to adoption seemed even more expensive and onerous. A complicating factor was my husband's lack of enthusiasm for an adopted child and his desire for a genetic one, but when he suggested the possibility of surrogate motherhood, I felt a sharp repulsion at the idea of raising a child that was his and another woman's. So we let the matter drop.

The folktales that portray barren wives as bitter, envious, and vindictive are probably grounded in reality because of the traditional link between a wedded woman's status and the birth of sons. Beginning with the Old Testament, the history of humankind is full of examples. Among the most extreme are those in English history: The childless wives of King Henry VIII of England were beheaded or divorced; and although Catherine of Braganza, a dark-eyed Portuguese princess who was married in 1662 to Charles II, was unable to give birth to a live infant (she had one miscarriage and three stillbirths), the king refused to divorce her, but she was hurt and humiliated by the fact that he had sixteen children by eight mistresses whom she had to entertain.

Many of the unhappily childless struggle with a feeling of emptiness or lack of fruition, or the anxiety of remaining girlish, not entirely grown up. Although it is as likely for a male as a female to be infertile, psychologists and social workers report that women tend to suffer more from infertility, probably because of their early expectations and society's emphasis on maternity as the cornerstone of femininity. The assumption of fecundity remains pervasive—the use of the words *reproductive rights*, for instance, usually means the option *not* to exercise them—so that those who cannot conceive or carry often feel shock, shame, and narcissistic injury. One woman I interviewed admitted to living with a sense of "background sadness" that erupted unexpectedly. Many infertile women find going to baby showers deeply painful. Others often feel like unwilling outsiders or reluctant nonconformists, and they are unprepared for a way of life without children, an otherhood of unimagined possibilities. Margarete Sandelowski, a nurse who has worked with infecund women, reports that many of these women form an unhappy sisterhood marked by jealousy when one gets pregnant or hostility when another decides to accept childlessness. They can feel enraged, irrationally so, at abortion-rights activists, child abusers, reluctant mothers, and the deliberately childfree. They also complain about contradictory messages from feminists: that some feminists celebrate maternity, yet others imply that it is egocentric or elitist for women to want their own genetic issue when so many abandoned children already exist.

Sterility or infertility, when they are understood as barrenness, can still arouse primordial fears: Canadian writer Margaret Atwood's novel *The Handmaid's Tale* imagines a terrifying future in which older, wealthy, infertile wives covet the babies of younger, enslaved, natural mothers. Of the more than five million American couples who are having difficulty giving birth, more than half seek fertility interventions every year. Infecundity has declined slightly since 1965 among females in their thirties, but it has risen among younger women for a number of reasons, including the prevalence of venereal diseases. Such women sometimes invest the so-called empty womb with great emotional meaning and pursue pregnancy with a sense of primal urgency. The two-billion-dollar-a-year fertility industry can, ironically, prolong the pain of the infecund by unrealistically raising their hopes, since very costly fertilization procedures succeed infrequently. Now that it is technically possible to carry a child in utero after menopause, the struggle to bear can be virtually interminable, obliterating other aspects of life.

The situation is made worse because the unfruitful woman is often blamed by conservative voices in the culture for her childlessness. She may internalize these accusations and guiltily regard her infecundity as punishment for misdeeds or mistakes. In the nineteenth century, barrenness was linked to female education and, hence, women's emancipation, based on the outdated belief that blood used by the brain was unavailable to the womb. In this century, Freudian psychiatrists have regarded sterility as an unconscious manifestation of a woman's neurotic fear of her female nature. Now, in a similar kind of censure, the infertile woman who puts off pregnancy to get an education or to become financially secure is considered the culprit and blamed for self-centeredness. It is even worse if she enjoyed her eroticism during her single years; an acquaintance of mine, who was rendered infertile by pelvic inflammatory disease, remarked to me sadly that she was a victim of the sexual revolution, not, as was actually the case, the victim of a neglectful gynecologist.

Some of these emotions are underscored by a woman's religion or ethnicity; in Hispanic cultures, for example, motherhood is esteemed as the essence of womanhood. When Mexican painter Frida Kahlo was unable to bear a child, she identified with the martyrdom of the Virgin Mary, the "Mater Dolorosa." The starkness and force of the imagery in Kahlo's self-portraits is largely attributable to her extreme grief over her three miscarriages. Her 1932 depiction of a life-threatening miscarriage at three and a half months, *Henry Ford Hospital*, is set against the drab cityscape of Detroit, where the homesick artist was living with her husband, Diego Rivera, while he worked on commissioned murals. The painting shows a naked, vulnerable body lying on a bloodstained bed, and a face that resembled her own with a tear running down its cheek. Red ribbons, like umbilical arteries, extended from the empty uterus to various images evoked by the miscarriage—an orchid, a male fetus, a broken torso, and a sterilizing instrument. As an unwilling nullipara, the artist was confronted by the need to conceive herself "in an entirely uncharted space, both literally and figuratively," according to one art historian.

Although Kahlo, who had broken her pelvis in her youth, remained in physical and psychic pain for the remainder of her life, she immediately understood the positive implications of her predicament. In a revealing lithograph she made the same summer as *Henry Ford Hospital*, another look-alike female nude is split down the middle: The left side of the picture shows a hideous fetus whose umbilical cord tightly binds a woman's leg; the right side contains a weeping moon, along with uterine blood from the miscarriage that fertilizes new plant life, and two arms—one making a strong fist, the other holding an easel. The image clearly indicates that the death of the unborn child has generated new life both in nature and in art; the fist also shows the artist's expression of courage, and the easel her understanding of her vocation. It was during that time, in the aftershock of her mother's death and her realization that she would never be a mother herself, that Kahlo initiated her mature and compelling style as an artist.

Despite Kahlo's earlier insight about how to resolve her suffering, she remained morbidly obsessed by dead children, an unwholesome fascination that may have been related to her degenerating health and disappointing marriage. In any event, she kept a human fetus preserved in a jar of formaldehyde in her bedroom, and she slept under an old picture of a lifeless, flower-bedecked baby, one of the innocent *angelitos*, or little angels, in the mortuary portrait tradition. Her compositions also remained haunted by death. Five years after making the lithograph, she painted *The Deceased Dimas*, a boy dressed for burial with a crown on his head, as well as *Me and My Doll*, a sardonic rendering of a painted madonna with toy baby. A decade later she painted *Self-Portrait with Monkey*, a macabre play on the mother-and-daughter theme in which both the woman and animal wear golden hair ribbons; the painting is particularly disturbing, since the wild creature's paws are near the painter's neck, suggesting that the woman's thwarted desire for a child might cause her to be choked to death.

Likewise, Henrik Ibsen's 1886 play *Rosmersholm* depicts an unfruitful but blameless wife, who feels so worthless because of her barrenness that she kills herself. Another woman who was unable to exorcise her grief over childlessness was the early-twentieth-century writer Susan Glaspell, who did not dare get pregnant because of health problems. A college-educated New Woman from Iowa, she lived in Greenwich Village, where she wrote fiction and drama about childless, sensitive, restless, and discontented females like herself. Married to George Cram Cook, manager of the Provincetown Players, and stepmother to his two children, she moved with him to Greece before his sudden death. In a posthumous memoir about him, she wrote bitterly that she would have traded the "greater intensity" of their marriage for biological children. Adding that she imagined that writing novels was not as gratifying as creating life, she admitted that when mothers remarked that her books must be like children to her, she would glance at their babies' diapers drying by the fire and wonder if they really thought she felt that way. It is painful to read her self-pitying regrets and to realize how often such feelings result from the loss of choice about childbearing.

One friend of mine, who discovered her infertility after she married for the first time around the age of forty, suddenly began to yearn for a child, imagining that she would love it the way she had never loved before. She experienced her visceral feeling as "a raw need to love," she said. "There was something about the fantasy of a mother and a baby that encapsulated a beautiful rosy image of love that was untouchable by anything else." It is possible that her desire for an infant, repressed while she was single, was suddenly released by being married. Over time, as she gradually understood the genesis of her grief—her connection of unconditional devotion with maternal passion— she realized that there were plenty of children and adults in her life whom she could adore and care for intensely, and this insight released her from her need to be a natal mother. "That was my baby crisis," she explained. "That was my crisis of love."

The intentionally childfree tend to be secular, but the inadvertently childless are more likely to be influenced by religious faiths like Roman Catholicism, which strongly advocate procreativity and traditional family life, even allowing childless unions to be annulled. Church fathers base their teachings on the Old Testament command that believers be fruitful and multiply as well as on the belief in the sanctity of unborn life. To make matters worse, a number of biblical stories indicate that barrenness is a sign of God's displeasure or indifference. In the New Testament, the apostle Paul also preached that the pain of childbirth saved women from original sin.

Recently, however, some infertile women associated with orthodox or fundamentalist Christian faiths have turned to the Bible for affirmation of themselves as women without children. They recognize that Jesus, who had a welcoming and nonpossessive way with youngsters, and a number of other biblical personages had no progeny, among them Miriam, a prophet; Deborah, judge of Israel; Mary and Martha, who took care of Jesus; and the traveling tent makers, Priscilla and Aquila. They also note that Rachel, a biblical woman who expressed great grief at her inability to conceive—"Give me sons, or I shall die"—died instead from giving birth to her seventh child. They have discovered, as well, a biblical passage (Isaiah 54:1–3) that suggests that those without progeny can instead be symbolic or spiritual givers of life: "Sing, O barren, thou that didst not bear; break forth into singing, and cry aloud, thou that didst not travail with child: for more are the children of the desolate than the children of the married wife, saith the Lord. Enlarge the place of thy tent, and let them stretch forth the curtains of thine habitations: spare not, lengthen thy cords, and strengthen thy stakes; For thou shalt break forth on the right hand and on the left; and thy seed shall inherit the Gentiles, and make the desolate cities to be inhabited."

For women who have always wanted to be mothers, infertility is a cruel blow, and their route to equanimity is an arduous one. Those who remain painfully unresolved tend to confuse their sadness with their worry about lack of womanliness or the stigma of childlessness. Others find ways to dissipate their grief, like the woman who deliberately abolished the dead child of her imagination, a creature she associated with a sense of victimization, or like those who recall their original ambivalence about parenting, which caused them to postpone it until sterility set in. One couple marked the end of an unsuccessful struggle with infertility with a memorial service for a phantom "Isaac," then felt resolution, relief, and a "readiness to get on with life." Jean and Michael Carter, a gynecologist and English professor, respectively, who fought infecundity for five years, made a transition from what they called being childless to being childfree by embracing it, they explained, "as a positive, freeing thing." Whatever the reasons for not giving birth, researchers have observed in recent years, almost everyone eventually adapts to life without natural children with few lasting regrets.

Regardless of how the infertile adjust to childlessness, most do not get over their outrage at neglectful parents. Children often have difficult childhoods in our country; despite rhetoric to the contrary, they are devalued by grown-ups and government policy alike. In the nation's collective guilt toward the youngest Americans, the childless are falsely accused as the ones who dislike children. It is bitterly ironic that those who are reluctantly without offspring are often included in this categorization. In light of this, it is important to take a look at the role of children in the culture, both in the past and in the present.

Over the centuries, our understanding and appreciation of children has changed. French historian Philippe Ariès theorized that until the concept of childhood was established in the seventeenth century, children were treated like undersized adults and put to work. Another historian, who read old family diaries to detect attitudes toward girls and boys from the sixteenth through nineteenth centuries, found that most young people were enjoyed, even if they were considered troublesome at times. Then, as families moved off their farms in the nineteenth century, the economic value of the child declined, especially after the passage of child labor and compulsory education laws. As more middle-class children survived early childhood and needed expensive schooling, parents had fewer of them. Paradoxically, after they became less valuable economically, they became more important emotionally. The sentimentalization, even the "sacralization," of childhood happened during this time, along with the creation of children's literature, the study of pedology, and, eventually, the development of child psychology.

A century later, in March 1974, as the United States birthrate fell sharply, *Esquire* magazine headlined a cover article, "Do Americans Suddenly Hate Children?" What was happening, as we have seen, was that young couples, freed by modern contraceptives and encouraged by new opportunities, were putting off parenthood. Meanwhile, the old wives' tale about a baby strengthening a marriage came into question. Social scientists concluded that the birth of an initial infant disrupts the marital bond by replacing a stable duo with an unstable trio; the closeness of a mother and child is often at the expense of rapport with a spouse. Echoing my concerns in the 1970s, one feminist thinker explained that when a man and woman revert to a more traditional division of labor after the arrival of a baby, the housewife's power often declines, while the breadwinner's increases. The evidence indicated that offspring can keep a mother and father together for the sake of the family but not necessarily because of their greater happiness together. In other eras, adults had murdered or abandoned unwanted progeny, so effective birth control was certainly an advance over cruelty to children. In fact, the antinatalist attitude of the 1970s was actually more antiparenthood than antichild, and it was brought about by widespread socioeconomic changes.

Although the United Nations designated 1979 the Year of the Child, and it was followed by a decade of pro-family propaganda in America, child assistance programs were decimated during the 1980s. As more than half of all mothers with preschool-age children entered the job market, only a fifth of the ten million children in out-of-home care were in the few licensed day-care centers—most of the rest were cared for informally in baby-sitters' or the children's homes. Other signs of social stress and neglect of children were apparent: The poverty rate for families with school-age children surged, along with the number of births to unmarried mothers, youngsters placed in foster care, and children living in one-parent households. Children's cognitive test scores dropped, while juvenile crime and teenage suicide rates rose. Reports of physical and emotional abuse of children tripled and hit record levels. By the early 1990s, the social well-being of American youngsters had declined because of sharp increases in child poverty and child abuse, driving the nation's overall social well-being to its lowest point in two decades. The Council on Families in America observed around the same time that "the current generation of children and youth is the first in our nation's history to be less well off—psychologically, socially, economically, and morally—than their parents." It is evident that children are endangered in America, but not necessarily by nonparents.

By the late 1980s, despite a decade of pronatal propaganda, parenthood as well as childbirth was being seriously questioned, according to data published in *The Journal of Marriage and the Family*. Half of the six hundred young couples questioned in a study rated freedom of movement, leisure time, and a wife's job opportunities as equally or more valuable than raising children. Time alone with a spouse was scored as *more* important than child rearing. The respondents appreciated the prospect of sons and daughters as "love objects," means to "marital and family bonding," and "important buffers against loneliness and impersonality," but they were apprehensive about children's absorption of their time, energy, and money. In the end, they gave parenting "only a slight edge" over other aspects of life.

Young children, of course, can be appealingly childlike or maddeningly childish. While humorist W. C. Fields, who had no offspring, got away with calling himself a "misopedist," or child hater, a nullipara finds the accusation distressing because it is rarely true and because it evokes the anti-mother caricature. Only a minority of the intentionally childfree tell sociologists that they dislike kids; Sharon K. Houseknecht, in her review of scores of studies about deliberate nonparents, found that almost as many women were worried about bringing youngsters into an anti-child culture as objected to them. Still, parents as well as nonparents who resent or feel uncomfortable with puerile behavior certainly exist.

Often the childless with strong aversions to parenthood are those who have had retarded, deformed, or disturbed siblings. Some reject what they regard as the vicarious living of parenting. Many are uninterested in living child-centered lives or incapable of adjusting to a child's pace. Some admit to wondering if they have the patience to meet childish demands. (One group of young single women seeking tubal ligations included those who imagined that a child with insistent needs would be "a persecutor.") Others are afraid to recall and relive painful childhoods through the eyes of their own offspring. A few avoid raising youngsters because they fear arousing their own repressed childlike qualities, such as spontaneity or openness. Some of these rationales, of course, appear neurotic, immature, or narcissistic. But if someone has little tolerance for children, the lesser evil is not becoming a parent.

I have always found the company of little children either immensely enchanting or utterly boring. So I am probably implicated in the adult tendency to overvalue or undervalue youngsters. As a young girl I was certain that my brother a decade younger than myself, a boy with huge dark-blue eyes and black eyelashes, was the most adorable and sweet-tempered creature on earth, but I rarely took care of him. And an old family movie shows my sister and me at ages two and ten, respectively, wearing hair ribbons and party dresses, romping on a Sunday summer afternoon at the country home of my step-father's parents. At first I am seen pushing a small blond girl on a swing, then asking her to step on my shadow as I dance across the lawn. Finally I pick her up and place her in her grandmother's arms. The celluloid minutes were typical of the playfulness and gentle teasing, not the obligation of baby-sitting, that shaped my relationships with my much younger siblings, affected by my mother's desire to spare me any responsibility for their care.

Some of my adult experiences with children have reminded me of my early attitude toward kids. In recent years, I have hosted a winsome young African-American girl from the Bronx and enabled her to go to summer camp. When she was seven or eight, it was immensely gratifying when she expressed her joy about being in my garden by drawing an exuberant picture of a tiny smiling girl dwarfed by huge red and purple flowers and a gigantic yellow ball of sunshine. One time I was pleased and hopeful for her when, after observing me at my desk, she announced that when she grew up she wanted to become "an office lady." But when I reviewed entries in my journal, which were written during the initial days of her first visit, I remembered that the demands of this lively little girl had made writing at home virtually impossible, and I quickly dropped any lingering idea about adopting a child of my own. Now that my young friend, who is now my goddaughter, has become older and we are attempting to get beyond our generational and cultural differences, I find her endearing when she enjoys herself but annoying when she is moody. Our relationship has made me feel humbled by the reality that, at least for me, it is far more difficult to create a daily loving rapport with a living child rather than with an imaginary one.

As we near the end of the twentieth century, a majority of Americans are no longer living with children, making it possible for many of them to forget or ignore them. Yet a number of nulliparas may feel that something is missing, and they may want to nurture certain children, children of choice. I read about one woman who finally decided against motherhood after realizing she did not have enough time for the children she already knew. Nightclub singer Josephine Baker was in her late forties when she began to gather children from many races and nationalities into what she called the "Rainbow Tribe." A nun explained her choice of celibacy by saying that she wanted to shepherd many more children than she could give birth to herself. And novelist Gail Godwin has written about "collecting, through a process of elective affinities, a little family of children I hope to know all my life"; but she has admitted that although she was charmed by these children, when "chaos" broke out she was glad to withdraw "back into childlessness." Two decades ago Lucia Valenska described the debate about the words *childless* or *childfree* as merely rhetorical: "Clearly, with or without children, women are not free in our society. Even more important, as long as children exist, it is a delusion to speak of being free of them. They are still all out there, impatiently clamoring for recognition and support." Whatever our attitudes toward infants, toddlers, or youths, it seems reasonable and right to be concerned about them. It is important for those of us without children to regard youngsters as children of us all, whether that means tending them ourselves, voting for school bond issues and pro-child political agendas, or valuing their childlikeness.

Not everyone without offspring has the chance for enduring friendships with children, but childlike virtues are available to everyone. The potential for growth, genuineness, and creativity is around us as well as within ourselves. Appealing qualities of childhood are invested in dream children, but they also reside, more realistically, in existing children, in our memories of ourselves as youngsters, and in our mature personalities as adults. Whether our desire is for childbirth or rebirth, our core characters are composed of our earliest memories and private histories, which old photographs can help us remember. I recall a black-and-white picture that my mother snapped of me at around the age of four, after she had carefully dressed me for a visit to my father in a tweed coat with velvet collar and a beribboned Scottish cap. Seated on my small suitcase with a baby doll in arm, I had an innocent and trusting look on my face as well as one that appeared eager for adventure. When I look at the old snapshot now, it generates memories of pride and confidence, pleasure and wholeness that I felt in my earliest years. By connecting to the girls or boys we once were, it is easier to get more enjoyment, paradoxically, from both children and childlessness. When we realize that childfullness can be part of everyday life, for instance, any envy or sadness we may experience in the presence of young people evaporates.

Besides the real child of our memories or the phantom child of our imaginations, another kind of young creature is represented by the eternal child or *puer aeternis* archetype, one that is given divine form in various religious traditions as the child-god Hermes, the child Krishna, and the Christ child. The archetype also appears in myth and literature in many cultures: French aviator Antoine de Saint-Exupéry created a charming eternal boy in his children's book *The Little Prince*, a naive child who evidently represented his alter ego and possibly an unborn son as well. The author described (as well as rendered in watercolor) an ingenuous young prince with a trusting and idealistic persona, who talks wistfully about stars and roses and is unable to comprehend the world of grown-ups. Like his small hero, Saint-Exupéry in his own life was unable to reconcile his unrealistic dreams with earthbound realities, and he died tragically at a young age while piloting a small plane over North Africa. Lacking such counterbalancing traits as reliability and wisdom, the *puer* or *puella aeternis* can move too easily from enthusiasm to recklessness.

The power of this archetype, in its good and bad aspects, is compelling to many adults. For some, it is simple nostalgia for what one nonmother called "a time of gingerbread, magical spirits, and enchanted lands." For others, it represents a powerful drive to return to the best in oneself. Childlike sincerity translated into an adult idiom, for instance, enables a person to be natural and truthful as well as expressive and purposeful. Sometimes youthful virtues, including that of playfulness, are especially treasured by those whose difficult childhoods made it impossible for them to be childlike when they were young. My mother has observed that I was too grave as a child, and I sometimes wonder if my willingness to be childless was affected by my being a late bloomer and by my belated ability to dream, explore, create, and enjoy myself. In our quest for renewing experiences in adulthood, it is typical for nulliparas to search for them in love relationships, through chosen work, or with children of choice.

Mothers often anticipate parenthood as a way to keep them in touch with such appealing virtues: One woman without children imagined that the existence of an "invisible child" within herself, which she described as the quality of enthusiasm, might disappear if she did not give birth to a child; another explained that she hoped that having a baby would infuse her life with "energy, directness, and anarchy." Such hopes may be unrealistic, however, since the responsibilities of parenthood can destroy the ebullience of a young adult. After taking on the care of a young uninhibited creature, a mother or father often needs to counterbalance such behavior with discipline and authority for the sake of the child's safety. In other cases, youthful qualities like impulsiveness and impishness in a mother or father can struggle for ascendency with those of their offspring. Parents can also get into the habit of allowing their progeny to express youthfulness for them and, as a result, they can become cut off from their own sense of wonder.

Some potential parents have expressed the hope that parenting would allow them to recall and relive aspects of their own childhoods and heal old childhood wounds. The desire for a child can, in fact, be a disguised urge to nurture ourselves, our abilities, and our imaginations—and one that can be satisfied by doing so. Stanislav Grof, a psychiatrist who has no children, has advised others without children to heal childhood pain through honest introspection and creativity. One nullipara, who wanted to revive aspects of an earlier self, decided to write a memoir of her girlhood. After Irena Klepfisz decided against motherhood, she discovered her old doll and became tearful; it made her remember how, as a little girl, she had cared for it the way she had wanted her mother to care for her—"it was not a baby that I envisioned, but rather myself, five or six years old, cradling the doll in my arms and rocking it gently to sleep." Likewise, at a time when I was re-creating my life between marriages, a woman friend told me about her dream that I had given birth to a daughter who strongly resembled me; evidently the imagined look-alike child symbolized her perception that I had developed a renewed or reinvented self.

In fact, nulliparas may more easily retain youthful virtues by *not* becoming parents. Certainly their delight in their freedom, flexibility, and free time are frequently mentioned as reasons to remain childfree, according to sociologists. Men and women without children also tell interviewers about their passionate involvement in original work that demands inspiration and inventiveness as well as many hours alone. Such absorption is antithetical to the activities involved in taking care of a family. In fact, the creative process often needs to be protected and nurtured much the way a child does. Alfred Stieglitz liked to call Georgia O'Keeffe "The Great Child," believing that his wife was the incarnation of an open and natural female sensibility that would be destroyed by the cares of motherhood; he also regarded her renderings of immense blossoms and gorgeous abstractions as their progeny, highly charged images that emerged from intimate and erotic moments between them.

As a matter of fact, some adults without genetic offspring retain an acute ability to enter into children's imaginations. Interestingly, many authors of famous juvenile books and inventors of legendary fictive youths were or are childless. Danish storyteller Hans Christian Andersen comes to mind, as does the British dramatist J. M. Barrie, the author of *Peter Pan*. The authors of the classic children's books, *Alice in Wonderland* and *Mary Poppins*, were also without children. In this country there was Theodor Seuss Geisel, better known as Dr. Seuss, whose first wife was infertile; an only child who, as an adult, rarely felt comfortable around children, he believed that his fanciful inventiveness might have been subdued by the realities of fatherhood. Regarded as a man who was "a child at heart—rascally, optimistic, impulsive"—he had an imaginary child called "Chrysanthemum-Pearl." Other American writers without progeny have imagined memorable child protagonists in their novels, notably Louisa May Alcott's March sisters in *Little Women*, and more recently Ann Beattie's poignant young boy in *Picturing Will*. (It is interesting to note that a number of books about bad or bestial children, such as William Golding's *Lord of the Flies*, were written by parents.)

Nulliparas in the visual arts may also imaginatively and empathically explore aspects of being children; one of them has even entered creatively into the experience of giving birth. At an early age artist Judy Chicago decided against mothering for a career in art. When she turned forty, however, she found herself astonished at the paucity of natal imagery in Western art and began to research a huge "birth project" by watching women in labor and studying creation myths. Always attracted to images of iconographic voids, often regarded as uterine symbols, she created numerous representations and renderings of the joy and pain of bearing and being born. Then she had scores of needleworkers stitch her images, working in the traditional female needlecrafts of smocking, beading, batik, crochet, quilting, and embroidery. When challenged on her credentials as a childless woman, the artist responded by asking why being crucified was never a prerequisite for painting crucifixions. The project allowed the artist to experience childbirth symbolically, then translate it into metaphors for other forms of creation, perhaps in some final resolution of her own emotions about her unexperienced motherhood.

In storytelling, the absence of offspring in a union between a man and a woman often indicates a severed connection with the natural order, like an emphasis on intellect over instinct. The theme of the barren king and queen in fairy tales usually precedes the birth of a marvelous child who repairs the break, according to Jungian writer Marie-Louise Von Franz. In one version of the story, a childless royal couple adopt a daughter who, by attracting a crude beggar woman and child, reconnects them to naturalness in their personalities. In our own lives, when the dream of a flesh-and-blood child fades, whether we are organically fertile or not, or whether we are parents or not, we can experience the birth of a "symbolic radiant child" within ourselves, in the words of Jungian disciple Jeremiah Abrams. So at its best, the *puer aeternis* archetype represents lifelong vitality and the ability to renew oneself at any age.

LIVING WITH MEN, IMPROVISING THE WAY

The men in women's lives—grandfathers, fathers, friends, brothers, bosses, boyfriends, lovers, husbands—have a powerful impact on whether or not women conceive children. Virtually no research has been done on the male influence on a female's maternity, even though some sociologists, including Kathleen Gerson, have observed that it is the most important influence of all. Sometimes the male pressure or point of view is pernicious, and at other times it is benign or positive. In my case, I grew up with little faith in the male desire to parent because of my father's desertion: Once, when I expressed my doubts to an older woman about raising a fatherless child, she could not comprehend my reluctance and impatiently snapped that all mothers essentially raise children by themselves; I knew then that she had not lost her father. But as a young woman I was also uncomfortable with young men who professed patriarchal views, because I wanted to write and retain my senses of self-direction and adventurousness. Years later, as I did research for this book, I discovered that my trepidation about trying to combine writing and child rearing without a cooperative partner was warranted, and that lack of co-parenting is a widespread

problem. I also learned that males without children were as varied about why they avoided parenthood as their female counterparts, but they were more at peace with themselves, as well
as happier with the established American practice of childless
marriage.

Like the goddess Athena, who was born from her father's
head, some young daughters want to emulate their fathers, particularly if they are the more contented, more admirable, or
more affectionate parent. Such a daughter may identify with the
achieving, not the parental, part of her father's life, often with
his encouragement. He may make her feel as though she is different from her mother and other females, even that she is made
for something better than motherhood. In a survey of studies of
intentionally childfree women, sociologist Sharon Houseknecht
discovered that many respondents were the accomplished
daughters in the family, raised to be independent and to succeed outside the home. Evidence suggests that when a father,
or even a mother, encourages an eldest daughter in a family of
girls, or an only child, to have high aspirations at work, she is less
likely to become a mother. Undoubtedly this is also because she
is faced with the old dilemma of family versus career.

It is also true that a daughter can dread motherhood if her
father devalued her mother as a mothering woman. Nulliparas
in one contemporary study had fathers who dominated and de-
graded their mothers; the daughters felt psychologically unable
to give birth until they had resolved the emotional link between
inferiority and maternity. The woman with an abusive or absent father may worry about re-creating the pattern that made
her own childhood unhappy. The writer Anaïs Nin expressed
the anxiety of the unfathered daughter while addressing her
unborn love child, which she had decided to abort: "You ought
to die because in this world there are no real fathers, not in

heaven or on earth. . . . It would be better to die than to be abandoned, for you would spend your life haunting the world for this lost father, this fragment of your body and soul, this lost fragment of your very self." Although Nin's apprehensions may seem excessive (she was not married to her child's father), they were also grounded in the reality of being abandoned in girlhood by her father, a Spanish musician.

In fact, Nin's concern about creating an essentially fatherless child like herself is a serious issue for daughters of divorced parents, who today are among the third of American children who live apart from their male parents: In fact, half of these youngsters have never visited their father's new home, and a fifth have not seen him in five years. In the 1990s, there remains a pattern of male flight from marriage and fatherhood, resulting in a sharp rise in female and child poverty. Certainly the soaring birthrate for single mothers suggests that more men than women are rejecting parenthood. Six decades earlier, Nin pessimistically predicted to her fetus: "For as soon as you will be born, [like] as soon as I was born, man the husband, lover, friend, will leave as my father did." She went on: "I love man as creator, lover, husband, friend, but man the father I do not trust."

My earliest experience of paternalistic warmth came from my maternal grandfather, a kindly, bearish, genial man who smelled strongly of pipe tobacco. When I arrived at his home for Sunday dinners with my family, he would take me onto his lap, put his arms around me, brush the top of my head with his bristly chin, and read a children's book to me in a loud gravelly voice while I leaned contentedly against his chest. But I often felt peril in the presence of my stepfather and stepgrandfather, both of whom represented to me the harsh aspect of patriarchy. A telling incident comes to mind: When I was eight or nine, I used to find refuge in my stepgrandfather's library, where he kept his collection of pristine leather-bound volumes of *Life* magazine. Instead of being pleased that I was expanding my horizons through the pictorial drama, the fierce old man would enter the room from time to time to see if I was removing the heavy volumes by pulling on, and possibly bending, the bindings; luckily my long slender arms could reach in and push out the big books from behind, and I escaped punishment, if not suspicion. When a girl grows up with little faith in the protective aspects of paternalism, it can make her think long and hard about becoming a mother. In fact, in the early 1970s, sociologist Bernice Lott found that pro- and anti-liberation women had similar feelings toward their female parents, but those who felt their male parents had given them insufficient care and attention were less likely to want children. My warmhearted maternal grandfather was less a presence in my life than other father figures, so for me positive aspects of paternity were overshadowed by negative ones.

I have no memory of living with my father, only snapshots of him on military leave during the Second World War: One of them is of a tousled, laughing blond man lying in bed and holding me, a tiny infant wrapped in a pale blanket. After he returned overseas, he wrote a letter to my grandmother about how good my birth had been for my mother and himself, but tellingly, he also observed that he had a hard time believing that he actually *had* a daughter, since he had been away from home for so long. A few years later, still grinning, the young navy officer attempted to hold me for a photographer, only this time I was a squirming, protesting toddler reaching for my mother, who stood miserably by his side, the fate of the marriage already evident on her face. After the Armistice, when he broke away from the tight, traditional bonds of the large extended family in Providence and moved to Vermont, I always felt a little desolate about the lost relationship with my father. Although divorce was fairly common in postwar America, I was the only pupil in my class with an absent father, a fact that humiliated me, and one that I never knew how to explain. A classmate's father had died in the war, and sometimes I wished I could say that mine had also been killed, because it would make his desertion appear less deliberate.

Even before my mother remarried when I was five and a half, it became clear to me that my stepfather had no interest in being a substitute father to me. I can remember shyly singing him a song with the words *my father* in it and being disappointed by his dismissive laugh. On my mother and stepfather's wedding day, I appear in photographs as a withdrawn, worried, fingernail-biting flower girl in a long ruffled organdy dress with a wreath of rosebuds on my head. After the wedding, when my mother told me not to mention my genetic father because it bothered her new husband, my sense of shame increased. I had been named for my father, Laurence, so both my given and surnames were constant reminders that I was another man's daughter. I silently grappled over which male's last name to use, briefly trying out my stepfather's surname as a middle name, then resolving to keep my birth name as a loyal link to my biological father. I also struggled over which man to call Daddy, finally deciding on my stepfather, since that was what my little sister and brother had started to call him. Meanwhile, on the rare occasions that I saw the individual I covertly referred to as "my real father," I stubbornly refused to call him any name at all out of shyness and confusion as well as anger at his abandonment.

When my real father and I saw each other every few years, we would look at each other with identical hazel eyes and be rendered mute by the emotional barriers between us. His rural

Vermont life had a rough masculine texture to it that was unfamiliar to me: rifles and shotguns, old bird decoys, big open fires, meals of venison and game, barking hunting dogs, rough talk and laughter, flowing beer and scotch. Sometimes I felt an intense blood bond or father-longing that invoked or met a silent emotive surge within him, but our feelings remained unexpressed in the tense, silent, keyed-up atmosphere between us. At other times I felt revulsion at the sight of his two forefingers, severed in a woodworking accident, or the smell of alcohol on his breath and body. Still, I continued to yearn for closeness with him, and when I became a teenager, I wanted to ask him if he had minded not having a natural daughter nearby as much as I had missed having a real father. Sensing my desire and determination to break through his reserve, he seemed afraid to be alone with me. He never overcame his boyhood shyness; in fact, it metastasized into a deep inhibition against intimacy with everyone in his life. Still, my urge to reach the person who was my father remained tenacious, insistent, and unresolved until his death.

One day in the early 1980s, I noticed my father's birth date on a silver porringer and realized that he was about to turn seventy. I sent him a birthday card, and on my next birthday he responded, telling me about his delight in taking up bass fishing the previous summer. It was only a few months later that his liver cancer was diagnosed, and as he lay dying, I spent a day with him in his hospital room, where he was sober at last, tethered to his bed by an intravenous tube. I searched for the right words to say to him, and finally I said I was sorry that we had never had a father-and-daughter relationship. Thinking of his feisty masculinity, intellectual interests, and gift for woodworking, I added that I was proud to be his daughter. He responded by whispering that he was proud of me too. It was a reconciliation of sorts, but one that was too little and too late to affect my confidence in fathering and childbearing, since by then I was over forty.

When my father's safe-deposit box was opened after his death, it contained the long, loving, paternal letter he had written to me two months after my birth, on the day that his warship departed the West Coast for the Pacific war zone. A tender explanation of why "your Daddy had to go," the letter told me to save his words until I was older, because "if anything should happen to me, I wouldn't be able to tell you these things." It is sadly ironic that, although he survived the war, the letter would be locked away and he would become dead to me as a person. The letter also contained expressions of love for my mother, which he probably was unable to voice or even write to her, since he admitted being hurtfully inexpressive. He wrote about his and my mother's "appreciations," which he hoped I would eventually share—old houses, antique furniture, the devotion of a dog. In retrospect, I was glad that I had voiced my pride in him on his deathbed, for he had written to me four decades earlier that "I hope you'll be proud of your Daddy. Of one thing I can assure you, I will do my utmost to make you proud of me."

My mother had pasted this letter in my baby album, but after my father's return from the Pacific, he apparently tore it from the book and took it with him to Vermont, perhaps ashamed of his promise to settle down after the war with my mother, me, and his English setter "with the sureness that I will never have to leave again." Since I was deeply disappointed by his departure, from that age I was disinclined, like Anaïs Nin, to regard males as dependable parents, despite my stepfather's loyalty to our family. Yet since my father had kept the heartfelt letter carefully safeguarded all his life, it obviously held meaning for him, probably in regard to his lost youth or hope or love. Certainly it was an abandoned part of his personality, a caring and expressive aspect that eventually was dominated by a withdrawn, masculine persona. When he was dying, however, I realized I was mourning a relationship that had no grounding in reality; when I asked my father's other child, a half brother in his twenties whom I barely knew, what kind of father ours had been, he told me about a man who had often been distant and critical by day, drunk and cruel by night. Yet if I had read the letter in girlhood, it might have intensified my grief over my missing father, but it also would have comforted me to know that my young father had loved me.

At the end of the 1960s, when I moved from Providence to Manhattan, feminists were openly questioning the institution of marriage: I remember reading in wonderment a fiery handout titled "Fuck Marriage, Not Men" at the consciousness-raising Congress to Unite Women in the autumn of 1969. I had no intention of following that advice but, as I look back, the revolutionary rhetoric underscored my long-standing skepticism about matrimony. The ethos of feminism supported my rebelliousness, and only momentarily during my twenties did the lack of a husband evoke the same shame as the absence of a father.

At the time I was subliminally aware that in novels penned by women there were depictions of the archetypal good-hearted male, also portrayed as the-man-who-could-understand, the masculine presence who offers an enriching and enabling love. During my girlhood, I had been very intrigued by and mildly infatuated with some of my eight uncles and stepuncles, who, besides my maternal grandfather, had inspired the wish in me that someday I would find a man like one of them to love. Two of the uncles never married—an impassioned painter who settled in the Italian countryside and a suave bachelor who inhabited café society; the others had wives and children but, although they were sporadic presences in my life, I sensed their warmth for me both as a female being and a family member. In an option that was unavailable to my New England maiden ancestors, I was groping toward trying to separate heterosexual love from the institution of marriage with children.

In my wait for the-man-who-could-understand, I was drawn to men who, like myself, were doing creative work, and were usually unprepared for the role of co-parent or paterfamilias. In my thirties I feared imposing an indifferent father on a child; not only would it have revived my childhood pain, it would also have caused the child to suffer as well. In my second marriage in my forties to a warmhearted man who was also a writer, I was more emotionally inclined to take on parenthood, but it was less physically and practically possible to do so. This man viewed having a baby as less a realistic option than a romantic idea, part of its appeal being another chance at life for him. Even though parenthood was less a priority than writing for both of us, it was surprisingly difficult to dismiss; a primal urge to get pregnant seemed at times to be a tangible embodiment of our closeness, but after a pregnancy scare at forty-seven, my feelings of relief were as strong as those of sadness. In the end, however, my experiences with males who were unwilling or unable to take on fatherhood created an undertow that pulled me away from childbearing. As I looked into the experiences of others, I realized that for a woman to do it all, she needs a partner who will also do it all, the kind of man who remains in the minority.

In numerous myths, males produce progeny from their

mouths, ribs, and heads, but any womb envy this suggests has rarely been extended to raising children: The traditional division of labor between the genders—the male at work and the female at home—is so deeply ingrained that most men view the care of children as a natural female obligation. Patriarchs have always expected females to be the psychological "Other," the vehicle for qualities like selflessness that they do not wish to express and the performers of tasks like child rearing that they do not wish to undertake. At the turn of the century, A Childless Wife admitted that there were fewer enlightened "new men" than educated "new women," but she remained naively optimistic that females could change their recalcitrant mates. Around the same time, writer Floyd Dell admitted that young male idealists like himself were not known for their participation in family life. "We did not entertain the notion of balancing the heroism or the sacrifice of our sweethearts by some heroism or some sacrifice of our own in the way of an effort to reshape this sorry scheme," he wrote. "There were no works of imaginative literature to make us feel that we should. But there were an increasing number of imaginative writings . . . which enabled us to think very well of ourselves, and even to regard our laissez-faire, do-nothing selfishness as a pattern of social heroism."

Several generations later, in the 1970s, most fathers of young children remained uninterested in baby care. In 1973, when paternity leave was first offered in school systems in New York, Berkeley, and Seattle, only a handful of young fathers took advantage of it. Little seems to have changed in the following decades. Unpaid paternity leaves of absence are not an option for most men, either for financial reasons or for fear of being regarded as unserious at work. While men are doing more fathering, it is usually due to economic necessity: About 20 percent of preschool children are cared for by their fathers while their mothers are at work, but this is because the men are unemployed, work part-time or night shifts, or because the families cannot afford baby-sitters. Yet in the last two decades, many female sociologists, psychologists, and philosophers have recognized an urgent need for male parents to get involved in the hands-on chores of child rearing for reasons ranging from simple fairness to the psychological health of mothers and children. Sons raised only by mothers, for instance, tend to associate females with nurturing and come to fear autonomy in their girlfriends and wives (but not necessarily in their daughters).

Fathers who do try to be active parents are often treated as pariahs by men and women alike. When James Levine, director of the Fatherhood Project at the Families and Work Institute in New York City, taught preschool children in the 1970s, he was continually asked: "What do you *really* do?" He found it difficult to describe the satisfactions of caring for small children unless he could point to the rewards of money or prestige, like what one might get from being a priest, pediatrician, school principal, or child psychologist. In his 1976 book *Who Will Raise the Children?*, Levine advocated reforms to teach boys about what he called "direct caring" for youngsters (as opposed to providing for them materially), but he admitted that child tending encouraged a form of openness that was a disadvantage in a competitive career. He also acknowledged that deeply involving young fathers in child rearing would require an unlikely social revolution, elements of which would be paid parental leaves, shared domestic duties, home-based jobs, wage parity between the genders, and part-time professional work. When one father in the 1990s attempted to put in fewer hours at work to help care for his child, he found that the price was putting his career on hold, renting instead of buying a house, and feeling isolated from other men. Finding little support for his efforts, he and his wife ended up making the usual "complementary" contributions to the family, presumably like the customary arrangement of the husband providing money and the wife doing housework.

In recent years, as men read best-selling books like Robert Bly's *Iron John*, about the so-called new masculinity, which decry compliant "soft men" and urge them to get in touch with their lost fathers, many feel justified again in retreating from daily work around the house. The reality remains that even if mothers hold full-time jobs, they still do most of the domestic work. As males left farms for factories during the past century and a half, females stayed home and provided a stable, comforting family life; but now that women are leaving home for the office, no one is making it easier for them, the sociologist Arlie Hochschild has observed. Despite much evidence to the contrary, she optimistically called men's passivity on the home front a "stalled revolution."

It appears, in fact, that the upcoming generation is headed for a gender conflict. A 1994 poll of teenagers taken by CBS and *The New York Times* found that boys prefer the old-fashioned family (whether or not they have employed mothers), while their female counterparts are far less traditional, strongly desiring careers and egalitarian relationships with men—and even willing to have out-of-wedlock children if necessary. While the young girls want to share the breadwinning role, the teenage boys told pollsters that they are unwilling to share household chores. Even more ominous for the prospect of peace between the sexes, while the male youths consider themselves superior to girls, the young females view themselves as the boys' equals. Caroline Whitbeck has observed that many women like to think that if males were properly encouraged, they would dedicate themselves to parenting, but it may not be so: "It may be a hard and somewhat terrifying possibility that a chasm may separate our own thought from that of the masculinist culture."

Men can sire progeny without knowing it; women, of course, cannot give birth without being aware of it. Perhaps because of men's greater detachment from pregnancy, many of them are more objective than women about the pros and cons of parenting. It is interesting to note that my hesitations about parenthood were underscored by a number of male friends and professionals who were fathers, men who spoke to me frankly from experience the way few mothers have done: For instance, a close friend, who is also a writer, warned me against imagining that children would give my life a sustaining purpose; a gynecologist joked that it would be a loss if my genes were not passed on, but then he became serious and observed that everyone did not need children; and an internist described parenthood as both terrible and wonderful, then warned me against it if I valued my privacy or my time. Since these fathers had no real stake in whether or not I had a child, I found their observations very interesting, somewhat disheartening, and impossible to dismiss.

Domestic inequity is one reason that over the years some women have, in effect, gone on a "baby strike," refusing to have children until their men promise to help out. "Wipe out the children, let the race decrease, unless better conditions for the mothers could be found," declared the mother of two, Dora Russell, in the 1930s. My teenage idealism about social justice led to my interest in feminism, which, in turn, resulted in my belief in gender egalitarianism, even around the house; in the absence of such equity, I was worried about becoming a mother. Apparently I was not alone. Without a participating partner, the psychic costs of motherhood appear greater to many women than any possible rewards, according to Kathleen Gerson. Deliberately childless wives often do not even mention in interviews the expectation that their husbands would help with any potential children. And some confided to questioners that they feared that their resentment toward an unhelpful spouse would destroy their marriages. In fact, the happiest marriages are those in which partners share housekeeping equally, Arlie Hochschild has reported, a more common practice among those with the lighter domestic burden implicit in childlessness.

When I was younger, I was somewhat resentful of men who rejected fatherhood, but as I got older and recognized my own pleasure in being childfree, my attitude changed. I also learned that some males are childless by default because, like their female counterparts, they delayed marriage, never married, divorced, or discovered they were infertile. Men resist fatherhood for a wide variety of other reasons as well, some more realistic than others. In his thirties, my boyfriend feared losing himself as well as me to parenthood. I noted in my journal that during one of our talks "some of his real fears emerged: He'll be trapped in his job, I'll get fat and ugly, the kid may be deformed"—anxieties that I did not share. If males are married and intentionally childless, they are exceptional, since few find like-minded women, and most dutifully go along when wives invoke the right to be a mother. The minority of men who feel and act differently, who decide firmly against a pro forma or even participatory fatherhood, who stay single or find a wife who feels the same way, offer interesting rationales and perspectives that differ somewhat from those of nulliparas. Many justify and enjoy nonparenthood more readily than females, perhaps because, being unaffected by the potent motherhood myth, they evaluate it more easily on its merits. Understanding the nature of nonfatherhood, in fact, sheds light on nonmotherhood.

In some ways male and female experiences of nonparenthood are alike. Just as caricatures taint female childlessness with images of the ironhearted anti-mother, they color the male version with violent and fearsome anti-life overtones. In mythology, for instance, Hades, the only major Greek deity who is not a father, is the God of death and darkness. Literature is also replete with instances of the linkage between male sterility and moral depravity. Shakespeare's anti-hero Macbeth, who caused the deaths of the young sons of his rival for the throne, was haunted by his inability to produce progeny, and the language of the tragedy is scattered with phrases like "fruitless crown" and "barren sceptre" as well as images of winsome male children and symbolic child apparitions, like a bloody boy and a crowned child holding a living tree. In the last century, French novelist George Sand, the mother of two, wrote to her colleague Gustave Flaubert that his childlessness was the penalty for his being too independent. All this is a difficult legacy for childless men to inherit, some of whom may take this troublesome heritage to heart: One deliberately childfree husband observed that although it did not feel unnatural to be without issue, he wondered if it was irresponsible or immature.

In contemporary America, the insidious imagery has little to do with reality, as sociologists and psychologists tell it. Nonfatherhood is usually a considered decision, and nonfathers bare little relation to the negative stereotype of the sterile male. Even Freud, who was interested in Shakespeare's treatment of the theme of childlessness in *Macbeth*, was frustrated at being unable to associate the condition with punishment or illness in the drama. Psychological tests indicate that married nonfathers

are healthy if unusual individuals who are very satisfied and effective; other research agrees with and elaborates upon such
findings, adding that these males tend to be iconoclastic, creative, and ambitious. Men who have opted out of fatherhood
often give as a reason the desire to do risky, unremunerative, or
absorbing work. Flaubert, for example, who remained unmarried, lived with his mother, and kept his mistresses at arm's
length so he could write, remarked that he would rather "jump
in the Seine with cannon balls on my feet" than take on fatherhood. (In contrast, a writer who fathered children, Jean-Jacques
Rousseau, banished each of his five infants to a foundling hospital so that their upbringing would not interfere with his work;
Italian composer Giuseppe Verdi did the same, and both men
postponed marriage to common-law wives so that their bastard
children could be legally abandoned.)

Some nonfathers view traditional marriage with children as
an enclosure, particularly when they face the prospect of sacri-
ficing their interests and inclinations to support a family, something that has overburdened the fathers of many childless men.
In a 1970s study of vasectomized men in their late twenties,
most had concluded that fatherhood would conflict with a
compelling personal agenda. The vocations of men without
progeny are often extremely satisfying and high in prestige,
even if economically unpredictable, like being in the arts. Besides working for gratification, nonfathers also like being able to
leave unrewarding jobs, and some do indeed change positions
more often than fathers. Others want to work for moral principle even if for poor pay; one observer has suggested that parents
sometimes use children as "an excuse to retreat from commitment" by avoiding such jobs in altruistic fields. One man without children, who constantly travels to developing countries in
an effort to preserve the threatened animals and forests of the

earth, rightfully believes that his efforts are more life-affirming than fathering a few more children in an overpopulated planet.

The charge of immorality is leveled most pointedly at homosexual and bisexual males without children, but such accusations are symptoms of bias and ignorance. (Social scientists who have studied willingly childless men during the past few decades have almost without exception concentrated on married men or those who have undergone vasectomies, because their lack of offspring is more inexplicable than that of homosexual men.) Like lesbians, some gay men are more interested in fatherhood than others because of their personalities and family backgrounds. Homosexual couples may hope that they can adopt, but it is often an unrealistic wish: Although a few homosexual men have gotten through legal and other hurdles and adopted children, others worry about being regarded as child molesters if they succeed. There is also the ever-present worry of all gay parents about bringing up children in a homophobic society; if parents or siblings do not accept their homosexuality, for instance, gay partners cannot join family gatherings, a poor milieu in which to raise children. Like their straight counterparts, many homosexual men who are reluctantly childless miss the interrelatedness of family living and mourn its absence, especially if their fathers enjoyed fatherhood. And if the family surname ends with them, they may regret letting down a male tradition. Like other nonfathers, they may also worry about having no descendants to inherit their possessions and to remember them after they are gone.

Childlessness in men is not, necessarily, a symptom of pathology, and, in any event, there are ways to transform it, just as there are with women. Males who cannot father children because of infecundity sometimes must deal with masculinity issues, but studies show that they usually do not suffer the same

degree of depression as infertile females. Still, symbolic fatherhood is a valuable option; it is interesting to note that George
Washington, the "father of the country," had no biological offspring but raised two young male relatives. A study of infertile
husbands in the 1980s found that a minority reacted by becoming self-absorbed and taking up body building, health foods, or
macho sexuality. Most adjusted somewhat better, however, and
pursued interests in cars, houses, and boats. But the best-
adapted, who also had the happiest marriages, developed strong
involvements with others, particularly with adopted children.
Evidently, relating to young people is important for gay as well
as straight men. One graduate student, who interviewed eleven
homosexuals ranging in age from their mid-thirties to mid-
fifties, discovered that the men's senses of loss about not having progeny intensified with age unless they developed fatherly
friendships with the sons and daughters of friends and relatives.
Another man did not want children during his first marriage;
divorced in his thirties, he did not think much about fatherhood until he happily remarried at the age of fifty, but by then
he and his wife were unable to conceive. He felt regret, envy,
and intermittent sadness as he saw friends, as well as actors like
Woody Allen, Warren Beatty, and Jack Nicholson, father their
first children in their fifties, believing he had missed the "very
narcissistic" but short-lived experience of being the adored center of a small person's life. Gradually, however, he realized that
his work as a psychoanalyst was eminently paternal, as were his
relationships with a large extended family.

An old but often unspoken reason that males avoid fatherhood is their fear of losing girlfriends and wives to motherhood—if not to death during childbirth as in the past, then to
their absorption in child rearing. The loss of a woman can be
very threatening indeed: Simone de Beauvoir has observed that

nature represents for woman what woman represents for man—a refuge for rest, renewal, inspiration. Men may feel rivalrous even with unborn offspring: The biblical Elkanah, husband of the barren Hannah, asked: "Am I not better to you than ten sons?" Such men may have suffered as children from lack of parental attention or from excessive sibling rivalry, so that when they marry they do not want to compete for the attention of their wives. In other cases, reluctant fathers-to-be are *pueres aeternas* who cannot manage their own lives, let alone take on responsibility for another's. One of the reasons that Anaïs Nin had her difficult and dangerous abortion in the 1930s was because her lover, the writer Henry Miller, "remain[ed] the child himself who does not wish a rival," she wrote in her diary. Recently, a research project detected that some men's deep fears of loss were aroused by their wives' pregnancies, resulting in rage, anxiety, ambivalence, or flight.

The hope for a high level of closeness and companionship with one's mate is actually an ancient reason to avoid having progeny, one that has been noted in the Old Testament by rabbinical scholars: "So that [wives] might lean on their husbands despite their beauty." Husbands in childfree unions over the last century have testified that the purpose of the marital tie is the enjoyment of an intimate and intense relationship with a wife. In 1901 Ida Husted Harper noted that while wives are blamed for lack of heirs, husbands often do not want them either; she cited as examples a man whose first wife had died in childbirth and a banker who lost his wife's company after their son's birth. Many men welcome the prospect of a partnership with a woman who wants, above all, to remain his friend and lover. In the early twentieth century, Floyd Dell wrote about looking for a "Glorious Playfellow"; tired of manipulative but overtly submissive women, he wanted "to find in woman a

comrade and an equal . . . because it promised to be more fun
. . . what men desire are real individuals who have achieved
their own freedom." New York artist Wanda Gág, who chose
art over children around the same time, discovered to her surprise that many of her male friends easily endorsed her choice.
Regardless of the reasons, men without children report that
nonfatherhood within marriage is highly agreeable: Sociological
surveys dating from the 1950s consistently describe childless
husbands as happier than fathers.

Another historic reason for the nuptial arrangement without
progeny is that it allowed a young wife to retain her health and
appearance. The Bible says of Sarah, the beauteous barren wife
of Abraham, that "the whole ninety years that [she] did not bear
she was like a bride in her canopy." During Reverend Foster
Barnham Zincke's travels in America in the mid-nineteenth
century, he heard young men justifying childlessness on the
same ground—that they "did not wish to have their wives, during the whole period of their good looks, in the nursery." The
reverend admitted that there was cause for concern, explaining
that the harsh climate and hardships of life rapidly destroyed female beauty. According to the reverend, the spirited young wife
asks, why "should I prematurely dilapidate myself by having half
a dozen children?" What appeared to the churchman as evidence of feminine vanity and frivolity may also, of course, have
been the attempt by young women to retain the independence
of their prenuptial girlhoods as well as the avoidance of the
physical perils of pregnancy. The old accounts are unclear about
whether this aspect of nonmotherhood was to the man's or
woman's advantage, but it seems likely to have benefited both.

Men who claim their time and earnings for themselves realize that they can be labeled selfish, but nonetheless they do not
necessarily place a harshly negative connotation on the charge,

if they admit it at all. When sociologist Sharon Houseknecht analyzed a group of childfree males, she found that almost three quarters readily cited as reasons their desires for freedom and self-fulfillment. Compared to nulliparas, nonfathers also find it easier to admit openly that they like having fewer expenses or dislike what one of them called the "anarchic" characteristics of children. Although such males seem to exemplify the anti-life image of childless men, many are often caring and concerned in their work and relationships. In some instances, it is they who go along with their wives' desires not to have children, although they could imagine being fathers if married to someone else. In fact, the partners of childless women often play important supportive roles; he is often the "giver of permission," as well as the one who absorbs jokes about his potency as well as criticism for condoning his wife's supposed abnormality.

In other cases, liberal or idealistic men who believe in gender equality or co-parenting are sometimes more reluctant to undertake fatherhood than traditional males who feel no obligation to share child care. Opting for childlessness often seems more honorable to many of them than taking on halfhearted or irresponsible fatherhood. Such an attitude appears to be a mature evaluation of oneself and a genuine concern for children. In fact, one analysis found no difference between married fathers and married nonfathers in terms of emotional maturity, defined as the success of their marriages and overall happiness and adjustment; instead, researchers found that the men's personalities differed between the two groups, with the latter appearing more eager for experimentation and inclined to independent thought. Whether these characteristics were a cause or a result of a way of life without children was unexplored. But the men's open and straightforward acceptance of a choice they regarded as best for themselves was cited as a measure of good mental health.

☙

Males who do not want to have children but wish to marry have long sought to bring into being an oxymoron—the childless marriage. In earlier centuries, matrimony without progeny was called an unfruitful union; intentional conjugal childlessness was regarded as insubordination to the natural, social, or religious order, yet it still happened because of personal inclination, religious faith, and a wish to retain family property. The marriage without children was common enough among some classes that English poet and prelate John Donne felt the need to preach against it in 1621: He proclaimed that when secular young men and women decided before wedlock to avoid pregnancy, their nuptial union was "no marriage, but an adultery." (He took this harsh position even though, a few years earlier, his own beloved wife had died while giving birth to a stillborn infant, their twelfth child.) While early Christian spiritual marriages were celibate, more recently, of course, men and women have had erotic intimacy without conception, allowing different concepts of matrimony, like that created by Ella Lyman and Richard Cabot. Over the past two centuries, women novelists who have sketched the quest for companionate marriage have often expressed the enduring female yearning for "equity, authenticity, Eros" in conjugal relationships, and contemporary evidence suggests that many childfree unions achieve these dreams.

By the end of the nineteenth century, American wives were having fewer children and even none at all. Some couples lived in hotels or boardinghouses, a way of life that seemed irresponsible to Reverend Zincke. He observed that this apparent "absence of natural feeling" about children was due to the "expenses and annoyances of house-keeping," and because residential hotels charged a dollar a child. He wrote disapprovingly that "childlessness allows comfort, society, amusement," and that such wedded pairs "cannot give up their autumn excursion, they cannot give up balls, and dresses, and concerts, and carriages." His picture contradicts other evidence that most of the childfree were hardworking and of modest means, like the social worker who called herself A Childless Wife. It also ignores the reality that others were high-minded. Ella Lyman Cabot, for one, believed that the consecrated marital union was primarily one "in which we can be of greater service to God" besides reproducing, as she wrote in her courtship letter to her future husband. The Cabots, whose marriage lasted from 1894 until Ella's death in 1934, decided that forging intimate and idealistic "spiritual bonds" between themselves was more important than raising children. They obviously assumed, like Charlotte Perkins Gilman and other feminist reformers, that there was an inherent conflict between marital and parental relationships. It is interesting to note that many recent sociological surveys indicate that nonparents, compared with parents, spend more time together, make love more often, express more affection and agreement, and share more interests and conversation.

The English churchman appears to have been especially annoyed by the fact that the newlyweds and other childfree nuptial pairs seemed to be enjoying themselves and not mourning the absence of "little blessings." Several generations later, A Childless Wife underscored this observation, denying in her 1905 article that she and her husband were "lonely and full of heart-longings, as childless people are supposed to be. We are happy—actively happy and full of the joy of living, not passively content." Likewise, in 1919 a historian named Arthur W. Calhoun acknowledged the "more persistent happiness of couples without children"; he recognized that they "can be all to each other" and escape the toil, cost, and tiredness of parenthood. "The man is able to give his wife a more satisfying companionship, and looks forward to the day when he can retire on a decent fortune and jaunt about the world with her." Some of this childlessness was situational and some perhaps the result of temperament—including those who particularly thrived on intense attachment and attention from nuptial partners. In any event, this long-lasting desire for gratifying marriages also motivates two out of three modern nulliparas.

Even today, when nonparents attribute their marital harmony to not having progeny, parents prefer to believe the childfree are either fraudulently fulfilled or satisfied *despite* not having offspring. In fact, nonparents with the best marriages seem to provoke the most hostility because they challenge the old assumption that children bring happiness to matrimony. Nonparental unions tend to resemble parental ones in the years before offspring are born or after they leave home, when parents report high levels of communication, egalitarianism, and camaraderie. They also tend to stress individual development for the benefit of society. "Our relations must always be such that neither would suffer any diminution of freedom or opportunity for development," A Childless Wife vowed idealistically at the turn of the century. In one study of successful long (but not necessarily childless) marriages, the common explanation was that the spouses allowed each other to grow and change. If this is important, then the childfree often have an advantage.

Equity in marriage (in terms of role similarity instead of role equivalence, or lack of the traditional division of labor) often appeals to those who opt out of parenthood, like Richard

Cabot, who, inspired by the arrangement of Harvard president Charles W. Eliot and his wife, argued for a childfree marital union on the grounds of gender fairness. "If there are no children there is no need why the housekeeping should not be evenly divided between husband and wife, either on Pres. Eliot's plan (the husband keeping house half the year and the wife t'other) or, dividing the daily work the whole year round. Once [you] get on this basis[,] the whole distinction you draw between the amount of sacrifice on one side and the other falls to the ground. We enter and we continue absolutely equal." His fiancée agreed, and she even advocated an androgynous ideal: "I do not think that men and women will stand on an equality in this matter of freedom for impersonal ends, till women are equally the wage-earners and men the nurses and comforters." Today the typical pattern among childless couples is that the wife earns more than usual and the husband less, resulting in closer parity in earnings and more marital egalitarianism. A Childless Wife believed that if she gave up her salary, it would damage her marriage: "Our marriage is now the union of two equals," she explained. "We believe that makes its happiness." Decades later, a 1981 study on the equity of parental roles during early, parenting, and empty-nest years found that, while males always had the advantage, parity increased as progeny left home and, in effect, made the marriage childfree.

One "evil consequence" of matrimonial unfruitfulness, warned Reverend Zincke, expressing a widespread view, was that as the married couple aged "there [was] no tie between them," and they often divorced. Ignorant or unaware of other bonds between husband and wife, he was voicing another common assumption made about childless unions. It is a view that continues today, even though most modern marriages are more fragile for a number of reasons, including married people's increased longevity, their high expectations for matrimony, and emphasis on their own individualism. Some current statistics show wedded people without progeny separating at a higher rate than parents, but the figures are misleading because many marriages fail in the early years before a wife gets pregnant. In fact, the overall divorce rate of childfree marriages is lower than for couples with more than two children. Childlessness does not cause divorce, but nonparents are freer to leave unhappy unions. They are also more likely to remarry, indicating the importance that marriage holds for them as the pivotal emotional experience of their lives.

Sometimes the absence of offspring is a symptom of marital difficulties. I know from my own experience that marriage without children can be, in its own way, uniquely complicated, since in its early years partners must deal with issues like pronatal pressures and the ever-present possibility of pregnancy. Also, the childfree nuptial arrangement can be strained because, paradoxically, its intensity and exclusivity can generate or exaggerate any existing tensions. Certainly that was the case with Georgia O'Keeffe's marriage to Alfred Stieglitz, a nuptial partnership without children that was characterized at various times by passion and inspiration as well as anger and alienation. I have learned from my own relationships and those of others that trying to redefine and expand traditional sex roles in the way that childless marriage allows can be perilous as well as exhilarating. This was the issue with my distant cousin Roger Baldwin, the civil libertarian, and Madeleine Zabriskie Doty, a social worker and children's advocate, who were married in 1919 by socialist Norman Thomas. Idealists, they tried to forge a free and equal relationship by sharing expenses and housework. They disagreed, however, over the nature of freedom within marriage, whether it should be intellectual or social and, not surprisingly, their unstable union remained without children and eventually dissolved.

Women's literature includes themes of marital enclosure and suffocation, leading females (albeit usually mothers) to madness or suicide, like in Kate Chopin's *The Awakening* and Sue Kaufman's *Diary of a Mad Housewife*. Yet childfree marriage has been for me a way to avoid the pitfalls of the institution of marriage in my search for more independence and intimacy. Once I was incorrectly assumed to be single by someone who remarked that I had "so much air" around me, meaning, I suppose, an aura of independence. At another time, when feeling unhappy in a relationship, I felt the frightening sensation of being unable to breathe. Those who venture beyond old gender definitions are sometimes able to be themselves more genuinely, resulting in deeply revealing and gratifying relationships. It is certainly a way of relating that has always interested me. Once I observed in my private pages that "I find the thought of living with someone involved in development, an inner journey, very exciting—while living with someone who doesn't acknowledge the inner life is very lonely and boring and frustrating." Recently, I felt hopeful after reading that psychologist Susan Bram found that the nulliparous women she had studied felt utterly feminine, as they integrated desires for affiliation with ones for achievement, as they moved toward "sex role transcendence." When I have faltered at this challenge, however, being nulliparous has enabled me to reinvent my life again.

SEVEN

RECOGNIZING OUR WOMANHOOD, REDEFINING FEMININITY

Even though there are more women, married and unmarried, without children today than ever before, little serious or sustained thought has been given to the meaning of femaleness outside of motherhood. Misperceptions abound: Mothers sometimes suggest that nulliparas are not real women or that we cannot really love unless we have given birth. Such attitudes are uncomprehending and hostile, of course, reflecting the enduring divisions among women. But if those of us without children also associate womanliness exclusively with motherliness, our efforts to claim our feminine birthright will be difficult. We may wonder if we are truly womanly, or we may question how to relate to the ancient pattern of women's lives. Doubts like these can make our struggles for self-acceptance intense, confusing, and interminable, since we are indeed intentionally or unintentionally violating epochs of female experience and even the laws of nature itself. There are, however, a number of ways we can affirm our femaleness outside of motherhood: We can recognize that our nonnatal bodily experiences validate us as whole and even vibrant female beings; relationships with family and friends, as well as connections to the natural world, are also

affirming. Although femininity and maternity have been en-
twined since the Garden of Eden, the nature of woman in all its
dimensions can be better understood by examining its varied
expressions in the lives of nulliparous females.

Growing up in the 1950s in a patriarchal New England family, I was given the perplexing message that my budding femininity was both unimportant and dangerous. On the one hand,
it seemed negligible because there was no real recognition or
appreciation of it, but on the other hand it appeared perilous
because after pubescence my mother warned me that I could
become pregnant extremely easily. I felt I had to hold myself in
abeyance, certaintly not venture to flaunt my young body,
which now contained a strangely invisible female power. I was
also bewildered by womanly images that seemed unappealing
or incomplete, like the wounded nature of my mother and the
invincible demeanor of my grandmother.

One day in the early 1960s, when I was in my late teens, I felt
a sudden shock of understanding about another kind of
femininity when I saw a magazine photograph of First Lady
Jacqueline Kennedy holding a sleeping infant and wearing a
fashionable Chanel suit, a matching pillbox hat, and immacu-
late white gloves. She appeared to me as a gorgeous modern
madonna. While her persona exuded exquisite taste, grace,
charm, and elegance, it also appeared elusive and unattainable:
As the president's wife, the First Lady's regal presence was supported and protected by immense power, wealth, and class as
well as by a large White House staff. Hers was also a ladylike
look fresh out of the 1950s, one that influenced and confused
the girls of my generation. One of our group, Susan Brownmiller, expressed her conflicts about that particular type of femaleness in a book called *Femininity*; she described it as an
artifice that was playful or tyrannical by turn—a little bit, she

wrote, was amusing and useful as a survival strategy, but too much was restrictive and inhibiting, even "a desperate strategy of appeasement."

In the midst of these influences, I attempted to piece together an inclusive and positive female identity that embraced the First Lady's aesthetics, my mother's kindness, and my grandmother's strength, as well as the movie star Elizabeth Taylor's sex appeal. To add to the difficulty of this task, I pondered the motto of my girls' boarding school—"to think, to do, to be"—an idea that assumed no inherent conflict between intellectuality and active or passive femininity, a concept that indicated that clear thoughts and bold actions created a womanly life. My exposure to feminism further complicated my efforts to integrate everything I admired about womanliness. Gender typing, of course, has traditionally assigned inborn qualities to males and females, usually with the more admirable cerebral ones being assigned to men and the lesser emotional ones to women. As a young feminist, I naturally rejected those old stereotypes; while patriarchs attributed female inertia to knowledge of the inevitability of motherhood, I believed that any passivity reflected confining expectations: I understood that the young woman who is denied a promotion because she might become pregnant may find the prospect of child rearing more appealing than a dead-end job. When I attended the large neofeminist gathering in Manhattan in 1969, which raised far-reaching questions about many aspects of modern women's lives, words on a blue flyer went so far as to urge the liberation of all females from the conventional "Feminine Image" in order "to create a new and fully human concept of Woman." The invitation was intriguing to me. The following year, 1970, I saw a retrospective of Georgia O'Keeffe's work at the Whitney Museum and began to intuit a form of fierce femininity that enabled O'Keeffe to protect her painting hours and develop her talent, which in turn allowed her to express her tenderness and eroticism on canvas.

My desire to express my femininity was complicated because womanliness had usually been associated with willingness to bear and care for children or at least to engage in social mothering. Because of my feminist awareness, I did not believe that the reproductive role was essential to the attainment of a female identity; instead, motherhood seemed to be a natural if not inevitable *expression* of femaleness. (I linked it to my "feeling that I am a strong womanly woman.") But I was troubled because nonnatal femininity within marriage had long been regarded as a sign of a woman's evil or ineffectual character. Familiar roles help give the illusion of order and stability, so childless women, by establishing their femaleness outside of motherhood, inadvertently challenge old assumptions about biological law and feminine nature. The beautiful Queen Guinevere, for instance, the barren wife of King Arthur in the legendary tale of courtly love, symbolized to me a weak woman, an eternal maiden captivated by romantic illusion, since her seduction by Lancelot led to the dispersal of the knights of the Round Table.

Not giving birth can certainly be a crisis in feminine identity if a nullipara or a nulligravida regards herself and others as a female *manqué*, someone who has failed to fulfill herself. In fact, psychologist Mardy Ireland has described three kinds of women without children who experience differing and disturbing senses of absence—those who simply lack the desire for a child, those who miss having their own child, and those who mourn not being mothers. Philosopher Margaret Simons has rightly argued for "a philosophical justification for the choice not to be a mother. For it's my belief that for feminism to be really 'pro-choice,' a woman must be able to choose not to be a mother without losing her self-respect or her identity as a woman."

The birth of a baby can be, of course, a way to establish femininity: "I, who was never quite sure / about being a girl, needed another / life, another image to remind me," wrote the poet Anne Sexton, who gave birth to two daughters. "And this was my worst guilt; you could not cure / nor soothe it. I made you to find me." When mature womanliness is defined by maternity, it can make a woman feel compelled to have a baby, regardless of the cost to herself and those around her. Anne Taylor Fleming, a California journalist, has written about her failed efforts to become pregnant in her late thirties, which were motivated partly by her desire to end an identification with men and to find "some sense of reconciliation with my own femaleness." She said she "wanted to let go, swell up, take on flesh, to be fully female, fully fleshed female." In this way, when nurturant qualities are embodied by the female torso enlarged by pregnancy, natal motherhood becomes effectively mandatory, and nulliparas, as well as males, are undermined. This kind of thinking can lead to all sorts of distortions. One analysis of almost two hundred women seeking in vitro fertilization found that many of them overidealized the old-fashioned female role; its authors, sociologists Victor J. Callan and John F. Hennessey, theorized that the women's "exaggerated sense of femininity" (defined by qualities like warmth and expressiveness), along with their certainty that they would be excellent mothers, were psychological defenses or compensations related to their inability to conceive. Others have noted a completely different phenomenon: that a strong sense of femininity can transcend the usual female roles. Shirley Radl, a mother and author of *Mother's Day Is Over*, has recognized the possibility that childfree women have greater gender confidence because their femininity does not depend on motherhood.

What I did not know until recently, though, is that throughout the ages the elements of womanliness have rarely been agreed upon. Some theorists have long been suspicious of absolute assignment of sex-linked traits, regarding them as more political than hormonal. "What is now called the nature of woman is an eminently artificial thing—the result of forced repression in some directions, unnatural stimulation in others," wrote British philosopher John Stuart Mill in the nineteenth century. A hundred years later, social scientists have still not fully explored how nulliparous women experience their own femininity. But as the Freudian view of womanhood as a triad of passivity, masochism, and narcissism has been attacked, anthropologists and others have concluded that masculinity and femininity are more cultural stereotypes than universal principles. The view, for instance, that childlessness is a conscious or unconscious denial of womanhood is "simplistic," according to Boston psychiatrists Malkah T. Notman and Carol C. Nadelson. They have made the provocative point that childbearing in itself is not essential to feminine identity or personal self-esteem—what is important is the assumption of the *ability* to reproduce: "It seems that femininity itself (and masculinity as well) is a fluctuating and variable concept, intimately related to the awareness of the capacity to bear and nurture children, but not depending on this for realization." Although they did not apply their theory to the infertile, their thinking implies the importance of recognizing the procreative *purpose* of the body over actually reproducing.

In the years since I began to think about my femininity, no one concept of womanliness has emerged and gained dominance among feminists or any other group of women. In the

1990s the word *feminine* still carries narrow and negative connotations such as weakness and inertia for some people, while for others it suggests specialness and superiority. In my attempt to loosen the concept from its old moorings, I have found that it is sometimes preferable to use unusual words for womanhood like *muliebrity*, or to use those with negative connotations in conventional usage, like *womanlike* or *womanish*, in a deliberately affirmative manner. The writer Alice Walker has advocated the use of the word *womanist* for all positive and powerful female behavior—a term, she explains, that African-American mothers use to praise a daughter's behavior when it is "outrageous, audacious, courageous, or *willful*" as well as inquisitive, serious, and grown-up. Whatever it is called, the essence of our gender is eternal, if elusive, but at the same time, it is essential for those of us who are nulliparas to experience and express it if we are to achieve a sense of wholeness.

As we examine the nature of femaleness apart from motherhood, our physicality—rooted in the rhythms of nature by our menses, our eroticism, and other aspects of our corporeal beings—is very important. Every woman's body is troublesome, Adrienne Rich has stated, in "its clouded meaning, its fertility, its desire, its so-called frigidity, its bloody speech, its silences, its changes and mutilations, its rapes and ripenings." But the body of the woman without children has its own challenges: Whether we have girlish or motherly figures, we often struggle with nature either to avoid or to achieve conception; we may feel lingering sorrow for the unused reproductive mechanisms of our bodies; and we must contend with a heritage that condemns sexuality outside of maternity. Frida Kahlo's painting *Roots* has red veins emanating from an anatomy resembling her own,

which become green vines and branches in a dry, rocky landscape, indicating the barren artist's ambivalent view of the female torso as both helpless and nourishing. But as we examine
the reality of our authentic physical experiences, those of us
who are nonmothers realize that our physiques do not need
to be problematic simply because of their willed or unwilled
unfruitfulness.

At times, however, even those of us who are intentional nonmothers may mourn not using our wombs and breasts as nature
intended; sometimes we feel, regardless of the many ways we
use and enjoy our bodies, that they remain untested, under-
used, even immature. Bodily grief seems to exist for some who
have not experienced gestation, labor, and lactation. During
the year that Georgia O'Keeffe reluctantly realized she would
remain childless, she decided to devote herself to "magnificent
beauty" and rendered images of alligator pears resembling pregnant torsos. Once when I was in my twenties and visiting a
pregnant friend, I was surprised that her physicality, her evident corporeal expectancy, seemed more powerful than my
earnest efforts to develop a profession, which suddenly seemed
flimsy in comparison to the miraculousness of her swelling
stomach. Recently I interviewed a woman who had never
yearned for babies in her younger years, but after losing both
breasts to cancer, she spoke of her wistfulness about missing
out on nursing. A friend of mine who is adopted and without
offspring spoke of her desire for a biological bond with another
being. Another woman told me that she regretted being unable
to pass on her particular genetic imprint; such women, as well
as only children and those with half or stepsiblings like myself,
are indeed organically apart, but it is a fact that we can experience as either isolation, uniqueness, or something in between.

Inhabiting flesh that has never been with child or never given birth is different from having a body that has undergone one or more deliveries, yet it is a difference that is often invisible to others. In my experience, gynecologists' offices are full of statuettes and pictures of mothers and infants, as if the only activity of the female body is giving birth; I have often wondered at the lack of illustrations of amorous couples or graying menopausal women. (When we are not ignored, we hear only the negative side of childlessness—that it is one of the risks for breast cancer or heart attack.) If a childless woman has an obvious maternal physicality—large breasts and hips elaborately evolved for childbirth—it is a constant reminder of the reproductive mandate. But the inner reality does not always match the outer one for the quarter who worry about the health risks of pregnancy and delivery. Mothers tell us that bringing a child to term changes the figure irrevocably, while those of us who are nulliparas know that our bodies retain their familiarity. This can be comforting: In one recent study, young mothers were significantly less satisfied with their physiques than those who had not yet given birth. Nonetheless, it is unnecessary to be alienated from other females and our female legacy because we have not gone through labor. Although my mother delivered four infants and I delivered none, I identify with her physicality because I inherited her body: Our arms, legs, hands, and feet are identical except in regard to the fleshy changes caused by age.

In other ways, all females share important bodily experiences. The summer before I turned thirteen, I had a mysterious bellyache that soon resolved itself with my first menstral period. I became infused with wonder that my young body could produce a baby, but I was content to keep it as a potential, a promise. My mother told me that I now had "the curse," reflecting the widespread negative attitude toward menarche. The unhappily childless may be distressed to be reminded each month that they are infecund. But Elizabeth Corey, known as Bachelor Bess, a turn-of-the-century midwestern schoolteacher and homesteader, referred to her menses in letters home as a time of "celebration," apparently a reference to her freedom from childbearing. And for me monthly bleeding became a reassuring reminder of my healthy femaleness, the possibility of fertility, and my body's groundedness in nature. During menstruation, many women feel their bodies undergoing a tidal transition that is cleansing and recharging; each cycle is experienced and even enjoyed like a little gestation, moving predictably from premenstrual heaviness and moodiness, through menstrual aches, to postmenstrual vitality. In some cultures or castes, menstruating women go into seclusion either by their own volition or because of imposed taboos; my mother used to scorn her friends who took to bed each month as weak or foolish, but perhaps she would have regarded her periods as more than a curse if they had been times for rest and rejuvenation. Bleeding on a lunar cycle is sacred in some Native American tribes as a time of heightened female power due to the appearance of life-giving blood. In recent years, some young women, both those who have borne and those who have not, have advocated celebrating monthly menses with rituals, relaxation, and bright red clothing.

Many women, mothers and nonmothers alike, ground their feelings of femininity in another aspect of physicality—eroticism. Centuries ago, the sensuality of females was considered suspect because it was related to empowerment: The disreputable ladies in medieval literature were "almost always associated with female sexuality, assertion, and creativity," according to literary historians Sandra Gilbert and Susan Gubar. Nulliparas, married as well as unmarried, have a troubling history in this regard since female carnal desires outside of wedlock or motherhood have been regarded as profoundly immoral and dangerous. In the fourteenth century, Geoffrey Chaucer had his five-times-married, earthy, feisty, worldly Wife of Bath reveal that she "fear[ed] that her barren sexuality resembles wild fire, destructive and insatiable."

Three hundred years later, prelates and poets continued to worry about the supposed unnatural eroticism of nonmothers: In 1616, for instance, Ben Jonson criticized a court lady for preferring lovemaking over mothering in his poem, "To Fine Lady Would-bee," in which he accused her of using contraceptives: "The world reputes you barren: but I know / Your 'pothecarie, and his drug sayes no." The poet gratuitously tries in verse to reassure this lady that she will soon forget the pain of childbirth, and that she can restore her faded looks with paints. When she expresses reluctance about losing her freedom and pleasures, he is less sympathetic: "Oh, / you live at court: / And there's both losse of time, and losse / of sport." Finally, he cruelly admonishes her to write on her "wombe" that it is actually a "tombe" because of her buried but unborn children.

In nineteenth-century America, in the wake of modern ideas about the importance of erotic gratification, a few rebels practiced free love, but often with the result bearing out-of-wedlock children. It was widely assumed that woman's strong sexual nature was satisfied and kept in bounds by motherhood, a view related to the biblical belief that her original sin is redeemed by the pain of childbirth. "At the end of the nineteenth century, we were told that when a woman enjoys sex but declines motherhood, she is worse than a beast," says psychologist Louise Kaplan. "We were warned of the terrible evils that might emerge from the Pandora's box if women did not contain their sexual fires and murderous potentials in the tender eroticism of motherhood."

There is another tradition, albeit a more hidden and libertarian one, that severs the customary link between sexuality and procreativity. It exists, of course, among homosexuals. Among married heterosexuals it has ancient roots in the Old Testament and the Jewish tradition, which teach compassion for the barren wife and assert the husband's obligation to have marital relations with her. Only a few radicals in the last century, like anarchist Emma Goldman and suffragette Victoria Woodhull, openly declared that women had the right to amorous passion outside of marriage and motherhood. As Freud's writings about the female libido began to circulate in the twentieth century, Margaret Sanger became motivated in her drive for legal, inexpensive, and reliable contraception by her belief in a woman's right to erotic fulfillment without the fear of pregnancy.

Testimony from women is conflicted about the relationship between maternity and sexuality. Historically, while some wives were motivated to avoid childbearing to protect their looks and, presumably, their sex appeal, others found maternity to be the only expression of their erogenous natures. And today some women find desire enhanced when they do not fear an accidental pregnancy; others enjoy lovemaking that holds the possibility of conception. One nonmother I interviewed sadly recalled that her use of the birth control pill had devalued and diminished her sexuality by severing it from the life-giving power of potential birth. "I blindly defied nature, and nature evened the score," she observed, adding that the pill had suppressed her ovulation for twelve years before she discovered that pelvic inflammatory disease had left her infertile. And while a number of young mothers believe that parenthood interferes with amorousness, others tell us that pregnancy enhances their eroticism. They state that gestation increases the vascularity and therefore the sexual responsiveness of the pelvic region; some have called childbirth the biggest orgasm of all.

While the verity and extent of the evidence is speculative, it is certain that the female libido is strongly affected by a woman's attraction and attitude toward her partner. This view is illustrated in mythology by the story of the nymph Daphne, who turned herself into a tree to avoid being raped by Apollo, suggesting a blocking of her eroticism out of fear and outrage. Love is a powerful aphrodisiac, and testimony from happy childless marriages in the sociological literature suggests that many partners are more sexually active and pleased by their sex lives than parents. Regardless of its childbearing status, there certainly can be immense enjoyment of one's own or another's body as objects of desire; in my experience, the fact that my womb was never used precisely as nature planned has made little difference.

For nulliparas of earlier generations it often remained difficult to disregard centuries of cautionary teachings about carnality apart from maternity. Sometimes they downplayed sex or retreated from it altogether, especially if they were unmarried. Georgia O'Keeffe, born in the Midwest in the Victorian era, was deeply discomforted by erotic interpretations of her gigantic floral stamens and petals. (One reviewer wrote that her early charcoal abstractions of forms within forms simply revealed that she wanted to have a baby.) Virginia Woolf noted that women of her generation felt inhibited about writing about the body's desires and that she, herself, had not revealed the truth about her own "experiences as a body." Although Woolf predicted that no female would write honestly about her sexuality for years, it was only two generations later that Erica Jong, while still childless, wrote the explicit and high-spirited *Fear of Flying*. Although the judgmentalism toward, if not disparagement of, nonmaternal eroticism seems to have eased in secular society, even today nulliparas are suspect, as if they are perverting or denying their sexual natures: One young woman who did not want a baby was told by a boyfriend that she was opting for "self-castration," as if she were undergoing a clitoridectomy, or female circumcision.

The ways women's bodies are perceived and the ways we live in them are often surprisingly divergent. Erik Erikson has described what he calls the empty or disappointed womb, but he seems unaware that the uterus, vacant or not, is an active organ with its menstrual and sexual sensations; he has also ignored spiritual, intellectual, and imaginative interpretations of what he regards as female inner space. Another psychologist, Mardy Ireland, has more recently noted that the nonpregnant womb can be viewed as a metaphor for "holding and bringing forth"—if not an infant then an emotion or an insight from the fermenting unconscious. Instead of living with the idea of an empty inner space, all women—especially childfree ones—can hold it as a symbol of internal fecundity, inner richness, and the possibility of renewable life whether we are sexual or celibate, with or without child.

A body that has never been pregnant can be regarded as potent, still in anticipation, invested with self-potential and self-possession. From the skeletal to the circulatory systems, the female torso is prepared for a pregnancy every two years for three decades, allowing women who suppress their fertility the possibility of using all their physiological energy and endurance for lovemaking, dancing, running, or other forms of bodily exertion. For me, the digging and planting of a garden are a ritualistic, instinctive, harmonious, absorbing form of physicality in which I have learned to compensate for my lack of upper-arm musculature by dragging, dropping, and rolling heavy objects, as well as by using tools—for example, angling a crowbar to coax large rocks from the ground. Whatever the many ways we use our bodies, it is important for those of us who have never given birth to experience them as womanly, sensual, strong, energetic, and even eloquent.

Another aspect of womanliness besides our physicality is our sociability—the web of human relationships that enhance and enrich our lives. As a writer and, I suppose, an introvert, my mind's eye instinctively turns inward; but whereas my trade and an aspect of my nature call for quiet apartness, another part of me seeks connection, company, love. Affiliations, in fact, are especially important to counteract the isolating effect of writing, an intense activity that demands the utmost attentiveness. Yet, paradoxically, my alliances with female friends have helped me to understand and justify my need not to be with others at times. Although this kind of withdrawal has been called uncaring and, hence, unfeminine, I have found that as I express myself, and inevitably my womanhood, through relationships with everyone around me, my femininity is constantly revealing itself. Others' needs and desires—as well as intrusions—both deepen my inner resources and expose my limitations. As I listen, care, and try to comfort, I draw on old lessons learned at my mother's knee and new insights arrived at as an adult. This is a nurturing and sustaining stance that I enjoy today, one that takes a slightly different form with every person; it is also a response that demands much imagination, tact, insight, and patience. It is the outward, social face of personhood, one that has long been associated with femininity. It is also an attitude available to mothers and nonmothers alike, and one that links nulliparas to our womanly legacy of nourishing maternal figures.

In the past, unmarried women often lived in extended families or they gathered together as social workers in settlement houses, as nuns in convents, or as faculty at women's colleges. Some single females developed intense friendships, living together for years in "Boston marriages," which were sometimes erotic in nature. Others waited until middle age to marry and entered into childless marriages. Even so, most women who did not want children never married, and at times they suffered from a lack of intimacy; in the spring of 1828, for instance, when New England novelist Catharine Sedgwick was thirtynine and in low spirits after turning away another suitor, she wrote that her "solitary condition" felt "unnatural" and lonely since she was "first to none"; then, however, she quickly recovered and acknowledged that she was "second to a great many" relatives and friends. Despite such moments of doubt, spinsters in the nineteenth century were much more likely to write in diaries and letters about the deep pleasure they took in their unwed states, and in the strong alliances they created within the female sphere. In that pre-Freudian era, they apparently did not feel that chastity was a difficult burden to bear in light of the dangers associated with childbirth.

In our era, when so many nulliparas live alone or among unknown neighbors in large cities, most of us feel a strong need for community. It can be a desire for a communion of the spirit or psyche, in which communication takes place by long-distance telephone or even by computer, or for an actual neighborhood or town in which to relate to others. Those of us without children often form "friendship families," according to Berenice Fisher, a professor at New York University, especially if we are single and live apart from our relatives. Experts have many theories about this desire for connection. Psychiatrist Martha Kirkpatrick, the editor of two books on women's sexuality, has observed that the quest for intimacy appears to be "an even greater imperative in the lives of lesbians" (who, of course, are less likely to have children) as "an unconscious effort to re-inforce or complete their feminine development." Relatedness is so important to women, in fact, that it frequently fuels the fear of childlessness. Certainly I feel that my lifelong desire for closeness with a partner, female friends, and certain children is intensified because I do not have progeny, particularly as I anticipate old age.

Relationships with males, of course, are extremely important to the heterosexual nonmother's ability or inability to enjoy her femaleness. Some men resist recognizing the essential female-ness of a woman who rejects the maternal role, particularly if she is successful at work; they may also turn on such women and call them unfeminine, when the issue is usually their own lack of strength. When I was in my forties, I confided in my journal that I was still looking for a relationship with a "manly man," one who would "allow the lightness and the femininity" to sur-face within myself, who would let me be soft and vulnerable with him. Having finally found such a man in my third husband, my womanliness now feels enhanced in a way that both strengthens my sense of self and enables me to discover myself in another way. Like Chaucer, who praised the independent, childless young widow Criseyde as "Wommanly," such men do not associate a woman's lack of maternity with a lack of femi-ninity and, in fact, sometimes they find an inverse relationship between the two. And, as studies have shown, most husbands in childfree marriages seem happy and well adjusted. Perhaps that is because some nonmothers regard their relationships with men as the most important ones of all. As a little girl, one of my friends fantasized not about mothering but about dancing with boys, and she viewed babies as expressions of romantic love, only to be considered after meeting the man of her dreams. This is the kind of woman who gladly remains without children in order to cement and celebrate a successful alliance with a male. Diarist Anaïs Nin, for one, felt it her destiny to be a muse and a mentor to men: "Nature connived to keep me a man's woman, and not a mother; not a mother to children but of men. Nature shaping my body for the love of man, not of child."

Nulliparas tend to be more androgynous than other women, more so than the ultra-feminine Nin, according to Sandra Bem, a research psychologist and the creator of a sex-role test. The word *androgyny* was coined by the early Greeks—from *andros*, male, and *gyne*, female—to describe creatures like the goddess Artemis who engaged in both warfare and midwifery. Today the term is often used to describe a psychological, not a physical, state that transcends gender definitions. More than a century ago Alexis de Tocqueville admired such breadth in American women who "often exhibit a masculine strength of understanding and a manly energy, generally preserve great delicacy of personal appearance and always retain the manners of women, although they sometimes show that they have the hearts and minds of men." (Still, he feared that without distinct gender roles there would be "weak men and disorderly women.")

Childless women also tend to express their empathy in the traditional way of symbolic mothers. In Joan M. Offerle's 1985 study, they were found to be nurturing through paid or unpaid teaching, and through work in environmental, civil rights, and humanitarian causes. One of them, a friend of mine, is a modern-day Artemis; she ministers to the members of her staff, but she also travels around the world for a group that restores sight to the blind in developing countries. I found my own style of social mothering when I served for six years on the volunteer ambulance squad in the village where I live, an activity that required diagnostic skill, ability at comforting, physical strength, and even bravery as we swooped in like ministering angels at all hours of the day and night to transport an elderly person to the hospital, stabilize the broken bone of a child, or rescue an injured person from a wrecked car. But all too often, our so-called caring work is ignored because we are not mothers.

Friendships with other females are also essential to our developing and ongoing senses of womanliness. But just as the concept of femininity contains inherent contradictions, so too, did my youthful friendships with other girls. Sometimes my interests simply diverged from those of typical teenage girls; at other times I was just more rebellious. When I went to boarding school in the late 1950s, I felt different from many girls because of my interests in politics and social issues; one spring weekend, for example, when many of my classmates headed off to dances at Ivy League men's colleges, I attended a Quaker seminar at a settlement house in Spanish Harlem. This pattern of going my own way continued as I got older: When I got to college in the Midwest, I did not pledge a sorority, because I was both weary of female milieus and suspicious of social pretensions.

After moving to Manhattan in the late 1960s, a few years after college graduation, I joined a consciousness-raising group. For the first time in my life, I began to deeply appreciate female friendships as I and other young women began to relate to each other in new ways, with greater interest in each other, and as more than rivals for male attention. Young, mostly unmarried, and all nonmothers, we started to talk openly and honestly about our parents, jobs, and love affairs. We were astonished to discover that so many of us had gone through similar, confusing, disturbing experiences, and by comprehending our commonality, we felt both bonded and freed. Over the years, as our lives changed, as some of us became mothers and others did not, we drifted apart. But the memory of our intoxicating connectedness remains.

Female friendship often draws on the practice of talking about ourselves and others in empathic ways; this instinct for common ground and comparable experiences expands our scope and knowledge as females. Women without children often have a quiet commonality in which we talk little about being nulliparous. Our presences, however, affirm each other's childlessness. I was once close to a woman with whom I shared a first name and an appearance so similar that we were taken for sisters; we shared a number of interests, such as books and travel, and an affinity for secondhand clothing shops. Paradoxically, because our personalities resonated so well together, she inspired me to recognize and refine my own style and expressiveness, as I probably did for her. My friendships with women with whom I am less akin are also eye-opening, since they force me to understand female attitudes and experiences that are less familiar. Recently, over a period of several years, a group of women who paint, sculpt, photograph, and write gathered in my home on Sunday evenings to talk about the ways the creative process intersected with their personal lives. Oddly and completely by chance, almost all of us were childless; we were motivated partly by a desire for collegiality, since we were creating alone in our studios and homes, and partly by a desire to receive inspiration, affirmation, and information from one another. The end result of all these exchanges with other women over the years has been greater enhancement and expansion of my sense of womanliness.

In the past, females habitually bonded because they were mothers, not because they were women; historian Gerda Lerner has argued that the paucity of women's intellectual history "has kept [women] for far longer than was necessary from developing a consciousness of their collectivity in sisterhood, not motherhood." Indeed, many childfree females have agonized over the way the demands of young motherhood cripple close friendships. As in the nineteenth century, when a first pregnancy raised the specter of death, today those of us without children usually expect a painful loss when a sister or a close friend announces that she is going to have a baby. The way many childless women tell it, the experience is a one-sided injury, one the new mother does not notice because she is so absorbed in her infant. Although a few nonmothers deliberately befriend mothers as a way to obtain children in their lives, most nulliparas remain, by necessity or preference, closest to friends who are also without young children, including those who have not yet given birth or whose offspring have left home. This is not because childlessness is a strong link between us, but because the natures of our daily lives are more alike. At times, of course, we arouse envy by being relatively unencumbered; and many parents assume that we dislike children or do not understand the pleasures of mothering.

The ideal for all women, it seems to me, is to embrace others while developing or preserving a strong sense of self. In their 1977 study of unmarried middle-management businesswomen, Margaret Hennig and Anne Jardim discovered that when these women reached their thirties, after years of putting their careers first, they became preoccupied with issues of femininity. Until then, they had been unable to combine their private lives and professional ambitions. As their positions became more secure, they tried to resolve their intensifying personal conflicts by putting their jobs on hold and spending more time on their appearances and friendships. Eventually, half of them married men who appreciated their Artemis-like natures: their competence in the world and their womanliness at home. Although none became natal mothers, many became stepmothers. As they became more at ease with themselves, most went on to even greater business successes. In contrast, those in the study who did not undergo this personality development remained locked unhappily in middle-management positions. From such testimony, it is evident that we must cultivate our womanhood, but do it authentically so as to contribute to our own growth and to the happiness of others.

While the femininity of childless women can be expressed through the body and through our relationships, it can also be expressed when we feel close to the natural world. Soon after I moved to the country, I had an ecstatic dream about looking down and discovering a lush, green paradise marked by a pattern of meandering rivers. "I felt great freedom in anticipation of wandering down the paths," I noted in my journal. Women have long been thought to represent creation, sometimes in the derogatory sense of being passive and instinctive "mother earth" beings, and although the association is a cliché, I certainly find that I enjoy outdoor activities as an essential aspect of my womanly life. I am not alone in this. Today, as the industrialized "gray world," to use ecologist Gary Snyder's phrase, threatens to destroy the natural green one, so-called ecofeminists have called for an ecological revolution to preserve what some call "sister earth," a phrase that suggests an ethical and egalitarian relationship with nature. My hours in my garden affirm me in a nonnatal femaleness, probably because gardening is something I learned from my mother, but also because it is nurturing and maturing in its own right, as it teaches lessons about proportion and persistence, fragility and endurance, disappointment and fruition.

Over the centuries, women's relationships with the natural world have been both enslaving and empowering: Nature may take over the female body for the purpose of perpetuating the species, but its gardens and forests have also provided her with solace and sustenance. And while medieval tapestries and old book illustrations have portrayed ladies within walled floral gardens, it is sometimes unclear whether they are imprisoned or sheltered. At any rate, the female allegiance to nature is a tenacious one: While in literature a male protagonist often journeys from court to a pastoral milieu and back again, a female frequently does the reverse, and finally settles into an enhanced version of the early natural paradise. I have done this in my own life—from Rhode Island to New York City and back to rural Connecticut. The intimacy and identification of women with nature is a persistent theme in fiction by women as well as in women's letters, novels, paintings, diaries, and notebooks. Georgia O'Keeffe, the daughter of a Wisconsin farmer, wrote to her friend Jean Toomer in 1934 that "my center does not come from my mind—it feels in me like a plot of warm moist well-tilled earth with the sun shining hot on it—" Using this as a metaphor for her sense of self, she went on: "It seems I would rather feel starkly empty than let anything be planted that can not be tended to the fullest possibility of its growth—worthy of its quality."

Virtually every female in my large extended family has a flower or vegetable garden, a personal green plot, that is either formal and restrained, wild and impulsive, exotic and expert, or dramatic and profuse. My mother has carved her flower garden from farmers' fields at the edge of the sea, with constant winds and occasional hurricanes as her challenge. Her garden is a hybrid of bright English exuberance and disciplined Japanese silhouette; she permits the spontaneity of some species by allowing a few perennials to seed themselves but participates in the harsh domination of others by severely pruning trees and shaping topiary. She is gratified when her sprigs and saplings generously forgive error and reward instinct, and her weeded and clipped beds and borders give her peace and pleasure. In her garden and in her greenhouse she also experiences mastery: She knows that her bushes and blossoms can be neglected, manipulated, even murdered without guilt; she regards non-thriving specimens like naughty children, but unlike real off-spring, she can brutally uproot them if they refuse to flourish. Like the lady of the beasts in the ancient tapestries, my mother welcomes toads, birds, insects, snakes, and other wild creatures into her domain. And like the fictional old woman who experiences moments of epiphany and ecstasy in nature, my mother is well rewarded for her efforts and her expressiveness amid her greenery, probably more so than in other aspects of her life. So as my mother's daughter, when I become covered with dirt while digging in a flower bed in the spring, I feel happily in harmony with her as well as with the life-generating force of nature.

A few years after reading the letter my father wrote to me shortly after I was born, but having forgotten his words about dogs, antiques, and historic houses, I bought a puppy and moved some family furniture into an old house on a village green in New England; I can only attribute this move to my gravitation to the similar "appreciations" that he referred to in his letter, not to any obeisance to him. At the time the back-yard was covered with snow; as it melted, I spent a season read-ing gardening books, watching, and weeding. In the following springs, summers, and falls, calling on some instinct of farmer forebears, I pulled rocks from the earth and replaced them with enriched soil; I planted, pruned, watered, uprooted, and edged. My garden became a source of rejuvenating joy that gave me inner balance when I needed it. It was even an escape at times:

When I was evasive with myself, my garden notebook became more detailed than my personal one.

My absorption in nature has had great resonance for me as a nonmother: When I became intimately acquainted with the goings-on in my garden, I noticed its profligate ways, its excess of seeds, its demands and dependencies, its cycles of growing and dying. I realized that nature is about more than propagation—it is also about blooming and tenacity, loss and adaptability. Ignoring the natural world, especially if we are not part of the ongoing generational reproductive process, can be perilous. We can become too intellectual or isolated or ignorant about the rhythms of life. Each year I find that my garden deeply involves me in physicality and instinct that complements intellectuality. I nudge along growing things by deadheading and clipping, mulching, composting, and fertilizing in a way that is the perfect antidote to the still, contemplative, cerebral act of writing. The colors, smells, and shapes of the beds and borders also provide continual creative pleasures during the long periods between publication of my books. A friend once perceptively observed that in my garden I actively participate in the earth's annual rebirth. Whatever the case, in my small rectangle of nature, I plant in the spring and cut down in the autumn with urgency and exhilaration.

Besides the world of nature, there are myriad other ways to relate to our female legacy apart from childbirth. In a family tradition of needlecrafters, my mother knits and stitches every day in a furious flow of creative energy that affirms my own sense of feminine creativity. Perhaps her masterpiece is a crewel bedspread of Adam and Eve in the Garden of Eden, a natural paradise full of berries and blossoms, birds on the wing, and bushy-tailed animals. Like other females in the family, I care deeply about creating a pleasing and comfortable home, one that reflects my aesthetic values. Other women without children in my circle also tend animals, embroider, cook, and enjoy other homemaking activities. We are, as I discovered in my research, like other nulliparas with atypical female lives who embrace some traditional womanly activities. In fact, literary critics have speculated that Emily Dickinson's gardening and household chores were rituals that calmed her unease about creating daring poetry; indeed, those ritualistic acts helped enable her poetry.

In the decades since I first struggled to understand femininity and to find my own, I have realized that the unwed women of New England experienced a rich and rewarding sense of womanliness outside of motherhood. In the Revolutionary War era, these nulliparous females viewed their sphere as "active, generative, and multifaceted," writes historian Lee Chambers-Schiller; one such woman, Mary A. Dodge, a Massachusetts writer who was also a governess, teacher, and journalist, believed that "whatever tends to enlarge the mind, as well as increase the sympathy, belongs to woman. Politics, art, science, all are hers, subject only to her choice, subordinate always to her freedom." Emily Dickinson expressed a more radical view—that the creation of art was the true fulfillment of womanhood, more so than marriage or maternity. The concept of the feminine also has broader meanings in different cultures and castes. The so-called divine feminine, a force that represents creativity or originality, exists in a number of spiritual traditions, including the Native American; in fact, Laguna Indians use the word *mother* for the most evolved person in the pueblo—whether a parent or not—because he or she inspires symbolic ritual rebirth. Furthermore, the Shaker concept of spiritual motherhood, which transcended biological maternity, invested celibate women with religious authority in the belief that so-called female virtues (like sensitivity, subjectivity, intuitiveness, and irrationality) made women more receptive than men to God.

Femininity, like other aspects of the self, is highly individual. For me, being feminine had little to do with the rigid pronatal gender rituals of the 1950s, like dancing school and the debutante cotillion. Femaleness was neither a flimsy construct nor narrow or restrictive, and it was more than a code of behavior. Early on I felt an unshakable sense of femaleness, even though I did not play with dolls very much but instead liked to ride my two-wheel bicycle no-hands around the block in my cowgirl outfit. True femininity, as opposed to female impersonation, is so deeply rooted in our psyches that it cannot be affected by whether or not we give birth. Furthermore, since we are female, everything we do must be, by definition, feminine. "If I am myself, I am feminine," declared a friend of mine, a childless wife. "I never *for a moment* thought that I had to have children to be a woman or to be feminine."

Femininity, I have concluded, is a sensibility that evolves in tandem with dreams and desires, a set of values influenced by hormones and upbringing, which may or may not involve motherhood. In my thirties, just before I left my job to become a full-time writer, my personal ethic was becoming more evident. At Christmastime 1977, motivated by seasonal sentimentality—and sounding like my mother's daughter—I noted in my private pages that I disliked "upward mobility, materialism at the expense of the human values of warmth, nurturing, kindness. The lack of kindness, especially, bothers me." Two decades later, I believe that my life in my fifties is a deeply feminine one, enriched as it is by my husband, my home and garden, my work, and the people, including a number of children, whom I care deeply about. Writing allows a full expression of what matters to me as a woman, and it feels very feminine to

work at home, where I can integrate writing with such pleasurable aspects of daily life as cutting flowers, making soup, walking the dog, working alongside my artist husband, drinking tea
with a friend, and greeting neighbors at the post office. I have
come to believe that femininity is expansive enough to encompass enabling others *and* expressing the ego. If we as childless
women can courageously accept all our inclinations and interests as unquestionably legitimate and womanist, we can enlarge
what it means to be a woman.

EIGHT

POSSESSING OURSELVES, DOING OUR WORK

While those of us without children want to feel grounded in our femininity, many of us also wish to establish important ties to the world of work. We usually choose our life's work carefully, or we feel compelled to do it; however we come to it, our trades and professions are usually integral to our identities and independence. "How good work is—work that has a soul in it! . . . In all human relations, the woman has to yield, to modify her individuality . . . but true work is perfect freedom, and full satisfaction," wrote Elizabeth Blackwell, an unwed and childless doctor and the first female physician in America, in 1860. Throughout the centuries, the desire for engrossing endeavors has been a motivation for childlessness, one that continues to this day, ranking right after the aspiration for marital happiness, according to sociologists. In Sharon Houseknecht's survey of nineteen studies about nulliparous women, 74 percent of the respondents cited the wish for meaningful work outside the home as a reason for refusing motherhood. Often the jobs that fascinate non-mothers are risky, demanding, unremunerative, or in some way difficult to combine with mothering. When the urge to undertake such occupations causes or contributes to a woman's childfree state, she is liable to be considered antisocial or selfish, since she stands in contrast to the selfless madonna myth. Yet if a nullipara involved in a serious calling can ignore outer and inner accusations of selfishness, she may be able to achieve a kind of expression and achievement that are as generous toward her culture as any maternal gesture toward a child.

Writing has been my chosen work since I took up newspaper reporting after college. I turned to journalism out of a sense of adventurousness as well as a wish for empowerment; since I was still shy and softspoken in my twenties, sometimes even having difficulty finishing sentences, a reporter's shield gave me license to go anywhere and ask anyone almost anything. Other, more hidden, reasons also made a career important to me. After my father moved to Vermont, he had little success as an owner of a small furniture factory, and his downward plunge, which led to his becoming an alcoholic carpenter without a hunting dog, antiques, or an old house, frightened me. And because I could never rely on him, I learned to depend upon myself and became, in effect, my own paternal parent at an early age. I realize now that I wanted to avoid and even, I suppose, redeem my father's disgrace by having my version of his name become visible in bylines.

In time I turned to writing books out of an urge for more independence and expressiveness. When I began my first biography, I planned to pack up my old Karmann Ghia and drive around the country for an undetermined number of months doing research and interviews, an odyssey that I obviously could not have undertaken with a child, although the desire for one had not died. "My fantasy of escape is with me again: taking off in the little green car with typewriter, notebooks and pens, tape recorder, sleeping bag, et cetera for the Southwest," I noted in my journal at the age of thirty-four. "I dream about a life in

New Mexico with an adobe house, hot sun, writing, fires, dog, baby." A biographer inevitably flattens his or her life for a while when illuminating someone else's, but, as Bernard Malamud suggests in *Dubin's Lives*, his novel about a fictional biographer of D. H. Lawrence, the vicariousness of the experience can eventually lead the author to expand his or her own existence. I certainly found myself affected by the values and viewpoints of O'Keeffe and Stieglitz, which gave backbone to my own. My need to write also became bound up with other psychic needs, and at forty I reflected: "The way I relish solitude and freedom, I wonder why I thought I should have a child. . . . The one thing I'm certain of is the beauty of feeling joyfully at home with myself, a feeling that comes about in solitude." To this day I find it deeply pleasurable to plan a workday, to have time to think and imagine, to be able to do my chosen work. I have never wanted anyone, not even a child, to violate this precious space.

A plethora of painful testimony exists about the anguish of being unable to use one's intellectual or imaginative abilities. One poignant example is the sentiment of illustrator and writer Mary Anna Hallock Foote, who wrote to another writer in 1888: "How do you *bear* it—Helena, my dear girl—that constant thwarting and suppression of that side of your Nature, so strong and imperative really and so hidden, except in your rare work, when you have time to work." Often in the past a young woman was unable to use her education or talents because she had small children. In the nineteenth century, educator Catharine Beecher believed that women's nervous diseases, especially among the gifted, were caused by enforced mental inactivity or the inability to use one's learning. Likewise, Ida Husted Harper darkly imagined in 1901 "what it means for a woman to give the core of her life, the beautiful years between twenty and forty-five, the time when the mental powers are at their best, when enjoyment in the pleasant things of the world is keenest, to the exacting demands of the nursery." She added: "It would drive a man insane."

Today, work outside the home varies immensely; it can be white, pink, or blue collar. The possibility of pregnancy, or an interrupted career because of motherhood, remain reasons to discriminate against all women workers, and most still earn less than men, including professionals. Degrading or badly paid jobs are poor alternatives to the prospect of staying home with one's children. Also, after children are born, parental priorities sometimes change, and women opt for undemanding jobs, assigned work, or opportunistic positions with good benefits. The woman with a routine job to make ends meet will not experience the same conflict between working and child raising as someone whose endeavors are deeply gratifying. Furthermore, the link between enjoyable employment and self-development is real, making the idea of parenthood problematic for ambitious girls: In 1985, for instance, a sample of teenage girls from poor southern families with the highest educational and professional aspirations of all their classmates, boys and girls alike, wanted no offspring. Other studies show that women who get the most pleasure from their careers are less likely to become mothers. "If I did not have an overwhelming desire to do other things, I probably would have had a child despite the difficulties," acknowledged one of them.

In past centuries, well-born women who worked outside the home were almost always engaged in unpaid or underpaid vocations, but their pursuits often gave them feelings of pride. Ellen Glasgow's fictional Dorinda in the novel *Barren Ground* discovered that labor "is symbolic of a woman's freedom to exist in direct relationship to the world and to unleash her full vitality." Similarly, Simone de Beauvoir made the point that employment often enables a woman to affirm her integrity rather than her vanity; "like an artist she [should] 'passionately lose herself in her projects,' in order to find herself in action and transcendence, rather than in what she appears to others to be." More recently, philosopher Sara Ruddick has used the word *workless-ness* for the painful periods when she was unable to do her scholarly research and writing; when she began to work again, she experienced the "satisfactory predominance of activity over passivity, of reality over fantasy, of creation over conception. It continues to astonish me that this single human ability to work brings so much additional pleasure, order, solace, and meaning to my life."

Work has surely made me organize my time, concentrate my mind, strengthen my will, and set a standard of wholesome engagement with others. After I began to freelance almost two decades ago, I noted in my journal that I felt elated by "my ability to *leave*, my ability to say *no*, to refuse to be bored or exploited anymore. Now that I've done it in one area, can I do it in others and do it again?" While writing at home, I realized that I had to protect my ability to work without distraction, which I called then "a fragile balance." Over time I have learned that by preserving my productivity, along with my energy, my eagerness, and even my earnings, I have learned to protect myself emotionally.

If it is well paid or well rewarded, labor brings empowerment. With the growth of manufacturing in the nineteenth century, the monetary value of women's work on the farm diminished. As early as 1832, English intellectual Harriet Taylor declared that women, for the sake of retaining respect and influence, should contribute directly to family earnings. Likewise, A Childless Wife wrote in 1905: "Whenever I learned the reason of the woman's submission it was always based upon the fact that she had children and no money, the existence of the one precluding the obtaining of the other.... I discovered that enough of money, rightly earned, can buy freedom, independence, self-respect and the power to live one's own life, and those privileges were a satisfactory synonym for happiness for me.... I decided that freedom, equality and self-ownership would come to the wife with her own pocketbook." Her view was not widespread, however, and during the years 1900 to 1940, only a quarter of American women—mostly the poor, unmarried, and childless wives—worked for wages. Since then, of course, more American wives and mothers have found jobs out of need or desire, including the wish to undertake highly valued and remunerative work. After the percentage of employed women rose to one third of all females during the Second World War, it dipped in the 1950s and 1960s before doubling to 60 percent in 1992. Meanwhile, social scientists have found that women working for pay have higher self-esteem than housewives.

Besides benefiting themselves, women often serve society when they use their energies outside the home; Margaret Mead, in fact, urged females to find "a divine discontent that will demand other satisfactions than those of child rearing." Instead of raising children, for instance, Ella Lyman Cabot of Boston wrote seven books on ethics and childhood education (and her husband taught ethics, wrote books on healing, and suggested visionary reforms in the field of medicine). Lydia Maria Child, a writer who was born in Massachusetts in 1802 and educated by an older brother, was married at the age of twenty-six to an idealistic but impractical lawyer; three years later she wrote to her mother-in-law that she wished to become pregnant, but she never did, probably because of her husband's impotence (she later referred in a letter to the "childlike" nature of his lovemaking). He was an affectionate and admiring partner, however, and she testified that "he always insisted upon thinking that whatever I said was the wisest and whatever I did was the best." But because of his ineptitude as a lawyer and sugar beet farmer and her intelligence and relative freedom as a nonmother, she left him for a number of years and moved to New York in the 1840s to edit an abolitionist newspaper, the *National Anti-Slavery Standard*. Developing her abilities out of necessity as well as opportunity and resolve, she wrote forty-seven books—stories, poems, biographies, histories—on topics from household economics to the history of women.

When maternity was aggressively proclaimed again in the 1980s, some mothers attacked female professionals for adopting "masculinist" values like competitiveness and tried to paint them as nonnurturing anti-mothers, regardless of the social value of their work. It seems misguided, especially after several waves of feminism, to reject so-called male qualities or to project them onto nulliparas. Some supposed masculine attributes, like expertise and assertiveness, are essential to protect humanistic ones; certainly few women can be stay-at-home mothers without being dependent on welfare or a partner's paycheck. Likewise, in the political or legal arena, when waging battles for the rights of children and others, it is important for women to be vigilant, rational, persuasive, and what is conventionally regarded as "manly."

Work is much more than labor to many nulliparas: It is an expression of themselves as well as an act of enablement. Frequently such women wonder if and how they can also be mothers. Many who are in the arts find that the creative process is especially difficult to integrate into family life: All too often the artist's need for apartness conflicts with the child's need for availability. Novelist Charlotte Brontë, for instance, wrote that it would be preferable to be a struggling factory girl with "mental liberty" than a comfortable governess with little chance to daydream in the company of her charges. Novelists and other writers seem to be most outspoken about this issue, probably because, by the nature of their work, they publicly articulate and publish their experiences and perceptions. Over the years, debate has raged among mothers and nonmothers, particularly in the professions, about the pleasures and penalties of combining creativity and child rearing. Although mothers often become defensive and nonmothers doubtful about the possibility of combining the two, it is interesting and important for women to have these discussions.

In the past, when women devoted themselves to one of the arts, it was often an act of assertion and of rebellion against childbearing. Emily Dickinson, who viewed marriage as a sacrifice of self and motherhood as a risk to life itself, believed that devoting herself to poetry was both an escape from such dangers and an expression of vibrant womanliness. Until well into this century, almost all distinguished female achievement in literature came from women without children, says Tillie Olsen, the mother of four daughters, in her book *Silences*. Surprisingly few writers besides Olsen have made this connection: In the 1950s, when patriarch Ashley Montagu urged separate gender roles in *The Natural Superiority of Women*, he found two unusual women worthy of special admiration—Queen Elizabeth I and Georgia O'Keeffe—but he seemed unaware that their accomplishments were related to their childlessness. Giving birth has always been more highly rewarded than other forms of creativity in young women, so the plight of the gifted girl is especially problematic. If her genius shows up early, she may be allowed to develop it, but one wonders how many females become mothers before their abilities are evident. Virginia Woolf, in *A Room of One's Own*, described the fate of an imagined girl genius, Judith Shakespeare, sister of the bard, who ran away at sixteen to the all-male London stage, became pregnant by a theater manager, and killed herself on a winter's night. Woolf asked: "Who shall measure the heat and violence of the poet's heart when caught and tangled in a woman's body?"

Once children are born, the conditions for creativity may diminish. Adrienne Rich has described the prerequisites of writing poetry or fiction when one is a mother in terms of uninterrupted hours and mental freedom. And whereas disciplined self-expression demands the intense focusing of energy, child rearing requires the patient dissemination of it. Georgia O'Keeffe worried that if she had to interrupt an oil painting to tend to a child's needs, the paint might dry and ruin a work-in-progress; and Louise Nevelson, who had a son in her early twenties, felt compelled to leave him with her parents in Maine when he was nine so she could study art in Europe. Furthermore, in contrast to biological or social mothering, the inward-looking nature of deeply inventive work can appear self-indulgent, particularly when it is highly pleasurable.

Like fellow poet Emily Dickinson, Adrienne Rich also believes that engaging in creativity is an unstable and subversive act: "If the imagination is to transcend and transform experience it has to question, to challenge, to conceive of alternatives, perhaps to the very life you are living at that moment." She goes on: "Now, to be maternally with small children all day in the old way, to be with a man in the old way of marriage, requires a holding-back, a putting-aside of that imaginative activity, and demands instead a kind of conservatism." For a young mother to put personal preferences on a par with family goals takes unusual courage and drive, especially when the choice is between doing work whose rewards are financially unpredictable or taking a position with a steady paycheck. For writers it takes "conviction as to the importance of what one has to say, one's right to say it. And the will, the measureless store of belief in oneself to be able to come to, cleave to, find the form for one's own life comprehensions," says Tillie Olsen.

Olsen has worried that the output of the growing numbers of women writers with children will be "impeded, lessened, partial"; mothering and creativity are essentially incompatible, she has observed from her own experience, because "in intelligent passionate motherhood there are similarities [to creativity], in more than the toil and patience. The calling upon total capacities; the reliving and new using of the past; the comprehensions; the fascination, absorption, intensity. All almost certain death to creation—(so far)." Since a mother of small children needs to be empathic and attached, it may be difficult for her to develop the necessary differentiation and distance from her offspring to be original and individualistic. French writer Hélène Cixous, in an essay that fervently calls for females to write in womanly voices, notes that "a woman is never far from 'mother.'" She continues: "There is always within her at least a little of that good mother's milk. She writes in white ink." If that is so, then Cixous implies that all women, perhaps even childless ones conditioned to be mothers, create with blinders on or without a genderless perspective related to all humanity. Perhaps this is why a friend of mine painted a series of portraits of her daughters in heroic poses; another one, when musing aloud to her young daughter about a writing topic and hearing the child suggest herself, spun out a series of stories for children starring a fictional character like the little girl.

Novelist Mary Gordon neglected her writing during her initial pregnancy: "It is impossible for me to believe that anything
I write could have a fraction of the importance of the child
growing inside me," she explained. When the infant was born,
she at first found it difficult to summon the energy, focus, and
discipline to write: "The thought of going back to work on [my
novel] makes me feel physically ill. Infinitely more enjoyable to
lie here in the haze and silence with a baby." After producing
both books and babies, Gordon has revealed that for her it is
"much easier to be a mother than a writer," and she called
motherhood a simpler and more enchanting existence. She
added that having children also deeply affected her objectivity
and orientation as a person: "I worry about the membrane that
my obsession with them creates between me and the outside
world," she wrote. "This is why a certain kind of childless
woman rightly fears what having children would do to her
moral life. There is nothing more absorbing than a baby, nothing more intoxicating, and, if things are going badly, nothing
more drowning. . . . So to decide to have children, especially in
this world, is perhaps not the highest moral choice. At some
points refusal is the highest morality, but it is not, has never
been, the kind of morality that most interests me." Her impli-
cation is that motherhood comes with moral blinders, like the
willingness to always put the interests of her own offspring before, say, those of needier children or important charities.

Other kinds of work may also be adversely affected by a
mother's mind-set. When her daughter was young, anthropologist Margaret Mead found that she lacked the impartiality,
originality, and creativity to study other children, even though
she was apart from her child for long periods of time, because
she could only judge other youngsters comparatively, particularly their intelligences. Nonetheless, Mead noted this as an in-

teresting personal phenomenon, a temporary and relatively unimportant setback in her career, but if she had had another child or two, her work as a scientist might have been seriously compromised. And although we now reject the nineteenth-century theory that a female's use of her brain damages her womb, a parallel remains today between education and child-lessness. When historian Elizabeth Fox-Genovese entered graduate school, she believed she was not only limiting her marriageability but also risking her motherliness. Her concern has a ring of truth to it: In 1990, when they were around the age of thirty-nine, 40 percent of the women in the Wellesley College class of 1973 (who matriculated when the number of females in American graduate programs doubled) had no bio-logical children. And in the 1990s, nonmothers continue to have the most education and the best-paid jobs of all American women.

Academic research can certainly absorb a woman's attention, but the demands of the tenure system also play a part in many female academics being nulliparous. It is said that professors who seek tenure and lawyers who want partnerships are less likely to be female parents than doctors, because the latter can build careers more quickly after early childbearing. By the time academic women win tenure, it is often too late for them to give birth, according to Mary Beth Montgomery, who inter-viewed women faculty in the field of social work in the late 1980s. Women scientists are also in a profession that makes little accommodation to family life. "There will always be the astrophysicist who has to spend weeks at a telescope on a mountain in Hawaii, the geologist who runs when the volcano blows, the biologist who has to give injections every three hours round the clock," reports Shirley M. Tilghman, a professor of molecular biology at Princeton University.

Some mothers abhor the prospect of choosing between the polarities of creating and mothering. German artist Kathe Kollwitz, in a memoir called *Life in Art*, described a period when both her young sons were away for Easter and she had more time to sculpt. She became depressed in their unfamiliar absence, however, and her work suffered: "Formerly, in my so wretchedly limited working time, I was more productive, because I was more sensual; I lived as a human being must live, passionately interested in everything." For her part, novelist Ursula Le Guin has praised the creature she calls the "housewife-artist"; while admitting that babies literally and figuratively eat manuscripts, she nonetheless has criticized the "heroic mode" of choosing childlessness for the sake of creativity, calling it a rationale for an unfortunate need to make a choice. Other writers, working in a notoriously solitary profession, have turned to motherhood with relief: Anne Roiphe, for one, found it an antidote to "the madness of loneliness" and a protection against "internal demons." After her daughter was born, Alice Walker observed that she felt more balanced, as if she had found another, less cerebral, center of creativity, one more connected to other women; mothering, she continued, made her feel more committed to her own life, including her urge to write. Her child also became a stable bond in a life of shifting alliances, a relationship that gave her welcome affiliation and affirmation. Like other African-American women who have historically worked for wages while rearing children, Walker found it easier than many of her white counterparts to combine what novelist Toni Morrison has called "the nest and the adventure."

In the past, when women's roles were more rigidly defined, some female novelists downplayed the pleasure they took in their supposedly self-indulgent creations, either because self-abnegation was expected, or because their literary vocation indeed isolated them too much. They wrote alone, of course, but usually without the intimacy of marriage or the approval of others. "My author existence has always seemed something accidental, extraneous, and independent of my inner self," admitted the unwed Catharine Sedgwick, who penned popular historical romances in an effort to create an American literature. "My books have been a pleasant occupation and excitement in my life.... But they constitute no portion of my happiness—that is, of such as I derive from the dearest relations of life." Likewise, Louisa May Alcott contrasted herself to her sister in a low moment and wrote: "She is a happy woman! I sell my children [books], and though they feed me, they don't love me as hers do." Ironically, Alcott got a chance to become a mother after her sister died in childbirth, and she adopted the infant, a namesake called Lulu. Unfortunately, whether because Alcott was unwell, middle-aged, or ill suited to the role, she was unable to be "playful and patient" with her niece, who lived with her during the last ten years of Alcott's life.

Tillie Olsen has wondered if women writers without children ever feel the price they pay to do their best work is too high—a "damnation"; the answer, at various moments, is yes and no. Some nonmothers are always happier nurturing ideas and images than small human beings. Others vacillate: A year before her marriage, Virginia Woolf wrote despairingly: "To be 29 and unmarried—to be a failure—childless—insane, too, no writer." After her wedding her doctors advised her not to get pregnant because of her fragile mental state; she had already suffered one nervous breakdown, and they feared her susceptibility to another. Her nephew and biographer Quentin Bell believed that her childlessness was always a source of grief to her, but her own words reveal an eventual dissipation of her sadness

through her creativity. During her thirties, she often felt inade-
quate and incomplete without a child, but it is possible that
those feelings were also aroused by the lack of a sexual relationship with her husband. In her late forties, as her aspirations and
accomplishments grew, she wrote that "I scarcely want children
of my own now . . . perhaps I have killed the feeling instinctively; or perhaps nature does." At the age of forty-eight, with
the completion of her innovative novel *The Waves*, she wrote
elatedly: "Children are nothing to this."

Too often the urge to do exciting work is considered a sign of
egocentricity in women, particularly when it exists outside of a
caretaking profession, like teaching, nursing, or social work. As a
result, the issue of guilt troubles many nulliparas; Anaïs Nin, who
took to heart this kind of criticism, worried that writing novels
sublimated her sexuality, demanded aggressiveness, and stimulated her rivalry. Certainly my childlessness was associated with a
character flaw years ago when an older woman I barely knew, who
was a mother, accused me of not taking the time to rear a child.
Although it is true that I did not want to turn my little white
writing room into a nursery, I did not feel that my reluctance was
unreasonable—I wondered why the would-be father was unwilling to turn over his den, since he had an office at work. Perhaps I
never felt guilty about any youthful self-centeredness because
being nulliparous was not entirely my choice: Instead, at times I
associated it with a sense of self-preservation and at others with a
sense of responsibility toward an unborn child.

A double standard in regard to selfishness is often applied
to females and males. Our foremothers who advocated voluntary motherhood or contraception were condemned for
being self-seeking. Suffragettes were similarly criticized when

they marched to win the vote. In the early years of this century, socialist Henrietta Rodman, who favored collective housekeeping arrangements, was accused of "monstrous egotism" for calling cooking, cleaning, and caring for clothing and children the "four primitive home industries." The accusation is often a cover for other concerns, such as worry that women will leave their traditional roles as comforters. "We see now, in the lives of women who have been called selfish or unwomanly or worse, a brave attempt to live a life for which there was no pattern," writer Carolyn Heilbrun has observed. Harvard professor Carol Gilligan has called womanly selflessness the female Achilles' heel, describing it as a lower moral stage for women than for men, because its prevalence among females cripples them, and it is less common among males. "Women are always being accused of being selfish," observed Joyce Nicholson, an Australian children's book author and mother of four. "All they ask is not always to be the ones who must be unselfish."

In Toni Morrison's novel *Sula*, the young heroine is an adventurous outsider who resists marriage and motherhood and pursues what she calls "Me-ness." When her grandmother urges her to have babies as a way to "settle" her, Sula replies: "I don't want to make somebody else. I want to make myself." Regarded as selfish, she is treated like a pariah and dies at a young age. The grandmother's voice expresses the misogynist view that, as Eve who was redeemed from sin by enduring the pain of childbirth, motherhood cures women of their natural narcissism. Therefore, it stands to reason that women without children remain if not sinful, at least self-absorbed. This is peculiar thinking in light of the existence of selfless celibate saints and other childless holy people in various cultures. It is interesting to note that Marguerite Duras, the Frenchwoman who wrote the novel *The Lover*, seemed to have experienced motherly love more strongly than romantic passion; in an example of maternal chauvinism, she has ardently described motherhood as a uniquely feminizing, even humanizing experience which is "the only opportunity offered a human being to experience a bursting of the ego."

The charge of egoism leveled against the childless can be extremely troubling; even the open-minded and eminently rational Ella Lyman seemed ashamed of the appeal of childfree wedlock, though she imagined that others were secretly sympathetic toward it. As mentioned earlier, in her 1893 letter to her fiancé, she expressed her concern that it was "wrong to speak of it freely" because such a marriage could be a retreat for the selfish and fearful, and it could even become widespread and "endanger the race." Since that time, many other women who have passed up motherhood have also worried about being considered egotistical, a charge that violates the powerful training we receive during girlhood to put others before ourselves. When one friend of mine misbehaved in childhood, for instance, her mother used to accuse her of not being patient or generous enough to be a mother. If such criticism is believed, it can invoke anxiety or guilt in a nullipara about being an egomaniac, an anti-mother, or just not nice enough. Internalizing this societal message, Italian writer Oriana Fallaci blamed her miscarriage on her "selfishness" for leaving a hospital where, immobilized, she felt boredom and rage, in order to return to the exhilaration of her work as a journalist.

So we remain extremely careful about offering complicated or controversial explanations for our childlessness. We learn to adjust our answers to the questioner, distinguishing casual from serious inquiries. If the questions seem implicitly critical, our answers often sound inherently antisocial. Whereas it is acceptable to imply that one's nonparenthood is caused by infertility, it is not all right to suggest that it originates in a taste for independence. It is reasonable to hint at a health problem, but not to an inordinate pleasure in self-expression. It is also understandable to suggest a concern for overpopulation, but not to reveal a distaste for the burdens of parenthood. It is certainly never all right to dislike the demands of young children. Consequently, those of us without children often feel the need to hide an enthusiasm for adventure or order or tranquility or romance. It is therefore welcome evidence, indeed, to learn that sociological research indicates that most of the childfree do not take the prevailing ethos to heart; they have good self-regard, often much better than that of parents.

Parenthood, in fact, can also be a way of indulging narcissism. In the last century, Catharine Sedgwick, invoking the objectivity of the maiden aunt, advised one of her nieces against "that mere extension of self-love with which some parents love their children." When mothers talk about their infants, they often describe beings of their own flesh and blood who are psychic extensions of themselves; they tell about falling in love with themselves in a child and falling in love with themselves as mothers. Although understandable, this intense identification with a baby can be considered, in the words of writer and mother Phyllis Chesler, "reproductive narcissism." Writer Mary Gordon has noted that the egoism of the infant is better known than that of the mother; maternal egocentricity is unacknowledged "because it is an egoism that reaches out, takes up another creature," but even so, that "makes it no less egotistical." Selfishness in the name of motherhood is sometimes not seen as selfishness at all. A survey of six hundred single recent college graduates found in one third of them "a strong pronatalist bias that was supported by narcissistic reasoning," but since it was the conventional choice of parenthood, the subjects were evaluated as desiring healthy self-fulfillment. There is nothing inherently wrong with that, as long as the same attitude is extended toward the childfree. Certainly when I considered becoming a mother, it was in the hope of personal rejuvenation: "Part of infusing my own life with richness is the urge to have a child—to give my own life the sense of wonder, reality, excitement, depth, beauty that it's been lacking," I confided to my journal when I was in my thirties. Then, when I was in my early forties, a transformation, a shift, had occurred that made me wonder if "I'm too old, emotionally, to have a child and sublimate my growing ego and desires."

Implicit in the accusation of self-centeredness leveled against those without children is the assumption that child rearing has greater moral value in a woman's life than any other activity. Generations ago, A Childless Wife challenged this preposterous presumption: If she and her husband had progeny, she reasoned, they would have to give up their altruistic but low-paid activities as social workers—she to raise children, and he to support them. "We question whether those people do right who destroy the social usefulness of their lives to produce children who are, at best, experiments. Is the only, or always the highest, duty to society the raising of children? Some children become a social curse; some are nonentities; only some are a decided benefit. When people are positively useful to their fellow beings, contributing definitely to the progress of humanity, should they not consider seriously before handicapping themselves, even with children?" She asked why even if their children "were as good, but no better, . . . should not we live out our lives and serve society now, instead of postponing such service a generation?" In response to the eugenicist argument that intelligent people like themselves should pass on their genes, she replied: "Often the family of a great man or woman is the only commonplace product of his or her life, making one feel that the energy spent in bearing or rearing such mediocre children might well have been used to better advantage."

I have come to understand from writing biographies of artists that introversion for the sake of creativity is not necessarily narcissism. When I was well into researching the life of Georgia O'Keeffe, I became troubled by the way she tended to brutally disregard people in order to ensure her solitary hours in the studio. In fact, I felt so distressed, and my own identification with her was so shaken, that I wondered if I could finish work on the manuscript. Finally I came to the realization that the painter's most important gifts to humanity were the transcendent images on her canvases, and I was able to complete the book. Afterward, when I brought up this topic during an interview with playwright Edward Albee, he remarked that it is not the artist who is selfish, it is art that is selfish in the demands it makes upon the artist. It is important to realize that, however gratifying, creative work can be agonizingly difficult to bring off. I have found that writing gives a feeling of absolute rightness when it is going well but painful restlessness when it is not. And the very nature of writing, by demanding the utmost clarity of thought and honesty of emotion, is always grueling and sometimes isolating. In the end, many of us in the arts hope that our novels, paintings, or musical scores will help enrich or enlighten the lives of others.

An exaggerated moral boundary exists between supposed egoless parents and egoist nonparents, whereas both can act either way within the frameworks of their lives. While social scientists have disproved the stereotype of the childless person as inevitably neurotic, it is true that some people do not nurture well—whether or not they have children—because of their immaturity or narcissism. But narcissists can be driven to give birth to a child (the urge to reproduce themselves) or not to give birth (no urge to take care of another). While no one can defend callous self-absorption or grandiosity, it seems that openly following one's interests can be ultimately less deceitful and destructive than, say, manipulating others for one's own ends in the guise of, say, saintly motherhood. Selfishness or selflessness are often in the eye of the beholder: Writer Isaac Asimov, the father of two, challenged the sincerity of pronatalists by reasoning that if children bring great happiness, then not having them is an act of supreme sacrifice. "Who do I harm by not having children?" Gael Greene asked in *The Saturday Evening Post* more than three decades ago, adding that giving birth "for the wrong reasons or for no reason at all or bringing [children] into an atmosphere of resentment and neglect is the greater selfishness." It has even been argued by Virginia Barber and Merrill Skaggs, authors of *The Mother Person*, that rejecting motherhood may be a more "benign selfishness" than gambling with another's life.

Those of us without children do not need to regard ourselves as egocentric; we can be proud of what we have done in life, not undermined by what we have not done. The woman without a child does not have to be a contemporary version of the nineteenth-century social mother in order to justify herself as a nonmother or to prove her femininity; she has as much right to pursue activities for the sake of satisfaction, gain, influence, or altruism as anyone else. Still, despite my own youthful nonchalance about being considered self-centered, I have been relieved to discover that sociologists and psychologists have firmly rejected the notion that the childless hold a corner on selfishness.

Work, identity, and independence are intricately intertwined for me. My girlhood desire to write became my adult need to write, and that pursuit has given me more self-sovereignty than usual in a woman's life. For as long as I can remember, I have assumed my right to my own trajectory (although I have not always wanted or been able to act upon it). Whether my attitude was inborn or implanted in early childhood remains unclear, but certainly by the age of six I was proudly determined to retain my birth name, even though it differed from the rest of my family's. Eventually other influences took hold: My exposure to feminism underscored my hope for financial independence, and the example of Georgia O'Keeffe illustrated the link between autonomy and creative work. I retain an insistent urge to explore and experience, then to retreat to reflect and write about these events, a rhythm that has appeared to me incompatible with rearing a child well. Female freedom has long been linked to nonmotherhood: Rabbinical commentary in the Old Testament acknowledges that the childless "pass the greater parts of their lives untrammelled." Today sociologists tell us that four out of five women choose childlessness for that reason: Radical feminist Jeffner Allen has provocatively urged women's "evacuation from motherhood" with a number of rationales, including the way in which motherhood precludes the ability to feel "open and free."

In British and American literature, heroines typically find the customary wife-and-mother role too restrictive for courageous acts. And throughout bildungsromans, or novels of development, fictional females experience freedom as the ability "to come and go, allegiance to nature, meaningful work, exercise of the intellect, use of the erotic capacities," aspirations that traditionally have been ridiculed and denied by patriarchal rules. The idea of a male sovereign self took root during the Enlightenment in western Europe, but the concept of female self-possession has always been seen, perhaps rightly so, as a threat to family stability. The individualistic ideals of the American revolution were not supposed to apply to women and, as Alexis de Tocqueville observed, the transition from girlhood to motherhood was one of submergence of self. But the existence of mythic figures like Artemis, as well as stories about heroines throughout legend and literature, indicates a persistent female longing for liberty.

In the nineteenth century, Anna Dickinson, an American actress and orator for reformist causes, gave voice to this view, insisting that "woman was *made for herself*—to round out herself. Let her live up to the full and make a complete woman of her in every respect." Likewise, turn-of-the-century writer Floyd Dell observed that educated young women "wanted something different—something for *themselves*. They wanted freedom only as a means to the increased satisfaction of a self-respect—or an egotism, if you will—too long cramped and chafed by masculine rule. They wanted Happiness—the happiness that comes from being a freely expressive and largely active personality." A half century later, Simone de Beauvoir wrote in *The Second Sex* that motherhood is "almost impossible to perform in complete liberty." Like Anaïs Nin and Oriana Fallaci during their accidental pregnancies, Doris Lessing's autobiographical character, Martha Quest, perceived the fetus growing inside her as the enemy within, a being who would derail her desire for self-possession. Over the years, a number of young mothers have given testimony to a grievous sense of loss of self, like Katherine Gleve, who, writing in 1987 in *The Feminist Review*, described "the relentless obligation and the necessity to respond which has deprived me of my own direction and brought the fear that I myself would be extinguished."

But little in psychological, feminist, or lesbian writings addresses a normal womanly interest in an adventurous way of life apart from motherhood. We are made to question this craving because of negative stereotypes of spinsters and suffragettes as well as descriptions of Freud's "castrating" and Jung's "animus-possessed" women (those with too many so-called masculine attributes). Many of us retreat from our wish for freedom because we are unwilling or unable to conceive of it as feminine. British biographer Antonia Fraser has observed that America is one of the few cultures that does not contain, in fantasy or reality, a celebrated equivalent of a virgin goddess or "warrior queen." Larger-than-life female archetypes of fiery maidenhood or bold leadership are rare in our society, either in the form of military leaders or angels of mercy, despite the prevalence of many powerful women, like anarchist Emma Goldman, spiritualist Mary Baker Eddy, politician Susan B. Anthony, and the numerous, nameless, independent girls and women who went to war, tamed the frontier, and traveled the world.

One little-known free spirit was Juanita Harrison, an African-American woman who was born around 1891 in Mississippi. A small, friendly woman with an olive complexion and long braids wound around her head, she created a life of adventure and pleasure for herself outside of marriage and motherhood. After seeing pictures of foreign cities in magazines as a young girl, she began her excursions at the age of sixteen as a lady's maid. In June 1927, when she was in her late thirties, she began to travel widely before settling down in Hawaii eight years later. There she acquired an orange tent, which she set up on the property of a congenial Japanese family near a native village full of music and hula dancing. "I want alway to be where wealth health youth beauty and gayness are altho I need very little for myself I just want to be in the midst of it," she wrote [*sic*]. "I have reversed the saying of Troubles are like Babies the more you nurse them the bigger They grow so I have nursed the joys."

Yet females often fear that a terrible price is paid for freedom—that it is dangerous to themselves as well as to their men and children—because there are few alternative stories. There is a frightening folktale about a gifted embroiderer whose autonomy and attention to her craft so enraged a male suitor that he turns her into a firebird and himself into an attacking falcon, whereupon the falcon kills the firebird; all that is left of her is a beautiful feather that drifts down to earth. Likewise, Chaucer's description of the childless widow Chriseyde has her struggling with whether or not to return the love of Troilus, which means risking her liberty and tranquility. In the sympathetic fourteenth-century account, Chriseyde states proudly that "I am myn owene womman," even though she is "an outsider in her own city, politically threatened, socially isolated, emotionally wary, sexually reluctant." She finally refuses her suitor, and later tellers of her tale portray her as a faithless woman who was punished by being forced into prostitution. Even novelist Henry James did not fully understand the dangers that independence presents to females in their imaginations. Like Tocqueville, he was puzzled by the way American women so easily gave it up, and at the end of James's novel *Portrait of a Lady*, the heiress Isabel Archer retreats from a life as a divorced woman back into an unhappy marriage; interestingly, the novelist has her giving birth to a son, a symbol of self-assertion, but one who dies in infancy.

Liberty has its limits, of course, as well as its risks. Anne Roiphe has written that, as a result of mothering, she grew "to value my wonderful individuality a little less and my common humanity more." Taken to extremes, individualism can result in license, exile, or loneliness. Negligent parenthood may result, as in the case of Ann Carson, who was born the daughter of a ship's captain in 1785; married off and made a mother at a young age, she became influenced by the ideas of Joan of Arc, Mary Wollstonecraft, and the Declaration of Independence and abandoned her family for the life of a petty thief, trading respectability for a disreputable but free and footloose life. In another case, Mary Moody Emerson, an unmarried, childless moral philosopher from Concord, Massachusetts, and the influential aunt of Ralph Waldo Emerson, wrote in 1817 that the price of independence was isolation, but one that she willingly paid: "Alass, with low timid females or vulgar domestics how apt is this [moral grandeur] to lose its power when the nerves are weak . . . but give me that oh God—it is holy independence—it is honor & immortality—dearer than friends, wealth & influence. . . . I bless thee for giving me to see the advantage of loneliness." For most women, independence seems best enjoyed alongside intimacy: Whereas many mothers gladly give up some autonomy for the sake of children, most nulliparas do the same for their friends and mates.

Still, childlessness allows for temporary, but invaluable, withdrawals in the name of work, acts of insularity that may threaten the status quo, if they allow the influence of society to recede and the power of reflection to take hold. One January, after my first book was published, I was still trying to resolve whether or not to get pregnant, but without a child to anchor me, I ventured from my busy, orderly, and predictable city life to a writers' colony on Ossabaw Island, one of the wild Georgia barrier islands. I was in "a period of gradually reawakening creativity alternating with times of frustrating stagnation," I noted in my journal, and I wanted to get back to myself and my work. I flew out of a gray and cold Manhattan to Savannah, then boarded a small private boat for the island, and watched it slowly come into sight—a low band of golden brown in the late afternoon light, dotted with grazing ponies. After docking I was driven down a curving road past flowering camellias and to a rambling stucco mansion. Two days later I noted: "I ventured for the first time through the thick semitropical jungle of giant palmettos and glossy magnolias and across stretches of low-lying salt marshes. . . . Every day tides rush in and fill up the stream beds, then retreat again, creating a rhythmic pulse to island life. As the flow of news from friends, newspapers, televisions, and radios is abruptly halted, I've lost interest in my former world. It has quietly slipped away, like a thick and detachable city skin."

Five days after my arrival on the island, I went on: "With this gift of uninterrupted time, I'm working steadily: I write for about four hours in the morning, lunch around one, walk for two or three hours in the afternoon, then write some more or read until dinner." The daily fast-paced walks gave me the liberating feeling that I was shedding my excess winter weight and getting closer to my bone, muscle, and nerves while, at the same time, Spanish moss– and vine-draped branches formed a glaucous green, sunlit, soft, tangled, protective awning above my head. A few days later I noted that "I am beginning to write in a personal vein now, perhaps an antidote to writing biography. The material forces me to recall old feelings and make new connections. It is going painfully slowly and gives me a rare tension headache, but I am able to follow this impulse here for several reasons. For one, its value is intuitively understood. For another, a distracting, stressful middle ground in my life is gone. I understand why doctors in the last century used to prescribe a change of scene for patients suffering from melancholia."

Retreats like the one I was engaged in often involve an introspective and instinctive search for direction, drawing upon experiences in nature for guidance. I explored the island's great stretch of deserted beach, where unbroken shells, like angel wings, lay with twisted sun-bleached trees, killed by the advancing salty surf, flung all over the sand like great silvery claws. "The moon, almost full, rose—a bloated, heavy, orange orb that emerged out of the sea," I observed. "Later, before dawn, a light shining in my eyes awoke me. It was the radiant moon outside my window, now bright white and on the other side of the sky." As the weeks passed, I wrote that "unexpectedly, a kind of numbness has left me, a shell has cracked and fallen away. I'm emotionally calmer, mentally freer, physically at ease—in short, happier. I remember, with a start, that I know how to laugh." As I prepared to return to the city, I vowed to retain my mood. "The island has opened me up, encouraged me," I wrote. "I feel I've become myself." Although such withdrawals are envisioned in female-penned novels as just as likely to lead to ostracism, victimization, madness, or death as to renewal, my experience on the Georgia island was the beginning of another life, one that included my final acceptance of being without children.

NINE

LOOKING AHEAD,
CELEBRATING OUR LIVES

We, the millions of women without progeny, have a long history, even a pedigree, as well as an atypical experience of womanhood. In terms of numbers, nulliparas and nulligravidas are slowly edging up to another historic high in America: A decade ago, 11 percent of all females aged forty to forty-four had no children, a figure that has risen to 18 percent. Who are we as we reach middle age? No longer maidens, but not yet matrons or matriarchs either, we are something else yet to be named. Occasionally we wonder if we are girlish or grown-up, as we exist uneasily on the edges of our extended families. When we look ahead, we sometimes worry about who will take care of us in old age. Without children, the idea of mortality also has an extra edge. Who will remember us? What will we leave behind? But above all, as we reach the age when we can no longer have children, it gradually dawns on us that no one notices whether or not we are mothers. It is time to value our nulliparous lives ourselves as well as to win respect from others and, in turn, to heal any rifts with mothers. After the age of fifty, at least for me, there has been the realization that it is finally time to put the issue of childlessness behind me and get on with the rest of my life.

Sitting around my fireplace on a Sunday evening a few years ago, ten or so female friends, ranging in age from their forties to their seventies, talked about why most of us had never given birth. The mood among us, as we sat in the small, spare room warmed by a fire, was one of safety, albeit with a slight under-current of tension. Engaged in a 1990s form of consciousness-raising, we had all lived through a far more militant era; now most of us were politically inactive and concentrated on our chosen work, as well as on our mates, gardens, and other activi-ties. A number of us had health or money worries, a few strug-gled with marital ennui or career anxiety, and one was involved in a custody battle over a child.

Although we had been meeting every week or so for months, that evening was the only time we decided to talk openly about our childbearing choices. As we spoke, the few mothers and the more numerous nonmothers among us regarded one another as if across a divide, from a distance, with curiosity, trying to com-prehend one another's experiences. The childlessness among us, we established, had little to do with lack of marital love: For the most part we were contentedly long-married or remarried, even much-married. Some of us without children had never heard the biological clock ticking, others heard it faintly or loudly, and most had heard it slow down and stop. Childlessness, oddly enough, was not a shared mode of existence, since we came to it for diverse reasons and experienced it very differently. In only two cases was the absence of offspring the result of early and adamant choices; one person knew as a young girl that she was, as she put it, "made for something else" besides motherhood; another woman was so determined to have her freedom that she underwent three illegal abortions without hesitation.

As we talked, there were moments between us of envy, guilt, worry, wistfulness, and gratitude. Infertility had not been an issue for any of us, although health problems had made several of us hesitate about getting pregnant. Mothers of grown and young children alike spoke sadly of miscarriages, abortions, and even an infant death. One of the mothers had first chosen religious celibacy in girlhood before becoming a devoted parent to an only child. As we spoke, it became apparent that most of us, mothers and nonmothers alike, had been deeply ambivalent about bearing children. Mothers recalled their surprise at the sudden rush of maternal feelings after the birth of a baby, and nulliparas described the ways they had drifted or struggled through their childbearing years without giving birth because of disinclination or inopportunity. For the most part, we probed one another's stories with compassionate understanding; one of the mothers was relieved that the nonmothers had few, if any, regrets. As the evening wore on, my realization was that, whatever our procreative differences, we had arrived at a time in life where our paths mattered very little.

I also realized that I felt deeply grateful for my life as it was, as well as a sense of relief at having eluded the absorption and, yes, the entrapment, of motherhood. I admitted that there remained an imaginary rapport between me and my dream daughter, a faint fantasy creature who lingered in my imagination as an alter ego as well as a little friend. I remembered too, that a decade ago, when I learned that my first husband had become a father to a daughter, I found the news difficult to bear.

And recently, I felt a surprising twinge of pain when I saw replicas of maternal figures in someone's sculpture collection: An ebony columnar Renaissance madonna nursing an infant at a full breast, a bronze female playfully balancing a baby on upraised feet, a metal maquette of an intimately and organically melded twosome, all exuding a mother-and-child kind of intimacy that I had known only as the infant. It was the experience that I had evoked myself as an art student years ago when I made a rudimentary madonna-and-child clay piece and gave it to my mother. At that moment I became aware that I had not found a perfect resolution to my old yearning, nor was it likely that I ever would. So I turned my eyes toward another female torso in the room—a piece with an open cerebral space that suggested the limitless, gestating imagination. Then I looked at renditions of other sculptural beings and painterly conceptions, like enraptured lovers and dancing gods, which suggested even more enriching aspects of life; ones that are meditative, erotic, exuberant. Many of the figures were placed around the room in front of paintings as if they inhabited still, shadowy, mysterious green landscapes, not unlike the one that I had once dreamed about, then made my own.

Some people, mostly mothers, have suggested that women willingly without children have been brainwashed, that child-lessness is actually anti-woman and pro-male, and therefore something immature *puers* or egotistical patriarchs will endorse. It is a charge that assumes that everything we do is merely compensation for not being mothers. It resonates with the criticism that we are victims of a "patriarchal injunction," in Tillie Olsen's words, a capitulation to male rules, a masculine way of life, as the price of female freedom. A poem by Margaret Atwood, "Spelling," written while the author was watching her small daughter play with a plastic alphabet, expresses this attitude. She wonders "how many women / denied themselves daughters, / closed themselves in rooms, / drew the curtains / so they could mainline words. . . . / I return to the story / of the woman caught in the war / & in labour, her thighs tied / together by the enemy / so she could not give birth." This at first appears to be a harsh, scornful judgment of the misguid-edness of those of us without children, given the circumstances in which mothers must sometimes raise daughters. But Atwood goes on to suggest the potency of a female's use of words and the importance of using them. "Ancestress: the burning witch, / her mouth covered by leather / to strangle words. / A word after a word / after a word is power." She concludes by asking: "How do you learn to spell? Blood, sky & the sun, / your own name first, / your first naming, your first name, / your first word."

The first part of the poem flies in the face of the evidence. In the past few years, social scientists have challenged the old belief that maternity is woman's natural pastime and that everything else is a substitute for it: Professor of social work and nonmother Carolyn Morell has pointed out that viewing every aspect of a nullipara's life "through the lens of this deficiency" dictates, for example, that her dog or cat is a child surrogate, but not the pet of a parent. Old folk sayings also suggest that the barren are spared knowledge of the pleasures of parenting; likewise, a contemporary researcher has proposed that psychologists who are parents may have trouble counseling those who are not because, as they imagine the absence of their own living children, they will feel more grief than do their analysands. But childbearing is also a great gamble, as some parents tell it, and nonparents are spared the possibility of parental bitterness and grief. Centuries ago the Greek playwright Euripides, who was also a father, made the point in *Medea* that for this very reason the childfree are more likely to be happy than parents.

Although nature did not originally intend members of *Homo sapiens* to outlive their reproductive lives by many years, the American female is now expected to live a third of her life after menopause. The onset of the change of life can mean a resurgence of sadness about the fallow womb, along with a sudden awareness of aging. It was not so long ago that physicians frightened spinsters with talk about how nature would punish them

for not reproducing: Their unused uteruses would decay (leading to disease and mental derangement), the climacteric would
be difficult (because organs had not been nourished by semen),
and their overall health would deteriorate (resulting in early
death). We know now that the midlife physical and emotional
crises experienced by some of these women resulted from societal conditions that made them feel unimportant, invisible,
and isolated.

Still, menopause is a time when unresolved sorrow may be
aroused within reluctant nulliparas who have not made peace
with the childlessness that they have, by then, lived with for
about a decade. In many cases this is because a woman was
unable to make a clear choice, like the one who arrived at
menopause with misgivings about her abortions, which she had
undergone because of her husband's financial problems and her
own pessimism about the future. And a friend of mine, who
had been infertile for nearly two decades, was dismayed to find
all her earlier grief returning as she faced a hysterectomy
around the age of fifty. But such incidents do not seem typical,
according to social scientists. In cultures that respect aging
women there is less menopausal depression—in fact, European
and other observers have called the syndrome a false one as
modern women's lives have expanded. Also, folk wisdom tells
us that the menopausal woman who keeps her vitalizing blood
for herself becomes more energetic, expansive, and expressive.
Furthermore there is no scientific data that prove that nulliparas have more difficulties at menopause than mothers. And
there *is* evidence that depression related to hysterectomy or the
onset of menopause is more likely to affect those invested in
motherhood.

Finally, it is interesting to note another aspect of the nulliparous existence at midlife. Especially before menopause,

many of us frequently feel younger than our years because no children of our own have placed us in an older generation. Instead of locking our steps with those of offspring born a couple of decades after us, we tend to mark our stages of life by people we have loved, work we have done, and places we have lived. Our emphasis is not on living vicariously through young progeny but on experiencing life directly. As a result, we often hold onto the perception that our potential is still somehow before us. The passage of time is also likely to affect us gradually and gently as we move imperceptibly from one transition to another with a minimum of generational upheavals. My sprouting nieces and nephews, for instance, make me feel that, like Alice in Wonderland, I have imbibed a magic shrinking potion, not that I have arrived at the age of a grandmother.

Affected by our strange sense of timelessness, those of us without children sometimes wonder if we are really grown-ups. Parenthood is often associated with the achievement of maturity, or, as the writer and mother Anne Roiphe has put it, with the growth of the "interior landscape," and with the assumption that parenting is invaluable for the parent. Certainly many young mothers exude a greater sense of purposefulness than their nulliparous peers, who are attempting to create unmapped lives. Because we are unaware of our heritage of symbolic mothers, who represent a superior form of motherliness and a special vision of womanliness, our doubts sometimes originate from within, but more commonly from without. We sense others' suspicions voiced either subtly or openly, that being childfree is equivalent to being childish. Sometimes we perceive that others try to infantilize us. We are vulnerable to the fear that we remain irresponsible *puellas*, eternal girls, simply because we are not mothers. Or we may identify with the perpetual daughter or the isolated female, both of whom are sidelined or marginal. "How do I stop seeing the world through the eyes of a daughter without becoming a mother?" one childless woman has asked. "How do I become a woman who did not give birth to children—but did give birth to herself?" When we look around, however, we find that there are a number of routes to full maturity and that such anxiety is unjustified.

The evidence linking maternity to maturity is equivocal, and it indicates that motherhood can be either strengthening or stifling, depending on a woman's personality and the circumstances of her life. Most mothers in a 1987 poll reported that rearing children enhanced their personal growth, but a minority did not: While seven out of ten said it was helpful in enforcing altruism and a sense of identity, two out of ten attributed their development to natural maturation, and one in ten called mothering regressive. Child tending seems to build self-confidence in some ways, but it erodes it in others. One theory holds that it is harder for a stay-at-home mother to mature if she is using her energy and imagination in only one arena; but this reasoning, of course, might apply to anyone engaged in a single activity. And any assumption that parenting and personal growth are contradictory ignores the fact that people often develop tremendously in their capacities for patience and responsibility while caring for children. Parenting surely provides the chance to become more mature, but not all mothers and fathers take advantage of it; neither does it necessarily improve relationships with one's own parents nor heal childhood traumas. About a decade ago, an Australian researcher suggested that it was the events of adulthood, not necessarily family life, that stimulated self-actualization. The old linkage between parenting and maturing may exist simply because most adults have always parented until they reached middle age.

One aspect of maturity, along with such virtues as being ethical and wise, is the inclination and ability to take care of others. Researchers into human development have identified various life cycles (though their studies generally assume the male or nonparenting pattern of uninterrupted work outside the home). Three decades ago, Erik Erikson outlined in *Childhood and Society* eight maturation stages, or "ages of man," the seventh being midlife "generativity," which he described as an interest in mentoring the upcoming generation. He called generativity a way of being, a generous turning outward, that enriches the personality, whereas its absence results in retreat, in the form of stagnation or pseudo-intimacy, as a person remains preoccupied with his or her own self-indulgent or infantile needs. Erikson, however, understood that simply wanting children or becoming a genetic parent was not, in itself, enough to achieve generativity. He also recognized that some of those who were without offspring either because of "misfortune" or unusual talents were able to achieve this level of psychological maturity.

Erikson was vague about what he meant by misfortune, but he was clear about the exceptionally gifted, who, as we have seen, have sometimes been excused from parenthood if their abilities were revealed early enough. He outlined the ways that acts or activities of generativity can take other, albeit inferior, forms besides parenting: Guiding, informing, or inspiring youngsters, he explained, can take place through the example of productivity or the influence of creativity. In 1991, for instance, an admirer of the dancer Martha Graham took exception to the statement in Graham's obituary in *The New York Times* that she left no immediate survivors: "This is not true. Every dancer, choreographer, artist, or musician is her immediate survivor. Every university or college dance department is her immediate survivor. Every child who has had a modern dance class is her immediate survivor. Every audience member who watched her dances performed is her immediate survivor." Religious celibates and saints, Erikson also recognized, express generativity through their selflessness and spirituality. Erikson's theory, however, leaves little room for the ordinary, nonpathological childfree person, certainly not for the female who chooses not to procreate.

Yet, as he suggested, exceptional individuals are different: I noticed that Georgia O'Keeffe intuitively expanded the meaning of the so-called empty womb through her work and transformed her understanding of the nulliparous experience in middle age. In the summer of 1943, during the Second World War, when she was fifty-five, she found a sun-bleached animal pelvic bone in the New Mexico hills and was taken by its curious, convoluted shape and oval hole: She repeatedly painted images of the whitish bone frontally, up close, and from the side, sometimes giving it the appearance of the curved wing of a great gull. There was a startling contrast between the empty pelvic birth canal surrounded by brittle bone and the soft, sensual undulating pink and blue voids she had painted earlier in life during the throes of her erotic attachment to Alfred Stieglitz, while she was still toying with the idea of getting pregnant. Yet the bony frame of the barren birth canal in the paintings also acts as a telescope—focusing the eye on the endlessly receding void of sky, or what the artist termed the "blue hole," her portrayal of an eternal spiritual force. With an evident awareness of war raging around her, the artist wrote in an exhibition catalog that the dry bones were "most wonderful against the Blue—that Blue that will always be there as it is now after all man's destruction is finished."

Mentoring is a matter of temperamental alikeness as well as the bond of blood. I, for one, have learned from women besides my own mother, like O'Keeffe, and in turn, I instinctively empathize with the concerns of certain little girls, like a niece who loves to read and dreams of becoming a photojournalist. As Erikson indicated, there are various ways to be generative; in the sociological data, nonparents report that they mentor at work, in marriage, and in other aspects of their lives. One older woman I know, who opted out of motherhood long ago, has assisted a number of younger creative people through small grants, money that otherwise might have been earmarked for her offspring. Such a variety of generative acts can be very beneficial: Margaret Mead, who favored individuality, urged everyone to appreciate dissenters like the childfree, and "to amplify the dissonance and turn them into specialists," instead of pressuring them to compromise or conform to convention. Accordingly, in the Native American tradition, asexual or homosexual males, who dress and live like females, have traditionally been praised as a valuable third gender who can best mediate problems between men and women. And when a Native American woman has no children, or when an older mother enters what is called the "Grandmother Lodge," she is expected to care about all the children in the tribal community, according to Brooke Medicine Eagle, a Crow Indian.

One of the dangers of being childless is the chance of becoming alienated from the upcoming generation, but today there is an important place for nonparents in the lives of underparented children in the human family. One of the themes of Ann Beattie's novels is the unraveling of the family, and her fictional childless adults and parentless children are symbols of this disintegration. But more than a decade ago, the United States Census Bureau defined a family as two or more people

related by blood, marriage, or adoption, a description that includes childfree couples. More to the point, single and married
nulliparas can be considered part of the modern extended family, which is composed of people of all ages from former and
present marriages. Mind-boggling in its complexity, it is nevertheless more and more common and, of course, familiar to me:
My unusual familial relationships have included stepgrandpar-
ents and an ex-stepmother, half siblings related to me through
both my mother and my father, a stepsister, stepnieces, an
ex-sister-in-law, and even an ex-aunt, to name a few. When I
married for the third time in my early fifties, it was to a man
with grown children and young grandchildren, expanding my
many roles to stepmother and stepgrandmother. Whether related by law, blood, or former affiliation, I try to get along with
everyone, since I cherish enduring relationships. While one
childless woman I know is pained that the generational line
ends with her, another (with whom I agree) feels that this is
true only in a literal sense, since there are so many ways to be
step, honorary, fictive, or blood kin to children.

It is widely assumed that the deaths of parents are especially
distressing to those of us who have not continued the family
bloodline; this is evidently true for the so-called perpetual
daughter, the never-married woman who lives with her parents
all her life and does not form other significant alliances. Among
those of us who have lived apart from our mothers and fathers
for many years, and who are presumably less dependent on
them, it is more usual for parental deaths to be experienced as
they are for everyone else—as losses of intense, irreplaceable,
emotional ties that go back to our earliest memories. Still,
some who have lost those primal bonds feel at times like aging
orphans, perhaps because they have not replaced the parental
relationships with those of their own progeny. One reluctantly

childless friend, who will have no genetic grandchildren, spoke to me of her sense of generational "thinness," a feeling of disconnectedness from humanity, as the rich texture of her family became flattened by the loss of older relations. "I sometimes feel like a star cut loose in the Milky Way," she sighed, but whether her feeling is unique to the childless is dubious. Although some of us with parents and without children may have resisted facing our chronological ages, doing so is essential to our maturation. As our aged relatives gradually die, it becomes important to act like elders with the children in our extended families.

❧

As long as a female is young and unmarried, her childlessness is unquestioned, even honored, since she represents the virgin archetype. When it is a matter of considered choice, however, the reaction is often different. The attractive lover of man, the Aphrodite or mistress type, is usually tolerated. But a nullipara who is old, isolated, or angry, or who is not sexual or maternal, runs the risk of being regarded as an anti-mother or an imperfect male and being cast out of the human family. Aware of this attitude, some of us, especially in our middle years, and regardless of whether we are married or not, confess to early-morning worries about who will take care of us when we are elderly, frail, or ill. One friend calls this fear the "primordial terror of childlessness," even though she knows it is not fair or even wise to consider young people as old-age insurance. But deeply embedded in the social contract is the unspoken expectation that if we take care of the young, then they will look after us when we are old. Indeed, many people become parents for this very reason. This concern with the future is associated with existential anxiety about being insufficiently connected to humanity, but it is often intensified in those of us who have ignored the genetic imperative; writer Irena Klepfisz's particular nightmare was one of exile—that without a natal child she might eventually become a homeless shopping-bag lady because of "an imperceptible loosening of common connections and relations."

As a young woman I experienced this fear after visiting an older female cousin, who was around seventy at the time, in a once-elegant part of upper Manhattan. As I walked in the door, I realized that she probably had very few, if any, visitors. Never married, this perpetual daughter had lived with her parents until their deaths, and now she was aging with a cat or two in a dirty, shabby apartment. She took me to lunch in a neighborhood cafeteria, and we struggled to make conversation about our relatives. After we returned to her home and I started to say good-bye, she abruptly thrust some old family coin silver spoons into my hands as if she never expected to see me again, or as if she imagined she were about to die. Already horrified by her apparent isolation and poverty, I was even more upset by this gesture, since she seemed vigorous, and, in fact, she lived alone for many years before moving to a nursing home. When I returned to my apartment on the Upper West Side of Manhattan, where I lived with my boyfriend, I felt terrified that if I did not marry and become a mother, I might eventually become as solitary as my cousin. Although she may not have been as lonely as I imagined at the time, she appeared to me to be a fearsome childless crone, slowly deteriorating on the fringes of society.

Afterward, I put the visit out of my mind. Recently, as I sifted through scores of sociological reports about the aging childless, I learned that one in five Americans over age sixty-five has no living offspring, and another one in ten is alienated from the ones they have. I read that even the presence of compatible children in an elderly person's life is no guarantee of care and companionship; one grandmother remarked that she found it surprising that while one young mother could take care of four little children, four grown sons and daughters could not take care of one old lady. In fact, aged parents often complain to social workers that their progeny are more likely to make requests than offer assistance. Parents may also feel neglected by busy or faraway sons and daughters. Mothers who had not seen their offspring recently often seemed more forlorn to interviewers than nonmothers; one study found that even poor or ill childless widows were not lonelier than widowed mothers. Even though parenting is considered the art of gradually letting progeny go, one mother remarked that, paradoxically, childlessness meant one less loss in life. In fact, social researcher Grace Baruch has written that a mother's disappointment in a grown child can be so debilitating that it can trigger midlife depression. Although I was certain that many of the elderly benefited from the care of their children and the company of their grandchildren, such testimony was not evident in these studies.

Marriage was more important than parenthood to well-being in old age, the data revealed. One study of widows age sixty to seventy-five indicated that, compared to other relationships, natal children had only a slight effect on their contentedness. Living in an institution, for example, is correlated to the lack of a partner, not the absence of progeny. These findings brought to mind another visit I had made, about a decade after meeting my elderly New York cousin, to a married cousin and her husband who had no offspring; both in their late seventies at the time, they spent summers in my great-grandfather Lisle's house on a hill in southern Vermont. The day I lunched with them, they had filled the old farmhouse with bouquets of summer wildflowers, and the ambience was charged with caring, intelligence, curiosity, and liveliness. I liked them tremendously and admired the simplicity and beauty of their home; in fact, I was so impressed with this Vermont cousin's "radiance, charm, vivacity, and fine taste," as I noted in my private pages at the time, that I even expressed my desire to be like her, to "be her descendant," as I put it. Her nulliparous old age was certainly more reassuring to me than that of my New York cousin.

From the sociological treatises, I also learned that after spouses, siblings are the most dependable relatives of the aged, and I recalled that my New York cousin had been an only child. Siblings may become even more important in the decades ahead; sociologists predict that members of the postwar generation, who tend to have more brothers and sisters than sons or daughters, will often end up living with their siblings in old age. (If a nullipara has no living siblings, nieces and nephews often arrange for their care when they become dependent, studies show, but they rarely give care themselves.)

What surprised me the most, in light of my encounters with my two older cousins, was data that suggested that women who had never had mates or children were the most contented of all in old age: They tended to be resourceful, self-reliant, and gifted at friendship. A sociological report concluded that aged never-married nulliparas saw fewer people every day than mothers, but this did not represent a change in their lives. Another group of women over age sixty who had never married reported rewarding relationships with chosen or "constructed" kin, including female partners, younger friends, or sometimes entire families. Unfortunately, an elderly person's friends of her own age may be able to offer only companionship, not care, during an illness because of their own fragility. When real need sets in, anecdotal evidence indicates, old people often are cared for by children of choice, paid or not; I knew that this had been the case with O'Keeffe and Nevelson. The importance of being able to depend on intimates or reliable younger people when one becomes ill or frail indicates the importance of group living arrangements either within or outside the extended family. All this testimony reassured me that my fate did not have to mimic my unmarried older cousin's bleak plight.

As I perused the sociological reports, I was also astonished to discover that most of the very oldest elderly live alone—more than half of all those over the age of eighty-five—whether they are childless or not. Being alone does not necessarily mean being lonely, I realized, perhaps partly because of the reputed introversion of old age. Further investigation suggested that most live alone to preserve their independence. One analysis, in fact, found that the happiness of the aged was inversely related to their dependence on their children. In my own circle, several aging mothers of childless wives without jobs have chosen to move to extended-care facilities with their peers, even though they could conceivably live with their daughters. I think often about my own mother, who lives with her husband four hours away, and with whom I am on the telephone more frequently than in her presence. When I am with her, she reminds me of the wise old woman in literature who exists happily by herself in nature; as in the ancient pattern, my mother lived in a city before settling into the country, where she wants to stay, tending her flowering plants in her greenhouse in winter and in her flower garden during other seasons.

Regardless of whether we are alone or not, there is a unique role for the nulliparous woman of age that can connect us to other generations. In childhood I devoured children's biographies of heroines like Pocahontas, Jane Addams, Louisa May Alcott, Clara Barton, and Amelia Earhart, stories that expressed the clear, unafraid, hopeful voice of the American girl who "has scarcely ceased to be a child when she already thinks for herself, speaks with freedom, and acts on her own impulse," as Alexis de Tocqueville observed. As the Frenchman and others, like Harvard professor Carol Gilligan, have observed, this voice tends to become subdued as a girl approaches the age of menarche and eventual motherhood. Perhaps those of us who are nulliparas have the potential to be outspoken at an earlier age because we have already learned to exist outside convention. But if we are reticent about why we are childless, we cannot be reliable guides for others: Once I found myself hesitant about being too influential when a young engaged woman confided to me that a priest was pressuring her and her fiancé to have children right after their wedding. Also, if we are evasive about the merits of nonmotherhood, we do not challenge or change others' ignorance about childlessness. By middle age, however, many of us have learned bold, firm, and positive responses. Perhaps in the last third of life we can abandon our earlier silence and recapture the courageous voice of early youth.

Evidence indicates that the happiness of older men and women has, above all, to do with the state of their finances, health, social lives, and spiritual well-being. The final and eighth stage of maturity, which Erik Erikson has called the achievement of "ego integrity," is the ability to accept the value and inevitability of one's life, which of course includes the experience or absence of pregnancy or impregnation. Although many childless women wonder when they are young if they will have regrets later, I have found no evidence of pervasive or persistent second thoughts, at least not more than women have about other paths in life not taken. And after studying a half dozen surveys that involved thousands of people, Grace Baruch was startled to find no documentation that motherhood enhanced a woman's well-being in middle age or in old age. Another researcher, in fact, observed that there are few differences between very elderly parents and nonparents in terms of loneliness, regrets, and acceptance of death in the last stages of life. As a result of all this evidence, I began to realize that raising a child for the sake of the future might not be a wise choice at all.

The living of a life, of course, inevitably shapes that life. If I had gravitated to motherhood and given birth on the usual biological schedule, I would have cared for my babies tenderly, devotedly, fiercely, the way my mother cared for me. Their needs would have felt more insistent than my own, and their importance would have been endorsed by both my mother's example and others' expectations. If I had become a mother at an early age, my desire for work of my own might not have been so clear or so urgent. Without being a mother, the act of writing became a way to breathe an essential kind of personal oxygen as I kept my journal, traveled, talked, observed, read, and reflected. If I had not been able to write, I would have felt darkly angry and inconsolable, perhaps without knowing why. If I had become a mother, surely my sense of self would now be different in ways that I cannot imagine. Instead, I have been molded by what can perhaps be called nulliparous time, innumerable moments that have allowed for marital love and meaningful work as well as certain indulgences, like remaining in my shadowy, sweet-smelling garden until nine o'clock on a June evening. As I approached the age of fifty, I began to feel a half-repressed sensation, an old feeling from my twenties of floating free. My way of life, now completely formed around nonmotherhood, or otherhood, had enabled me to sidestep some tricky gender issues, I realized, and I felt elated at enjoying feminine pleasures and masculine liberties. It was a sense of almost illicit privilege that felt delicious as well as a little dangerous.

Other nulliparas and nulligravidas in their middle years have shared similar feelings with me, and the sociological data have validated my impressions that many of them are relishing the rewards of uninterrupted careers and successful relationships. Researchers find that middle-aged women, mothers or not, base their feelings of well-being on mastery at work and pleasure in marriage; other aspects of life, like the presence of children, are irrelevant. This is so even if they are unwilling rebels: Roberta Joseph, a married psychoanalyst, realized that deciding *not* to become a mother "force[d] me into a particularly threatening form of nonconformity, which derive[d] not from a wish to rebel but from the realization that my prerequisites for happiness [were] outside the norm." When the biotic clock stops ticking around the age of fifty, many nonmothers feel like they have been through a refining fire, having gone through ordeals of uncertainty and longing that have finally resolved themselves in joy and relief.

Living as a misunderstood minority, isolated by our odd invisibility and the awkward silence about childlessness that exists in our culture, can hasten a kind of self-knowledge; this, in turn, can take us beyond desiring children as the urge for a child as a form of youthful self-realization diminishes. There's a Hindu saying: "What need have we of children, we who have this Self?" Like prepatriarchal virgins, many modern nonmothers are able to set their priorities and act on their instincts with élan. Some need all their strength and imagination to find a little independence and authenticity, like Juanita Harrison, the lady's maid who traveled the world before settling in Hawaii in an orange tent. One unmarried nullipara I know feels she has "secret social power," or a sense of energies retained; another spoke to me of her sense of elation and wholeness, triumphant emotions she rarely dares reveal because they challenge the rules about what makes a woman happy. Childlessness to such women can be called the practice of self-possession, or, as one social scientist described it in the heady days of the 1970s, "a woman's ultimate liberation." As the mother of author Alice Walker liked to say to women unable to bear: "If the Lord sets you free, be free indeed." Although few of us want to live outside the warmth of human relationships, the benefits of non-motherhood should not be disregarded.

Once I shared a Manhattan taxicab with a stranger, a frantic young mother with her newborn infant, who blurted out to me that she was overwhelmed by caring for her baby and another small child; she seemed frighteningly vulnerable as she indicated that she was misunderstood by her husband; although I suddenly felt immensely, but falsely, composed in her presence, I ached for both of us and for the pathos of our polarities. A number of women have called for an end to such differences between us, which can result in ignorance and alienation—the erroneous pity or envy of mothers toward the childfree and the irrational shame or superiority of nulliparas in the presence of mothers. In an attempt to respect our diversity, it is important to understand that while childlessness is affirming for some, motherhood is an act of assertion for others. Almost every sociological study indicates that the emotional health and happiness of mothers and nonmothers are essentially the same; what differs is their *perception* of parenthood—women tend to agree about the disadvantages of children but disagree about the rewards.

Two decades ago Letty Cottin Pogrebin, a mother and writer, attacked what she called the new "childfree aristocracy," but she also called for tolerance; repelled by both antinatalists and pronatalists, she expressed her yearning for an enlightened middle ground, for "a radical, visionary alternative." As a first step, philosopher Margaret Simons has suggested the combination of "the value of motherhood with the value of childlessness"—a blend of compassion and assertiveness in all women into what she called a "feminist maternal ethic." As my sister and I talk to each other more openly now, we agree that, all things being equal, it is preferable for the majority of women to have at least one baby as well as the proverbial book. There are hopeful signs that the dilemma of the old either/or choice may be easing. Some young scholars are moving beyond the debate over difference versus equality feminism to embrace both of them. And in the legal field, there is talk of giving pregnancy benefits to all women under the banner of equality of reproductive opportunity.

Paradoxically, the clear alternative of childlessness today makes childbearing more meaningful since, as Charlotte Perkins Gilman reasoned a century ago, advocating motherhood for all women devalues its importance. So understanding and elevating nonparenthood might make elective parenting more likely and even eliminate reluctant parents, reducing the epidemic of child abuse. And, to take a highly optimistic view, if parenthood became more of an option than a mandate, mothers and fathers might find that in an era of rapidly falling birthrates, more child and family assistance programs might be passed in Congress. In turn, it is even possible for those of us without children to regard pronatalism compassionately as understandable, if misguided, coercion in light of the difficulties of parenting, not an unjust attack on nonbreeders or indifference to the earth's ecology.

It is also true that the issue of the egocentricity of nonmothers is turned on its head in an endangered environment. One in three women without children cites overpopulation as a reason for not giving birth, according to sociologist Sharon Houseknecht, but she has expressed uncertainty about whether this concern is a motivation or a rationalization for such a personally significant choice as parenthood. Yet at least one such woman, Vicki Robin, has stated fervently that she decided to mother the earth instead of babies: "I faced up to the fact that the urge to procreate and pass on my genes in the face of population pressures and environmental crises was a little piece of insanity hard-wired into my DNA." Certainly the contribution of the childfree, acting conscientiously or not, should be acknowledged in the face of an exploding world population. Ecologist Jim Schenk, the father of two, has done so: "Let each of us honor someone who does not have children. . . . Let them know we believe they are courageous, even as we look at our own children and feel the tears well up in our eyes."

Can a person transcend nature by neglecting or refusing to reproduce without any pain or guilt? Several decades ago, a group of young single women who wanted tubal ligations worried about their decision's supposed unnaturalness; they were most likely unaware that two generations earlier the fiery Englishwoman Dora Russell had detected in her reading of history "a prolonged struggle on the part of the individual to free himself (and then herself) from biological slavery." By not bearing children we are defying an aspect of natural law, but as beings with brains we are also able to do so—the cognitive matter invented contraception, after all, giving the mind the chance to override the reproductive imperative of the body. It can be argued, therefore, that it is as human to transcend nature as it is to create life. Whatever the path each person takes in regard to childbearing, it is evident to me that life-generating and life-enhancing forces are morally equivalent. After fearing punishment for violating biological law, those of us without children find the reality of our lives liberating.

NOTES

ONE
FINDING THE WORDS, DISCOVERING MY WAY

p. 5. A *1983 British study* . . . *people.* Frances Baum, "Orientation Toward Voluntary Childlessness," *Journal of Biosocial Science* 15, no. 2 (April 1983): 153.

pp. 6–7. *Almost a century ago* . . . *children.* A Childless Wife, "Why I Have No Family," *The Independent* (23 March 1905): 654.

p. 8. *"To this day* . . . *themselves."* Berenice Fisher, "Affirming Social Value: Women Without Children," *Social Organization and Social Processes: Essays in Honor of Anselno Strauss* (New York: Aldine de Gruyter, 1991), 87.

p. 12. *Childlessness* . . . *mothers.* Elissa Benedek and Richard Vaughn, "Voluntary Childlessness," in *Women's Sexual Experience: Explorations of the Dark Continent,* ed. Martha Kirkpatrick (New York: Plenum Publishing Co., 1982), 208.

p. 13. *One 1955 study* . . . *instead.* Linda Silka and Sara Kiesler, "Couples Who Choose to Remain Childless," *Family Planning Perspectives* 9, no. 1 (January–February 1977): 16; quoting E. G. Mishler, C. F. Westoff, and E. L. Kelley, "Some Psychological Correlates of Differential Fertility: A Longitudinal Study," *American Psychologist* 10 (1955): 319.

p. 13. *The pronatalist bias* . . . *woman.* Lotte Bailyn, "Notes on the Role of Choice in the Psychology of Professional Women," *Daedalus* (Spring 1964): 236.

p. 18. *Meanwhile* . . . *Evening Post.* Gael Greene, "A Vote Against Motherhood," *The Saturday Evening Post* (26 January 1963): 10.

p. 23. *"a growing number . . . self-preservation."* Lucia Valeska, "If All Else Fails, I'm Still a Mother," *Quest: A Feminist Quarterly* 3 (Winter 1975): 52.

p. 24. *"once women . . . openness."* Judith Lorber, "Beyond Equality of the Sexes: The Question of Children," *The Family Coordinator* (19 October 1975): 465.

p. 24. *One survey found . . . them.* L. G. Pol, "Childlessness: A Panel Study of Expressed Intentions and Reported Fertility," *Social Biology* 30, no. 3 (1983): 318.

p. 24. *A decade later . . . peers.* Kristine M. Baber, "Gender-Role Orientations in Older and Child-Free and Expectant Couples," *Sex Roles* 14, nos. 9–10 (1986): 501.

p. 26. *Firestone . . . Snitow argued.* Ann Snitow, "What Feminism Has Said About Motherhood" (undated manuscript); also published as "Mother-hood—Reclaiming the Demon Texts," *Ms* (May–June 1991): 34, and as "Feminism and Motherhood: An American Reading," *Feminist Review* 40, (Spring 1992): 32.

p. 26. *Feminism . . . roles.* Mary-Joan Gerson, Jo-Anna Posner, Anne M. Morris, "The Wish for a Child in Couples Eager, Disinterested, and Conflicted About Having Children," *The American Journal of Family Therapy* 19 (Winter 1991): 334.

pp. 26–27. *Our Bodies, Ourselves . . . crises.* The Boston Women's Health Book Collective, *Our Bodies, Ourselves* (New York: Simon & Schuster, 1971), 154.

p. 27. *Bernice E. Lott . . . society.* Bernice E. Lott, "Who Wants the Children?," *The American Psychologist* (July 1973): 573.

p. 28. *"embodied . . . self-determination."* Adrienne Rich, *Of Woman Born: Motherhood as Experience and Institution,* tenth anniversary issue (New York: W. W. Norton & Co., 1986), 84.

p. 29. *"We are living . . . rules."* Ellen Herman, "Desperately Seeking Mother-hood," *Zeta* (March 1988): 73.

p. 31. *childless wife . . . still there.* Margaret Mead, *Male and Female* (New York: William Morrow, 1949), 231.

pp. 31–32. *Elayne Rapping . . . offspring.* Elayne Rapping, "The Future of Motherhood: Some Unfashionably Visionary Thoughts," in *Women, Class and the Feminist Imagination,* eds. Karen Hanson and Illene Phillipson (Philadelphia: Temple, 1990), 537.

p. 32. *"apologized . . . later.* Snitow, "What Feminism Has Said," 16.

TWO
EXAMINING THE CHOICE, WHY IT ARISES

p. 33. "*the agony . . . choicefullness.*" Dominie Cappadonna, "Dominie Cappadonna," in *Childlessness Transformed: Stories in Alternative Parenting,* by Jane English (Mount Shasta, Calif.: Earth Heart, 1989), 143.

p. 33. "*either monstrously . . . self-destructive.*" Ellen Willis, "To Be or Not to Be Mother . . . ," *Ms* (October 1974): 28.

p. 34. "*can present . . . resolve.*" Margaret Simons, "Motherhood, Feminism, Identity," *Women's Studies International Forum* 7, no. 9 (1984): 349.

pp. 36–37. "*birth control . . . empowered.* Black Women's Liberation Group, Mount Vernon, New York, "Statement on Birth Control," in *Sisterhood Is Powerful: An Anthology of Writings from the Women's Liberation Movement,* ed. Robin Morgan (New York: Random House, 1970), 360.

p. 37. "*In a large 1985 study . . . ambitions.* William F. Kenkel, "The Desire for Voluntary Childlessness Among Low-Income Youth," *Journal of Marriage and the Family* 47, no. 2 (1985): 509.

p. 37. *Carolyn M. Morell . . . childless.*" Carolyn Morell, *Unwomanly Conduct: The Challenges of Intentional Childlessness* (New York: Routledge, 1994), 19.

p. 37. *Karen Seccombe . . . women.*" Karen Seccombe, "Assessing the Costs and Benefits of Children: Gender Comparisons Among Childfree Husbands and Wives," *Journal of Marriage and the Family* 53 (February 1991): 191.

p. 39. "*Endlessly . . . again.*" Gerda Lerner, *The Creation of Feminist Consciousness: From the Middle Ages to 1870* (New York: Oxford University Press, 1993), 275.

pp. 39–40. *While few female novelists . . . choice.* Annis Pratt, *Archetypal Patterns in Women's Fiction* (Bloomington: Indiana University Press, 1981), 176.

pp. 40–41. "*In reading over the paper on marriage . . . outlandish.*" Richard C. Cabot to Ella Lyman, 11 June 1893, Ella Lyman Cabot Collection, Schlesinger Library at Radcliffe College.

pp. 41–42. "*Now I want to tell you . . . believe.*" Lyman to Cabot, 12 June 1893. Copyright 1995. The Ella Lyman Cabot Trust, Inc.

p. 43. "*we are only now . . . nonmotherhood.*" Jessie Bernard, *The Future of Motherhood* (New York: Penguin, 1974), 51.

p. 43. *Tina Howe . . . monologue.* Marilyn Stasio, "The Play's Her Thing," *Town and Country* (February 1993): 57.

p. 43. "*I was unable . . . instincts.*" Irena Klepfisz, "Women Without Children/Women Without Families/Women Alone," *Conditions, no.* 2 (1977): 72.

p. 43. *"It is because ... them."* Sara Ruddick, "Maternal Thinking," in *Mothering: Essays in Feminist Theory*, ed. Joyce Trebilcot (Totowa, N.J.: Rowman & Allanheld, 1983), 225.

p. 44. *"no children ... adult."* Lorie E. Hill, "The Baby Dilemma: How Homosexual and Heterosexual Women Are Handling This Decision" (Ph.D. dissertation, Wright Institute Graduate School, 1980).

pp. 47–48. *"I knew ... free."* Marjorie Dobkin, ed., *The Making of a Feminist: Early Journals and Letters of M. Carey Thomas* (Kent, Ohio: Kent State University Press, 1980).

p. 48. *"to reinvest ... being."* Elaine Showalter, ed., *Those Modern Women* (New York: The Feminist Press, 1978), 132.

p. 48. *"an indecent choice ... martyrdom."* Floyd Dell, *Intellectual Vagabondage: An Apology for the Intelligentsia* (New York: George H. Doran Co., 1926), 174.

p. 48. *"She must ... part."* Lorine L. Pruette, *Women and Leisure: A Study of Social Waste* (New York: E. P. Dutton & Co, 1924), 152.

p. 49. *"are seriously damaged ... breed."* Jean Ayling, *The Retreat from Parenthood* (London: Kegan Paul, Trench, Trubner & Co. Ltd., 1930), xiv.

pp. 49–50. *"has with good reason ... agony."* Rich, *Of Woman Born*, 160–61.

p. 50. *"Perfection ... womb."* Tillie Olsen, *Silences* (New York: Delacorte Press/Seymour Laurence, 1978), 31.

p. 51. *"could not tolerate ... question."* Jyl Lynn Felman, "Meditation for My Sisters: On Choosing Not to Have Children," in *Childless by Choice: A Feminist Anthology*, ed. Irene Reti (Santa Cruz, Calif.: HerBooks, 1992), 76.

p. 52. *"painful trade-offs ... compromises."* Sylvia Ann Hewlett, *A Lesser Life* (New York: William Morrow, 1986), 137.

p. 52. *"a hollow ... fruiting."* Frances McCullough and Ted Hughes, *The Journals of Sylvia Plath* (New York: Dial Press, 1982), 312.

p. 53. *"We should celebrate ... separatism."* Simons, "Motherhood, Feminism, Identity," 349.

p. 54. *A third ... defending it.* Baum, "Orientation Toward Voluntary Childlessness," 153.

p. 55. *A 1984 study ... childfree.* Susan Bram, "Voluntarily Childless Women—Traditional or Nontraditional," *Sex Roles* 10, nos. 2–3 (1984): 195.

p. 56. *"medieval maps."* Jean F. O'Barr, ed., *Ties That Bind: Essays on Mothering and Patriarchy* (Chicago: University of Chicago Press, 1990), vii.

p. 57. *Among the ambivalent ... way.* M. B. Sussman and S. K. Steinmetz, eds., *Handbook of Marriage and the Family* (New York: Plenum Publishing Co., 1988), 324.

p. 57. *"hard . . . self-discipline."* Janice Avenofsky, "My Turn: Childless and Proud of It," *Newsweek* (8 February 1993): 12.

p. 57. *"choice . . . childlessness.* Carolyn V. Morell, "Unwomanly Conduct: The Challenge of Intentional Childlessness" (Ph.D. dissertation, Bryn Mawr, 1990).

p. 57. *"a less dramatic choice . . . nonetheless."* Roberta Joseph, "Deciding Against Motherhood: One Woman's Story," *Utne Reader* (January–February 1990): 64.

p. 57. *"If a choice . . . all."* Melissa Ann Spore, "I'm Childless and Approaching Menopause," A *Friend Indeed* 8, no. 5 (October 1991): 1.

p. 58. *Those of us . . . regrets.* Baum, "Orientation Toward Voluntary Childlessness," 153, and Ronnie C. Lessor, "Deciding Not to Be a Mother," *Lesbians at Midlife: The Creative Transition,* ed. Barbara Sang, J. Warshow, and A. J. Smith (San Francisco: Spinsters Book Co., 1991), 84.

THREE

SEARCHING HISTORY, REMEMBERING OUR MAIDEN AUNTS

p. 59. *The Lisle Letters.* Muriel St. Clare Byrne, ed., *The Lisle Letters* (Chicago: University of Chicago Press, 1982), 13–17.

p. 61. *These early . . . "the feminine."* Charlene Spretnak, *Lost Goddesses of Early Greece: A Collection of Pre-Hellenic Myths* (Boston: Beacon Press, 1978), 35–36.

p. 62. *Some refused to marry . . . historians.* William Kenkel, *The Family in Perspective* (New York: Appleton, Century, Crofts, 1960, 1966), 74. Samuel Dill, Scott Nearing, and Nellie Seeds Nearing, *Woman and Social Progress* (New York: Macmillan, 1912), 134.

p. 62. *"childlessness . . . away."* Ludwig Friedlander, *Roman Life and Manners Under the Early Empire,* 7th ed., vol. 1 (New York: E. P. Dutton, 1908).

p. 63. *Constantina . . . childbirth.* Joyce Salisbury, *Church Fathers, Independent Virgins* (New York: Virago, 1991), 60.

p. 63. *"a revolt . . . self-definition."* Dyan Elliott, *Spiritual Marriage: Sexual Abstinence in Medieval Wedlock* (Princeton: Princeton University Press, 1993), 5.

p. 63. *Ecdicia . . . plan.* Salisbury, *Church Fathers,* 110.

p. 64. *"a profound spiritual rapport."* Elliott, *Spiritual Marriage,* 286.

p. 64. *"frictionless . . . friendship."* Elliott, *Spiritual Marriage,* 292.

pp. 64–65. *Parents . . . later.* S. Ryan Johansson, "Status Anxiety and Demographic Contraction of Privileged Populations," *Population and Development Review* 13, no. 3 (1987): 439–70; Pat Jalland, *Women, Marriage, and*

Politics 1860–1914 (Oxford, New York, and Melbourne: Oxford University Press, 1988), 254.

p. 65. *"out of reach . . . them."* Mary Callaway, *Sing, O Barren One: A Study in Comparative Midrash* (Atlanta: Scholars Press, 1986), 97, quoting from the *Treatises* of Philo, *De Posteritate Caini*, tr. F. H. Colson and G. H. Whitaker, Loeb Classical Library (Cambridge, Mass.: Harvard University Press, 1971), 135.

p. 65. *Margaret Cavendish . . . education.* Virginia Woolf, *A Room of One's Own* (New York: Harcourt, Brace & World, Inc., 1957), 64.

pp. 65–66. *"Ladies . . . children."* Sandra M. Gilbert and Susan Gubar, eds., *The Norton Anthology of Literature by Women: The Tradition in English* (New York: W. W. Norton, 1985), 72.

pp. 67–68. *Elizabeth Haddom Estaugh account.* Joyce G. Shepherd, "Quaker Lady from London," unpublished manuscript, May 1961.

p. 69. *"In America . . . silent."* Alexis de Tocqueville, *Democracy in America*, vol. II (New York: Alfred A. Knopf, 1985), 198–203.

p. 69. *quiet expectations . . . era.* Ellen Rothman, *Hands and Hearts: A History of Courtship in America* (Cambridge, Mass.: Harvard University Press, 1987), 64.

p. 70. *"most married women . . . bodies."* Judith Leavitt, *Brought to Bed: Childbearing in America 1750–1950* (New York: Oxford University Press, 1986), 14.

p. 70. *To be married . . . Emily Dickinson.* Toni A. H. McNaron, "Alone Among Her Peers," *The Women's Review of Books* 8, no. 8 (May 1991).

p. 70. *"the cult of single blessedness . . . their country and God.* Lee V. Chambers-Schiller, *Liberty, A Better Husband: Single Women in America: The Generations 1780–1840* (New Haven and London: Yale University Press, 1984), 207.

p. 71. *Shaker . . . submission."* Sally L. Kitch, *Chaste Liberation: Celibacy and Female Cultural Status* (Urbana: University of Illinois Press, 1989), 6.

p. 71. *"upheld . . . them.* Gladys Brooks, *Three Wise Virgins* (New York: E. P. Dutton Co., 1957), xii.

p. 71. *"season for gaiety."* Rothman, *Hands and Hearts*, 64.

p. 72. *"liberty . . . love."* Chambers-Schiller, *Liberty, A Better Husband*, 1, quoting earlier sources.

p. 73. *"unconditional love . . . behavior."* Lee V. Chambers-Schiller, " 'Woman Is Born to Love': The Maiden Aunt as Maternal Figure in Ante-Bellum Literature," *Frontiers: A Journal of Women Studies* 10, no. 1 (1988): 34.

p. 73. *"Little Aunty . . . mother."* Katharine Moore, *Cordial Relations: The Maiden Aunt in Fact and Fiction* (London: William Heinemann Ltd, 1966), 2, 94.

p. 74. *"intense struggle . . . domesticity."* Bruce Ronda, ed., *Letters of Elizabeth Palmer Peabody* (Middletown, Conn.: Wesleyan University, 1984), 3, 4.

p. 75. *Throughout history . . . suppress it.* Linda Gordon, *Woman's Body, Woman's Right: A Social History of Birth Control in America* (New York: Grossman, 1976), 70.

p. 75. *"great delectation."* Gilbert and Gubar, *Norton Anthology*, p. 20.

p. 77. *a large . . . present."* The Rev. Foster Barham Zincke, *Last Winter in the United States* (London: John Murray, 1868), 292.

p. 78. *"The society . . . stimulating."* Ida Husted Harper, "Small vs. Large Families," *The Independent* (26 December 1901): 3055–59.

p. 78. *"an unwilling motherhood . . . thing."* Carl N. Degler, *At Odds: Women and the Family in America from the Revolution to the Present* (New York: Oxford University Press, 1980), 204–205.

p. 78. *"all the . . . children."* Harper, "Small vs. Large Families," 3055–59.

p. 79. *Woman . . . earth."* George N. Miller, *The Strike of a Sex* (London: W. H. Reynolds, 1891), 54.

p. 80. *30 percent . . . century.* S. Philip Morgan, "Late Nineteenth- and Early Twentieth-Century Childlessness," *American Journal of Sociology* 97 (November 1991): 779. More than a quarter of the women in other northeastern states, compared to 6 to 8 percent in southern and western states with the exception of California, where 22 percent of the women were not mothers.

pp. 80–81. *Hollingworth . . . feeling."* Leta S. Hollingworth, "Social Devices for Impelling Women to Bear and Rear Children," *The American Journal of Sociology* (July 1916): 19.

p. 81. *"No woman . . . mother."* Margaret Sanger, *Woman and the New Race* (Elmsford, N.Y.: Maxwell Reprint Co., 1969), 94.

p. 81. *"not so much . . . babies."* Dell, *Intellectual Vagabondage*, 164–65.

p. 81. *"a heroic theory" . . . choice."* Dell, *Intellectual Vagabondage*, 172.

p. 82. *"a grand domestic revolution" . . . lives.* Dolores Hayden, *The Grand Domestic Revolution: A History of Feminist Designs for American Homes, Neighborhoods, and Cities* (Cambridge, Mass.: MIT, 1981), 295.

p. 83. *"would rather commit suicide . . . factories."* Arthur W. Calhoun, *A Social History of the American Family from Colonial to Present Times* (Cleveland: Arthur H. Clark, 1919), 250.

p. 84. *"if the feminist program . . . useless."* June Sochen, *Movers and Shakers: American Women Thinkers and Activists 1900–1970* (New York: Quadrangle/The NYT Book Co., 1973), 31.

FOUR
UNDERSTANDING OUR MOTHERS, ENLARGING MOTHERHOOD

p. 88. *"Mother's . . . identity."* Mardy S. Ireland, *Reconceiving Women: Separating Motherhood from Female Identity* (New York: Guilford Press, 1993), 129.

p. 88. *"mutilates" . . . "wildly unmothered."* Rich, *Of Woman Born*, 224–25.

p. 89. *Matrophobia . . . parent.* Nancy B. Kaltreider and Alan B. Margolis, "Childless by Choice: A Clinical Study," *American Journal of Psychiatry* 137, no. 2 (February 1977): 179.

p. 89. *Gloria Steinem . . . mother.* Gloria Steinem, *Revolution from Within* (Boston: Little, Brown, 1992), 191.

p. 89. *"Alone . . . her."* Nancy Friday, *My Mother, Myself: The Daughter's Search for Identity* (New York: Delacorte Press, 1977), 410.

pp. 89–90. *Wendy Haskell . . . itself.* Wendy Haskell, "The Role of the Mother-Daughter Relationship in the Choice Regarding Motherhood" (Ph.D. dissertation, Smith College School of Social Work, 1985).

p. 91. *"frightened . . . life."* Seth C. Beach, *Daughters of the Puritans* (Freeport, N.Y.: Books for Libraries Press, 1967), 22.

p. 92. *"It is understandable . . . assault."* Ruddick, "Maternal Thinking," in Trebilcot, 213.

p. 92. *"you'll have to struggle . . . disobedience."* Oriana Fallaci, *Letter to a Child Never Born* (New York: Simon & Schuster, 1975), 15–16.

p. 93. *Other childless daughters . . . coercive.* Sharon K. Houseknecht, "Voluntary Childlessness," in Sussman and Steinmetz, 369.

p. 93. *Virginia Woolf . . . children.* Elaine Showalter, *A Literature of Their Own: British Women Novelists from Brontë to Lessing* (London: Virago, 1982), 270.

pp. 94–95. *Constance A. Logan . . . them.* Constance A. Logan, "Voluntary Childlessness: Psychosocial Factors Related to Childbearing Choice in Career Women over Thirty" (Ph.D. dissertation, University of Cincinnati, 1987), 147.

p. 96. *in 1780 . . . mothers.* Elisabeth Badinter, *Mother Love: Myth and Reality* (New York: Macmillan, 1981), xix.

p. 97. *John Money . . . motherhood.* John Money and Anke Ehrhardt, *Man and Woman, Boy and Girl: The Differentiation and Dimorphism of Gender Identity from Conception to Maturity* (Baltimore and London: The Johns Hopkins University Press, 1972); Mary Anne Warren, *The Nature of Woman* (Pt. Reyes, Calif.: Edgepress, 1980), 335–38.

p. 98. *A twenty-four-year study . . . child.* G. F. DeJong et al., "Childless and One-Child, But Not by Choice," *Rural Sociology* 49, no. 3 (1984): 441.

p. 99. *In the early years . . . parents.* Hilda B. Ruch, "Ego Development, Marital Adjustment, and Selected Personality Characteristics: A Comparison of Voluntarily Childless Women and Intentional Mothers" (Ph.D. dissertation, East Texas State University, 1985).

p. 99. "*We learn . . . human being.*" Rich, *Of Woman Born*, 37.

p. 99. "*out of maternal practices . . . emotion.*" Ruddick, "Maternal Thinking," in Trebilcot, 213.

p. 100. "*These . . . bears.*" From *The Poems of Alice Meynell* (Scribner, New York: 1923, 1951).

p. 102. "*a willingness . . . structure.*" Mead, *Male and Female*, 225.

p. 102. *analysts . . . self-esteem.* Rosalind C. Barnett, Grace K. Baruch, and Lois Biener, eds., *Gender and Stress* (New York: The Free Press, 1987), 80.

p. 103. *Gael Greene . . . mothers.* Greene, "A Vote," 10.

p. 103. "*the silken chains of motherhood.*" Anna Quindlen, "Let's Anita Hill This," *New York Times*, 28 February 1991, 25.

p. 103. "*colossal . . . love.*" Olsen, *Silences*, 210–11.

p. 103. "*Emotionally . . . joy.*" Sara Maitland essay, in *Why Children?*, eds. Stephanie Dowrick and Sibyl Grundberg (London: Women's Press, 1980), 79.

p. 103. "*the compensation for feminine surrender.*" Showalter, *A Literature of Their Own*, 305.

pp. 103–104. *In the mid-1980s . . . ambivalent.* Louis E. Genevie and Eva Margolies, *The Motherhood Report: How Women Feel About Being Mothers* (New York: Macmillan, 1987), 407.

p. 104. "*an animal function.*" Gordon, *Woman's Body*, 104.

p. 104. "*Why especially . . . thought?*" Dora Russell, *Children, Why Do We Have Them?* (New York and London: Harpers & Brothers, 1933), 26.

p. 104. "*leaves out . . . truth.*" Jane Lazarre, *The Mother Knot* (New York: McGraw-Hill, 1976), vii.

p. 106. "*because the only mother . . . one.*" Marina Warner, "Pity the Stepmother," *New York Times*, 12 May 1991, 17.

p. 107. "*who denies . . . childcherishing.*" Mead, *Male and Female*, 231.

p. 108. *maiden aunts . . . mothers.* Chambers-Schiller, " 'Woman Is Born to Love,' " footnote number 20, 43.

p. 108. *George J. Annas . . . mothers.* Gina Kolata, "Reproductive Revolution Is Jolting Old Views," *New York Times*, 11 January 1994, 1.

p. 109. "*The unnatural mother . . . all.*" Charlotte Perkins Gilman, *Concerning Children* (Boston: Small, Maynard & Co., 1901), 277.

p. 109. "*For centuries . . . strengths.*" Rich, *Of Woman Born*, 252.

p. 109. *The poet . . . motherhood.* Rich, *Of Woman Born*, 248.

pp. 111–12. *A 1977 study . . . it.* Linda Silka and Sara Kiesler, "Couples Who Choose to Remain Childless," *Family Planning Perspectives* 9, no. 1 (January–February 1977): 6.

p. 112. *Another analysis . . . alternatives.* Lott, "Who Wants the Children?," 579.

p. 112. *"The result . . . children."* Lorber, "Beyond Equality," 465.

p. 113. *"All women . . . disappear."* Valeska, "If All Else Fails," 52.

FIVE

DREAMING ABOUT A CHILD, LOVING CHILDLIKENESS

p. 117. *"the small smiles . . . taken."* Connie Zweig, "A Father's Daughter," *Psychology Today* (September–October 1992): 23.

p. 118. *"All of me . . . me,"* Anaïs Nin, *The Diary of Anaïs Nin, Volume One, 1931–1934* (New York: The Swallow Press and Harcourt, Brace & World, 1966), 341.

pp. 118–19. *"As I looked . . . me."* Nin, *Diary,* 346.

p. 119. *"a little fish."* Fallaci, "Letter to a Child," 111.

p. 121. *"Now my little one . . . ours."* Margo Culley, ed., *A Day at a Time: The Diary Literature of American Women Writers from 1764 to the Present* (New York: The Feminist Press, 1985), 147.

pp. 122–23. *Margarete Sandelowski . . . exist.* Margarete Sandelowski, "Fault Lines: Infertility and Imperiled Sisterhood," *Feminist Studies* 16, no. 1 (Spring 1990): 35–51.

p. 124. *"in an entirely . . . figuratively."* Sarah M. Lowe, *Frida Kahlo* (New York: Universe, 1991), 65–68.

p. 126. *"greater intensity."* Susan Glaspell, *The Road to the Temple* (London: E. Benn, Ltd., 1926), 239.

p. 128. *Others . . . victimization.* Jo Ann Lordahl, *The End of Motherhood: New Identities, New Lives* (Deerfield Beach, Fla.: Health Communications, 1990), 43.

p. 128. *One couple . . . life."* Nancy G. Devor, "A Service for Isaac, Infertility, and Unrealized Dreams," *The Christian Century* (20 April 1988): 391.

p. 128. *"as a positive, freeing thing."* Jean and Michael Carter, *Sweet Grapes: How to Stop Being Infertile and Start Living Again* (Indianapolis: Perspectives Press, 1989), 52.

p. 128. *Whatever the reasons . . . regrets.* L. J. Beckman and B. B. Houser, "The Consequences of Childlessness on the Social-Psychological Well-Being of Older Women," *Journal of Gerontology* (March 1982): 243.

p. 129. *Another historian . . . times.* Linda A. Pollock, *Forgotten Children: Parent-Child Relations from 1500 to 1900* (New York: Cambridge University Press, 1983), 268.

p. 129. *"sacralization."* Viviana Zelizar, *Pricing the Priceless Child: The Changing Social Value of Children* (New York: Basic Books, 1985), 11.

p. 130. *one feminist thinker . . . increases.* M. Rivka Polatnick, "Why Men Don't Raise Children: A Power Analysis," in Trebilcot, 21.

p. 130–31. *By the early 1990s . . . decades.* "Researchers Say U.S. Social Well-Being Is 'Awful,' " *New York Times,* 18 October 1993, quoting "The Index of Social Health," of Fordham University social scientists, based on U.S. Census Bureau statistics about youths in sixteen categories.

p. 131. *By the late 1980s . . . life.* Arthur G. Neal, H. Theodore Groat, and Jerry W. Wicks, "Attitudes About Having Children: A Study of 600 Couples in the Early Years of Marriage," *Journal of Marriage and the Family* 52, no. 2 (May 1989): 313.

p. 131. *Only a minority . . . them.* Houseknecht, "Voluntary Childlessness," in Sussman and Steinmetz, 369.

p. 132. *One group . . . persecutor.* Kaltreider and Margolis, "Childless by Choice," 179.

pp. 133–34. *one woman . . . knew.* Cheri Pies, *Considering Parenthood: A Workbook for Lesbians* (San Francisco: Spinster Book Co., 1985), 136.

p. 134. *A nun . . . herself.* Marcelle Bernstein, *The Nuns* (New York: Lippincott, 1976), 103.

p. 134. *"collecting . . . childlessness."* Gail Godwin, "Hers," *New York Times,* 14 January 1982, sec. 3, 2.

p. 136. *"a time of gingerbread . . . lands."* Carol Anne Douglas, "Oh Dear, I Forgot to Have Children!," *Off Our Backs* (May 1992): 17.

p. 136. *One woman . . . child.* Berwyn Lewis, Nina Christesen essay, in *No Children by Choice* (New York: Penguin, 1986), 84.

p. 136. *another . . . anarchy."* Lucy Goodison essay, in Dowrick and Grundberg, 31.

pp. 136–37. *youthful qualities . . . offspring.* James Hillman, "Abandoning the Child," in Abrams, 83.

p. 137. *Stanislav Grof . . . creativity.* Stanislav Grof essay, in Jane English, *Childlessness Transformed: Stories in Alternative Parenting* (Mount Shasta, Calif.: Earth Heart, 1989), 65.

p. 137. *"it was not a baby . . . sleep."* Klepfisz, "Women Without Children," 72.

p. 137. *Certainly . . . sociologists.* Victor J. Callan, "The Personal and Marital Adjustment of Mothers and of Voluntarily and Involuntarily Childless Wives," *Journal of Marriage and Family* 49 (November 1987): 847.

p. 138. *"a child . . . impulsive."* Judith Morgan and Neil Morgan, *Dr. Seuss & Mr. Geisel* (New York: Random House, 1995), xviii.

p. 139. *In one version . . . personalities.* Marie-Louise von Franz, *The Psychological Meaning of Redemption Motifs in Fairytales* (Toronto: Inner City Books, 1980), 76.

p. 139. *"symbolic radiant child."* Jeremiah Abrams, ed., "Introduction: The Inner Child," *Reclaiming the Inner Child* (Los Angeles: Jeremy P. Tarcher, Inc., 1990), 1.

SIX
LIVING WITH MEN, IMPROVISING THE WAY

p. 140. *Kathleen Gerson . . . all.* Kathleen Gerson, "What Do Women Want from Men?," *American Behavioral Scientist* 29, no. 5 (May–June 1986): 619.

p. 141. *In a survey . . . home.* Houseknecht, "Voluntary Childlessness," in Sussman and Steinmetz, 369.

p. 141. *Nulliparas . . . maternity.* Patricia McBroom, *The Third Sex: The New Professional Woman* (New York: William Morrow, 1986), 98.

p. 141. *The woman . . . unhappy.* Benedek and Vaughn, "Voluntary Childlessness," in Kirkpatrick, 212.

pp. 141–42. *"You ought to die . . . self."* Nin, *Diary*, 338–39.

p. 142. *the third . . . years.* Ellen Goodman, "Finding the Missing Father," *Boston Globe*, 20 April 1992, 7.

p. 142. *In the 1990s . . . poverty.* Kathleen Gerson, *No Man's Land: Men's Changing Commitments to Family and Work* (New York: Basic Books, 1993), 6.

p. 142. *"For as soon as . . . did."* Nin, *Diary*, 339.

p. 142. *"I love man . . . trust."* Nin, *Diary*, 346.

p. 143. *Bernice Lott . . . children.* Lott, "Who Wants the Children?," 573.

p. 149. *"We did not entertain . . . heroism."* Dell, *Intellectual Vagabondage*, 174.

p. 150. *many female sociologists . . . children.* These women include Alice Rossi, Dorothy Dinnerstein, Nancy Chodorow, Jessie Bernard, Betty Friedan, and Sara Ruddick.

p. 150. *"What do you really do?"* James Levine, *Who Will Raise the Children?* (New York: J. P. Lippincott, 1976), 13.

pp. 150–51. *When one father . . . housework.* John Byrne Barry, "Daddytrack," *Utne Reader* (May–June 1993): 73.

p. 151. *a "stalled revolution."* Arlie Hochschild, *The Second Shift: Working Parents and the Revolution at Home* (New York: Viking Press, 1989), 215, 245.

p. 151. *A 1994 poll . . . equals.* Tamar Lewis, "Poll of Teen-Agers Finds Boys Prefer Traditional Family," *New York Times*, 11 July 1994, 1.

p. 152. *"It may be . . . culture."* Caroline Whitbeck, "Afterward (1982)," in Trebilcot, 185.

p. 152. *"Wipe out . . . found."* Russell, *Children*, 27.

pp. 152–53. *Without . . . possible rewards.* Kathleen Gerson, *Hard Choices:*

How Women Decide About Work, Career, and Motherhood (Berkeley: University of California Press, 1985), 137.

p. 154. *George Sand . . . independent.* Francine de Plessix Gray, "Chere Maitre," *The New Yorker* (26 July 1993): 82.

p. 154. *Even Freud . . . drama.* Victor Calef, "Lady Macbeth and Infanticide," *Journal of the American Psychoanalytic Association* 17 (1969): 528.

p. 155. *Flaubert . . . fatherhood.* Gray, *The New Yorker* (26 July 1993): 88.

p. 155. *In a 1970s study . . . agenda.* Philip Bellman, "Vasectomy and Childless Men" (unpublished manuscript, Reed College, 1974).

p. 155. *one observer . . . fields.* Jason DeParle, "Doing It for the Kids," *Utne Reader* (July-August 1991): 82, reprinted from *The Washington Monthly* (July-August 1988).

p. 157. *A study of infertile husbands . . . children.* Paul Berg, "Reaction to Infertility Provides Clues to Future," *Washington Post,* 21 July 1987, 5.

p. 157. *One graduate student . . . relatives.* Kevin Farrell, "The Psychosocial Adaptations of Middle-Aged Gay Men to Being Childless" (Masters dissertation, California State University, 1992).

p. 158. *"remain[ed] . . . rival."* Anaïs Nin, *Incest: From "A Journal of Love." The Unexpurgated Diary of Anaïs Nin, 1932–1934* (New York, San Diego, London: Harcourt, Brace, Jovanovich, 1992), 329.

p. 158. *a research project . . . flight.* Jesse O. Cavenar and Nancy T. Butts, "Fatherhood and Emotional Illness," *American Journal of Psychiatry* (April 1977): 429.

p. 158. *"So that [wives] . . . beauty."* Judith Baskin, "Rabbinic Reflections on the Barren Wife," *Harvard Theology Review* (January 1989): 101.

p. 158. *Ida Husted Harper . . . birth.* Harper, "Small vs. Large Families," 3055–59.

p. 158. *"Glorious Playfellow."* Dell, *Intellectual Vagabondage,* 139.

pp. 158–59. *"to find in woman . . . freedom."* Floyd Dell, *Women as World Builders: Studies in Modern Feminism* (Chicago: Forbes & Co., 1913), 20.

p. 159. *Regardless of the reasons . . . fathers.* Jessie Bernard; also George Denniston, "The Effect of Vasectomy on Childless Men," presented at the International Family Planning Association, Beverly Hills, Calif., October 1976; Angus Campbell, "The American Way of Mating: Marriage Si, Children Only Maybe," *Psychology Today* 8, no. 12 (1975): 37.

p. 159. *The Bible says . . . canopy."* Baskin, "Rabbinic Reflections," 101.

p. 160. *"giver of permission."* Barbara Hawkins, *Women Without Children: How to Live with Your Choice* (Saratoga, Calif.: R&E Publishers, 1984), 1.

p. 160. *one analysis . . . thought.* R. H. Magarick and R. A. Brown, "Social and Emotional Aspects of Voluntary Childlessness in Vasectomized Men," *Journal of Biosocial Science* (April 1981): 157.

p. 161. *John Dunne . . . adultery."* Jessie Bernard, *The Future of Marriage* (New York: World Publishing Co., 1972), 55.

p. 161. *"equity, authenticity, Eros."* Pratt, *Archetypal Patterns,* 43, 44.

p. 162. *He observed . . . carriages."* Zincke, *Last Winter,* 292–94.

p. 163. *"more persistent happiness . . . her."* Calhoun, *Social History,* 247.

p. 163. *Equity in marriage . . . parenthood.* Joan M. Offerle, "Voluntarily Childless Women: An Examination of Some Psychological Differences Between Early Articulators and Postponers" (Ph.D. dissertation, Virginia Commonwealth University, 1985), and other studies.

p. 164. *Decades later a 1981 study . . . childfree.* Robert Schafer and Patricia Keith, "Equity in Marital Roles Across the Family Life Cycle," *Journal of Marriage and the Family* 43, no. 2 (May 1981): 359–67.

pp. 165–66. *Account of marriage of Roger Baldwin and Madeleine Z. Doty.* Thanks to the Madeleine Zabriskie Doty Papers, Sophia Smith Collection, Smith College.

p. 166. *"sex role transcendence."* Susan Bram, *Sex Roles,* 195.

SEVEN
RECOGNIZING OUR WOMANHOOD, REDEFINING FEMININITY

p. 169. *"a desperate strategy of appeasement."* Susan Brownmiller, *Femininity* (New York: Simon & Schuster/The Linden Press, 1984), 15.

p. 171. *"I, who was never quite sure . . . me."* Anne Sexton, excerpt from "The Double Image," in *To Bedlam and Part Way Back* (New York: Houghton Mifflin Co.), 1960.

p. 171. *"some sense . . . female."* Anne Taylor Fleming, *Motherhood Deferred,* 62–63.

p. 171. *One analysis . . . conceive.* Victor J. Callan and John F. Hennessey, "Psychological Adjustment to Infertility: A Unique Comparison of Two Groups of Infertile Women, Mothers and Women Childless by Choice," *Journal of Reproductive and Infant Psychology* 7 (1989): 105.

p. 172. *"It seems . . . realization."* Malkah T. Notman, M.D., and Carol C. Nadelson, M.D., "Changing Views of Femininity and Childbearing," *Hillside Journal of Clinical Psychiatry* 3, no. 2 (1981): 187.

p. 173. *Alice Walker . . . grown-up.* Alice Walker, "One Child of One's Own: A Meaningful Digression Within the Work(s)," in *In Search of Our Mother's Gardens: Womanist Prose* (San Diego: Harcourt Brace Jovanovich, 1983), xi–xii.

p. 173. *Every woman's body . . . ripenings."* Rich, *Of Woman Born,* 284.

p. 175. *In one recent study . . . birth.* Susan I. Leitman, "The Relationship Between Body Image Attitudes and Women's Voluntary Childlessness" (Ph.D. dissertation, University of Detroit, 1990).

p. 176. *"celebration."* Philip Gerber, ed., *Bachelor Bess: The Homesteading Letters of Elizabeth Corey 1909–1919* (Iowa City: University of Iowa Press, 1990), lxvii.

p. 176. *"almost always . . . creativity."* Gilbert and Gubar, *Norton Anthology*, 7.

p. 177. *"fear[ed] . . . insatiable."* Priscilla Martin, *Chaucer's Women: Nuns, Wives, and Amazons* (Iowa City: University of Iowa Press, 1990), 39.

p. 177. *"The world reputes . . . children.* George Parfitt, ed., *Ben Johnson: The Complete Poems* (New Haven and London: Yale University Press, 1975), 53.

p. 177. *"At the end of the nineteenth century . . . motherhood."* Louise J. Kaplan, *Female Perversions: The Temptations of Emma Bovary* (New York: Doubleday, 1991), 408.

p. 179. *"experiences as a body."* Virginia Woolf, "Professions for Women," *Collected Essays,* vol. II (New York: Harcourt, Brace & World, Inc., 1967), 288.

p. 180. *"holding and bringing forth."* Ireland, *Reconceiving Women,* 138.

p. 182. *in the spring of 1828 . . . friends.* Mary Kelley, "A Woman Alone: Catharine Maria Sedgwick's Spinsterhood in Nineteenth-Century America," *New England Quarterly* (June 1978): 209.

p. 182. *Those of us without children . . . relatives.* Fisher, "Affirming Social Value," 87.

p. 182. *"an even greater imperative . . . development."* Martha Kirkpatrick, "Lesbians: A Different Middle Age?," *The Middle Years: New Psychoanalytical Perspectives,* eds. John M. Oldham and Robert S. Liebert (New Haven: Yale University Press, 1989): 141.

p. 184. *"Nature . . . child.* Nin, 346.

p. 184. *Nulliparas . . . test.* Susan R. Hoffman and Ronald Levant, "A Comparison of Childfree and Child-Anticipated Married Couples," *Family Relations* 34, no. 2 (1985): 197; also Judith Gass Teicholz, "Psychological Correlates of Voluntary Childlessness in Married Women" (unpublished paper, 1978).

p. 185. *But all too often . . . mothers.* Fisher, "Affirming Social Values," 87.

p. 186. *"has kept [women] . . . motherhood."* Lerner, *The Creation of Feminist Consciousness* 281.

pp. 187–88. *Hennig-Jardim study.* Margaret Hennig and Anne Jardim, *The Managerial Woman* (New York: Anchor Press, 1977), 140.

p. 189. *the female allegiance . . . paradise.* Gail David, *Gender and Genre in Literature: Female Heroism in the Pastoral* (London and New York: Garland Publishing, 1991), xiv–xv.

p. 192. *We are . . . activities.* Victor J. Callan, "Childlessness and Partner Selection," *Journal of Marriage and the Family* 45 (February 1983): 181.

p. 192. *"active, generative, and multifaceted."* Chambers-Schiller, *Liberty, A Better Husband*, 61.

p. 192. *"whatever tends . . . freedom."* Gail Hamilton, *Woman's Worth and Worthlessness* (New York: Harper & Brothers, 1872), 270.

p. 192. *Laguna Indians . . . rebirth.* Paula Gunn Allen, *The Sacred Hoop: Rediscovering the Feminine in American Indian Traditions* (Boston: Beacon, 1986), 27.

pp. 192–93. *"the Shaker concept . . . God.* Kitch, *Chaste Liberation*, 136–37.

EIGHT

POSSESSING OURSELVES, DOING OUR WORK

p. 195. *"How good work is . . . satisfaction."* Chambers-Schiller, *Liberty, A Better Husband*, 155.

p. 197. *"How do you bear it . . . work."* Carl N. Degler, *At Odds: Women and the Family in America from the Revolution to the Present* (New York: Oxford University Press, 1980), 387.

pp. 197–98. *"what it means . . . insane."* Harper, "Small vs. Large Families," 3055–59.

p. 198. *In 1985 . . . offspring.* Kenkel, *Journal of Marriage and the Family*, 509.

p. 198. *"If I did not have . . . difficulties."* Douglas, "Oh Dear," 17.

p. 198. *labor "is symbolic . . . vitality."* Carol Pearson and Katherine Pope, *Who Am I This Time? Female Portraits in British and American Literature* (New York: McGraw-Hill, 1976), 148.

p. 199. *"satisfactory . . . life."* Sara Ruddick and Pamela Daniels, eds., *Working It Out* (New York: Pantheon, 1977), 130.

p. 200. *"a divine discontent . . . child rearing."* Jane Howard, *Margaret Mead, A Life* (New York: Simon & Schuster, 1984), 286–87.

pp. 200–201. *Lydia Maria Child . . . lovemaking).* Deborah P. Clifford, *Crusader for Freedom: A Life of Lydia Maria Child* (Boston: Beacon Press, 1992), 84.

p. 201. *"he always insisted . . . best."* Beach, *Daughters of the Puritans*, 92.

p. 202. *Charlotte Brontë . . . charges.* Katherine Frank, *A Chainless Soul: A Life of Emily Brontë* (New York: Houghton Mifflin, 1990), 133.

p. 203. *"Who shall measure . . . body?"* Woolf, *A Room of One's Own*, 50.

p. 203. *"If the imagination . . . conservatism."* Rich, "When We Dead Awaken: Writing and ReVision?" (1971), *On Lies, Secrets, and Silence*, 43.

p. 204. *"conviction . . . comprehensions."* Olsen, *Silences*, 27.

p. 204. *"impeded, lessened, partial."* Olsen, *Silences*, 32.

p. 204. *"in intelligent . . . (so far)."* Olsen, *Silences*, 18.

p. 204. "*a woman is . . . ink.*" Hélène Cixous, "The Laugh of the Medusa," *Signs: Journal of Woman in Culture and Society* 1, no. 4 (Summer 1976): 881.

p. 205. "*It is impossible . . . me.*" Mary Gordon, "Having a Baby, Finishing a Book," in *Good Boys and Dead Girls and Other Essays* (New York: The Viking Press, 1991), 217.

p. 206. *And in the 1990s . . . women.* In 1992, 31 percent of all American women with graduate or professional degrees remained without children as did 26 percent of those with managerial or professional jobs, according to the U.S. Census Bureau.

p. 206. *By the time . . . 1980s.* Mary Beth Montgomery, "The Decision to Have Children: Women Faculty in Social Work," *Affilia* (Summer 1989): 73.

p. 206. "*There will always be . . . clock.*" Shirley M. Tilghman, "Science vs. Women—a Radical Solution," *New York Times*, 26 January 1993, 23.

p. 207. "*Formerly . . . everything.*" Olsen, *Silences*, 211–12.

p. 207. *Ursula Le Guin . . . choice.* Ursula K. Le Guin, "The Hand That Rocks the Cradle Writes the Book," *New York Times Book Review*, 22 January 1989, 1.

p. 207. *Anne Roiphe . . . demons.*" Anne Roiphe, "Can You Have Everything and Still Want Babies?," *Vogue* (December 1975): 152.

p. 207. *Alice Walker . . . write.* Walker, "One Child of One's Own," 361.

p. 207. *Her child . . . affirmation.* Marianne Hirsch, *The Mother/Daughter Plot: Narrative, Psychoanalysis, Feminism* (Bloomington and Indianapolis: Indiana University Press, 1989), 194.

p. 207. "*the nest and the adventure.*" Claudia Tate, ed., *Black Women Writers at Work* (New York: Continuum, 1983), 117.

p. 208. "*My author existence . . . life.*" Beach, *Daughters of the Puritans*, 32.

p. 208. *Alcott . . . life.* Elaine Showalter, ed., *Alternative Alcott* (New Brunswick and London: Rutgers University Press, 1988), xvii, xxv.

pp. 208–209. "*To be 29 . . . this.*" Olsen, *Silences*, 200–201.

p. 210. *Henrietta Rodman . . . industries.*" Sochen, *Movers and Shakers*, 20.

p. 210. "*We see now . . . pattern.*" Carolyn Heilbrun, "Discovering the Lost Lives of Women," *New York Times Book Review*, 24 June 1984, 1.

p. 210. "*Women . . . unselfish.*" Joyce Nicholson, *The Heartache of Motherhood* (London: Sheldon Press, 1983), 55–56.

p. 210. "*I don't want . . . myself.*" Toni Morrison, *Sula* (New York: Alfred A. Knopf, 1976), 92.

p. 211. "*the only opportunity . . . ego.*" Olsen, *Silences*, 210–11.

p. 212. "*that mere extension . . . children.*" Chambers-Schiller, " 'Woman Is Born to Love,' " 34.

p. 212. *"because ... egotistical."* Gordon, "Having a Baby," 217.

p. 212. *"a strong pronatalist bias ... reasoning."* Sandra L. Caron and Ruth L. Wynn, "The Intent to Parent Among Young, Unmarried College Graduates," *Families in Society* 73 (October 1992): 480.

p. 215. *"Who do I harm ... selfishness."* Greene, "A Vote Against Motherhood," 10.

p. 215. *"benign selfishness."* Penelope Dixon, *Mothers and Mothering: An Annotated Feminist Bibliography* (New York: Garland, 1991), reviewing Virginia Barber and Merrill Skaggs's *The Mother Person*, p. 11.

p. 216. *"pass ... untrammelled."* Baskin, "Rabbinic Reflections," 101.

p. 216. *evacuation ... free."* Jeffner Allen, "Motherhood: The Annihilation of Women," in Trebilcot, 315.

p. 216. *In British ... acts.* Pearson and Pope, *Who Am I This Time?*, 45–49.

p. 216. *"to come and go ... capacities."* Pratt, *Archetypal Patterns*, 29.

p. 217. *"woman ... respect."* Chambers-Schiller, *Liberty, A Better Husband,* 65–66.

p. 217. *"wanted ... personality."* Dell, *Intellectual Vagabondage*, 139.

p. 217. *"the relentless obligation ... extinguished."* Katherine Gleve, "Rethinking Feminist Attitudes Toward Motherhood," *Feminist Review* (Spring 1987): 39.

pp. 218–19. *"I want ... joys."* Culley, *A Day at a Time*, 225.

p. 219. *"I am ... reluctant."* Martin, *Chaucer's Women*, 165.

p. 219. *"to value ... more."* Roiphe, "Can You Have Everything?," 152.

p. 220. *"Alass ... loneliness."* Chambers-Schiller, *Liberty, A Better Husband,* 105, from Emerson Almanack, 1817 (7168, pp. 4–5), Houghton Library.

NINE
LOOKING AHEAD, CELEBRATING OUR LIVES

pp. 226–27. *"how many women ... your first word."* Margaret Atwood, from the poetry collection *True Stories* (New York: Simon & Schuster, 1981), 63–64.

p. 227. *"through ... deficiency."* Morell, *Unwomanly Conduct*, 89.

p. 227. *a contemporary researcher ... analysands.* Lila J. Kalinch, M.D., "The Biological Clock," in *The Middle Years: New Psychoanalytic Perspectives,* eds. John M. Oldham and Robert S. Liebert (New Haven: Yale University Press, 1989), 132–33.

p. 228. *European ... expanded.* Grace K. Baruch and Jeanne Brooks-Gann, eds., *Women in Midlife* (New York, London: Plenum Publishing Co., 1984), 7.

p. 228. *no scientific data ... mothers.* According to Margaret Mead, Dr. Carol Nadelson, and others.

p. 228. *And there is . . . motherhood.* Kirkpatrick, "Lesbians: A Different Middle Age," 147.

p. 230. *"How do I . . . herself?"* Zweig, "A Father's Daughter," 23.

p. 230. *Most mothers . . . regressive.* Genevie and Margolies, *The Motherhood Report,* 179.

p. 230. *an Australian researcher . . . self-actualization.* R. Rowland, "The Childfree Experience in the Aging Context: An Investigation of the Pro-Natalist Bias of Life-Span Developmental Literature," *Australian Psychologist* 17, no. 2 (1982): 141.

p. 231. *Erik Erikson . . . maturity.* Erik Erikson, *Childhood and Society* (New York: W. W. Norton, Inc., 1963), 267–68.

pp. 231–32. *"This is not true . . . survivor."* Harriet Lynn, "Letters to the Editor," *New York Times,* 12 April 1991, Sec. A, 28.

p. 232. *"most wonderful . . . finished."* Georgia O'Keeffe, exhibition catalog, An American Place, 11 January–11 March 1944.

p. 233. *in the sociological data . . . lives.* Bell and Eisenberg, 146.

p. 233. *"to amplify . . . specialists."* Mary Catherine Bateson, *With a Daughter's Eye: A Memoir of Gregory Bateson and Margaret Mead* (New York: HarperCollins, 1994), 166.

p. 233. *in the Native American tradition . . . women.* Walter L. Williams, *The Spirit and the Flesh: Sexual Diversity in American Indian Culture* (Boston: (Beacon, 1986), 2.

p. 233. *And when a . . . Indian.* Brooke Medicine Eagle, English, 36.

p. 234. *this is evidently true . . . alliances.* Robert L. Rubenstein, Baine B. Alexander, Marcene Goodman, and Mark Luborsky, "Key Relationships of Never Married, Childless Older Women: A Cultural Analysis," *Journal of Gerontology* 46, no. 5 (1991): 270.

p. 236. *"an imperceptible . . . relations."* Klepfisz, "Women Without Children," 15.

p. 237. *one study found . . . mothers.* Elaine D. Edgar, "Factors Which Impact on Older Widows' Loneliness: A Comparison of Childless Widows and Widows with Children" (Ph.D. dissertation, Ohio State University, 1989).

p. 237. *One study of widows . . . contentedness.* Beckman and Houser, "Consequences of Childlessness," 243.

p. 238. *data that suggested . . . friendship.* Gertrude Goldberg et al., "Spouseless, Childless Elderly Women and Their Social Supports," *Social Work* 31, no. 2 (March–April 1986): 104.

p. 238. *Another group of women . . . families.* Rubenstein, Alexander, Goodman, Luborsky, "Key Relationships," 270.

p. 239. *One analysis . . . children.* C. A. Bachrach, "Childlessness and Social Isolation Among the Elderly," *Journal of Marriage and the Family* (August 1980): 627.

p. 240. *Evidence indicates . . . well-being.* C. L. Englund, "Parenting and Parentage: Distinct Aspects of Children's Importance," *Family Relations* 32, no. 1 (January 1983): 21, and other studies.

p. 240. *Grace Baruch . . . age.* Grace K. Baruch, "The Psychological Well-Being of Women in the Middle Years," in *Women in Midlife*, 161.

pp. 240–41. *Another researcher . . . life.* Pat M. Keith, "A Comparison of the Resources of Parents and Childless Men and Women in Very Old Age," *Family Relations* 32, no. 3 (July 1983): 403.

p. 242. *the sociological data . . . relationships.* Sylvia M. Bitting, "The Consequences of Remaining Childless: Voluntary Childless Middle-Aged Women's Retrospective and Current Views, and Their Relationship to Life Satisfaction" (Ph.D. dissertation, California School of Professional Psychology, 1988); James E. Bell and Nancy Eisenberg, "Life Satisfaction in Midlife Childless and Empty-Nest Men and Women," *Lifestyle* 7, no. 3 (Spring 1985): 146; and Grace Baruch, "The Psychological Well-Being," 161.

p. 242. *"force[d] me . . . norm."* Joseph, 64.

p. 243. *"a woman's ultimate liberation."* Margaret Movius, "Voluntary Childlessness—In the Ultimate Liberation," *Family Coordinator* 25, no. 1 (January 1976), 57.

p. 243. *"If the Lord . . . indeed."* Walker, "One Child of One's Own," 364.

p. 243. *Almost every sociologial study . . . rewards.* Brenda DeVellis et al., "Childfree by Choice: Attitudes and Adjustment of Sterilized Women," *Population and Environment* 7, no. 3 (Fall 1984): 152.

p. 245. *"I faced up to the fact . . . DNA."* Vicki Robin, "To Breed or Not to Breed: Mothering the Earth," *In Context: A Quarterly of Humane Sustainable Culture*, no. 31 (Spring 1992): 23.

p. 245. *"Let each of us . . . eyes."* Jim Schenk, "To Breed or Not to Breed: Saluting the Childless," *In Context*, 22.

p. 245. *Several decades ago . . . unnaturalness.* Kaltreider and Margolis, "Childless by Choice," 179.

p. 245. *"a prolonged struggle . . . slavery."* Russell, *Children*, 15.

INDEX

Little Women (Alcott), 138
Logan, Constance A., 94
Longfellow, Henry Wadsworth, 67
Lorber, Judith, 24, 112, 113
Lord of the Flies (Golding), 138
Lott, Bernice E., 27, 112, 143
Lover, The (Duras), 210
Low, Juliette Gordon, 110
Lyman, Ella (see Cabot, Ella
    Lyman)

Macbeth (Shakespeare), 106, 154
Maitland, Sara, 103
Malamud, Bernard, 197
Male and Female (Mead), 107
Male parenting, 149–53
Married or Single? (Sedgwick), 39
Martha, 127
Mary, 127
Mary Poppins (Travers), 138
Maternal instinct, 95–98
Maternity leave, 22
Matrophobia, 89
McCarthy, Eugene, 20
Mead, Margaret, 31, 34, 102, 103,
    107, 111, 200, 205–206, 233
Me and My Doll (Kahlo), 125
Medea (Euripides), 227
Menopause, 227–28
Menstruation, 175–76
Mentors, 109–10, 233
Meynell, Alice, 100
Mill, John Stuart, 172
Millay, Edna St. Vincent, 48
Miller, George N., 78–79
Miller, Henry, 118, 158
Miriam, 127
Money, John, 97, 101
Montagu, Ashley, 202
Montgomery, Mary Beth, 206
Moore, Honor, 44
Morell, Carolyn M., 37, 57, 227
Morrison, Toni, 116, 207, 210
Mother Knot, The (Lazarre), 104
Mother Person, The (Barber and
    Skaggs), 215

Mother's Day, 100
Mother's Day Is Over (Radl), 34, 171
Mother Teresa, 62
My Mother, Myself: The Daughter's
    Search for Identity (Friday),
    89
Myrdal, Alva, 49, 100

Nadelson, Carol C., 172
Nancy Drew stories, 91
Nation, The, 49
National Alliance for Optional
    Parenthood, 26
National Congress of Mothers, 79
National Organization of Non-
    Parents (NON), 25–26
Native Americans, 176, 192, 233
Natural Superiority of Women, The
    (Montagu), 202
Nature, 188–91
Nazi Germany, 30
Nevelson, Louise, 91, 203, 239
New Right, 29
Newsweek, 22
New Testament, 127
New Woman, 81
New York Radical Feminists, 27, 33
New York Times, The, 24
Nicholson, Jack, 157
Nicholson, Joyce, 210
Nightingale, Florence, 44
Nin, Anaïs, 118–19, 141–42, 146,
    158, 184, 209, 217
Nixon, Richard M., 22
Nonfatherhood, 153–61
Notman, Malkah T., 172

O'Barr, Jean F., 56
"Obituary: Motherhood" (Peck),
    24
Offerle, Joan M., 184
Of Woman Born (Rich), 27–28
O'Keeffe, Georgia, 28, 37, 44, 84, 91,
    93, 138, 165, 169–70, 174,
    179, 189, 197, 202, 203, 214,
    216, 232, 239

ABOUT THE AUTHOR

LAURIE LISLE is the author of two biographies, the bestselling biography of Georgia O'Keeffe, *Portrait of an Artist*, and *Louise Nevelson: A Passionate Life*. She lives with her husband in northwestern Connecticut and Westchester County, New York.